TIL

DOROTHY GARO... ... From the moment David pulled up in a limousine outside her chic beauty salon, she was madly in love with the man who said he worked for the CIA.

BRANDI GAROFALO . . . After David Miller walked into her mother's life, the nine-year-old didn't trust him, but no one would believe her warnings, not even her mother.

JAYNE LEEBRICK MILLER . . . Married and divorced before she met David, she quickly wed the gentle ''attorney'' who promised her paradise but brought nothing but lies, deceit, and death.

BOB BROWN . . . An experienced private investigator, he uncovered the evidence that told Jayne her husband was a bigamist, a con artist, and a very dangerous man.

RICHARD LEEBRICK . . . He warned his daughter there was something phony about her husband, yet she refused to listen when he told her he feared for her life.

NO ONE SAW THE REAL DAVID MILLER.
THE FABULOUS LIAR. THE THRILL-SEEKER.
THE KILLER.
UNTIL NOW.

DEADLY PRETENDER

Other Dell Books by Karen Kingsbury:

MISSY'S MURDER
FINAL VOWS

DEADLY PRETENDER

The Double Life of David Miller

Karen Kingsbury

A Dell Book

Published by
Dell Publishing
a division of
Bantam Doubleday Dell Publishing Group, Inc.
1540 Broadway
New York, New York 10036

ISBN: 0-440-21507-2

Printed in the United States of America

Published simultaneously in Canada

January 1994

10 9 8 7 6 5 4 3 2 1

OPM

Dedicated
to:

My loving husband,
the greatest basketball coach in the world,
whose best lessons are not taught on a court.

My daughter,
whose laughter is contagious even amidst deadlines.

My little son,
who inspires me to keep striving
to make this world a better place.

Almighty God,
the Author of Life.
Thank you for helping me keep my perspective.

ACKNOWLEDGMENTS

Several people played a part in putting this book together. First, I would like to thank editorial assistant Mary Russell, whose research abilities are phenomenal and who was able to put her life on hold while she investigated parts of this book. And editorial assistant Debbie Salamone, whose reporting abilities were a great help to me in the final months.

Also, thanks to Richard and Janice Leebrick, Sandra Leebrick, and Jodee Bowen for helping me feel as if I personally knew Jayne Miller.

I would like to thank my husband, Donald, for providing a little levity and helping me in a variety of ways when it came to crunch time. There is no one I'd rather watch *Cosby* with. I love you always!

And to my parents, who continue to provide feedback and enthusiasm for my work. I love you both.

A special thanks to Amber Santiago, Carrie Foster, Sue Birkins, the preschool staff, and especially Cheri Brune, who provided loving care for my children so I could write.

Finally, I would like to thank my editors, Tony Gangi and Mitch Horowitz, for believing in my work and for being editorial geniuses. It is a privilege to work with you. Also a thanks to Leslie Schnur and Arthur Pine for giving me a chance three years ago.

AUTHOR'S EXPLANATORY NOTE

The events described in this book are taken directly from court transcripts and other public records and documents, as well as from numerous interviews with the many people involved. However, in many instances, to better communicate the story and the atmosphere surrounding the events, incidents and dialogue were dramatically recreated based on court testimony and other public records, and on interviews with various participants or other knowledgeable individuals.

Tom and Merritt Foster; Jayne's son, Dillon; Jake; and the names of several minor characters are all pseudonyms. The author has chosen to change these names and disguise the identities of certain of the people involved in this story. This has been done to preserve privacy. Any similarity between the fictitious names used and those of living persons is, of course, entirely coincidental.

1

Jayne Marie Miller learned that her husband was a big-amist on September 11, 1991. The oppressive Florida heat and dense humidity that afternoon was typical of the late summer days that caused people to wonder whether relief would ever come.

But a few days later on the morning of September 15, as Jayne drove toward her parents' home in nearby Sanford, weather conditions were the farthest thing from her mind. She made the drive five minutes faster than usual, parked her car in a swift, jerky fashion, and marched angrily up the walkway.

"I've had it," she announced as she entered the house. "I'm moving back to Los Angeles. It's over between David and me."

As Richard Leebrick walked tentatively into the room his eyes fell on his second-oldest daughter. Sometimes seeing Jayne made him remember how much he had aged in the past few years. Not that Jayne looked old. In fact, she was quite pretty, five-foot-three with bleached blond hair and sparkling brown eyes.

But she had turned thirty-three that year and the personal troubles she'd experienced in the past few years were beginning to show in the handful of extra pounds she carried and the tiny lines that had appeared around her mouth and eyes.

Life had not been kind to Jayne. Richard wished he could ease the pain that started when Jayne's first marriage ended in divorce years earlier, leaving Jayne with a son.

But the loneliness of being a single parent was nothing compared with the turmoil she'd experienced since marrying David Miller in February. He was a handsome, dark-haired thirty-nine-year-old man who talked of having a multimillion-dollar savings account. He seemed to all of Jayne's friends and family to be the perfect catch. The knight in shining armor Jayne had spent years waiting for.

But after a six-week period of bliss, David had begun acting strangely. There were unexplained business trips, strange alibis, and on many occasions concocted stories that had taken Jayne on an emotional roller coaster for the past several months. Because of this, Richard was not surprised by his daughter's statement that she'd had it. Jayne Miller was not one to be taken for granted nor taken advantage of and Richard knew there was only so much she would take before walking away from David and what was seemingly a life of lies.

"What's wrong, honey?" His voice was soft and compassionate as he walked over and put his hands on her slim shoulders.

"Dad, I found out something about David, something terrible. I've known for a while but I just couldn't tell you." Jayne's eyes filled with tears and her father leaned closer, angry that David had once again upset her. Richard had long since stopped believing David's endless tall tales.

"What did he do this time?"

"I don't know how to say it. I feel like I must have been crazy for ever trusting him."

Jayne lowered her head and began sobbing. Fighting to keep his anger toward David in check, Richard waited several minutes until Jayne was able to regain her composure.

"Dad." She paused, and Richard saw that she was gathering strength, struggling with whatever information she'd learned about her husband. "David has two wives."

For a brief instant, Richard resisted the impulse to laugh out loud. In her childhood days, Jayne had never been talented at telling falsehoods, and more often than not her parents would see through her stories before she could finish them.

But this time he knew instinctively that Jayne was telling the truth. He looked deeply into his daughter's eyes and slowly sighed as he sat down next to her.

"After everything that man has done to you, I have to say I'm not surprised, Jayne," Richard said bitterly. "You've checked into this, haven't you?"

Jayne nodded and allowed her father to wrap his arms around her in a way he hadn't done since she was a little girl. Minutes passed before either of them spoke.

"What are your plans?" Richard knew without a doubt that Jayne would seek revenge for having been taken advantage of. Unlike weak-willed or co-dependent women, who were routinely attracted to the wrong type of men, Jayne had always been strong enough to walk away from a harmful relationship.

Jayne's problem was in being too trusting. But now Richard was certain Jayne would do more than regain her composure. She would get even.

Jayne drew in a deep breath and sat a bit straighter on the sofa. "I'm moving back to L.A. on Tuesday, and after that I'm going to press charges. Actually, I'm going to start the process tomorrow. Before I leave." Richard could see the anger welling up in his daughter's eyes.

David had acted strangely since he'd known him. But lately he had even worried that the man might be dangerous. Despite his concerns, Richard knew Jayne would be all right. She would move back to Los Angeles and start her life over. Even after a blow like this.

Jayne shook her head in disgust. "It's a crime to have two wives at the same time. I've been in touch with a private investigator and we're going to meet tomorrow. He says he can help me make a game plan, so I'll know who to turn to and what steps to take."

Richard nodded but said nothing. Jayne had obviously given the matter considerable thought before admitting the truth to her family. Of course, with David's history the news wasn't terribly shocking, and at this point, after finding out that her husband was a bigamist, Jayne was not seeking approval for her plan.

"I won't rest until he's behind bars for this," Jayne promised, turning to stare out the front window. "But there's something I have to do first." She stood up and began walking toward the telephone. Richard waited for her to explain.

"David's things are still in your storage unit," she said. When Jayne and David began having serious trouble a few weeks earlier, Richard had allowed them to use his storage unit to store their belongings until they could work things out.

"I called him last night where he's staying and left a message telling him to be ready to get his things today," she continued. "I'm going there this morning and putting his things outside the unit." She picked up the telephone.

"Who are you calling?" Richard sounded worried. He believed that Jayne could take care of herself, but David had a temper and if he indeed had two wives, he was bound to feel cornered by Jayne's discovery. Richard resisted a wave of panic for his daughter's safety and quickly convinced himself he was overreacting. People like David weren't really dangerous, he silently chided himself.

"I'm calling David. He has eight hours to pick that junk up from in front of your storage unit or I'll have it hauled to the dump."

Richard joined his wife in the back room and tried not to listen to Jayne as she yelled a lengthy message into David Miller's answering machine. When she was finished, Jayne appeared in the doorway.

"I'm leaving."

"Honey, you're not going to see David, are you?" asked her mother. Richard had told his wife about David's other wife and she had been shocked. Now she was even more worried than her husband had been.

"No, don't worry, Mom." Jayne grabbed her purse from the counter. "I'm going to the storage unit now and by the time David gets there I'll be long gone."

"Okay," Janice Leebrick said uncertainly. "Now, you be careful. A man like that isn't stable. You don't know what he'll do."

"I know. I might have been in the dark for a while,

but if anyone knows what David's capable of, I do. I'll call you later.''

Jayne blew her parents a kiss and walked determinedly out the front door. As she did, she considered what she had just told her parents and decided it was the truth. She did know David. Better than ever. She knew him well enough to know that he was no longer the confident, self-centered liar he had once been. He was a broken man now, and in her opinion no longer a threat to her or anyone else. He had been found out and Jayne could tell from their last few conversations that the fight had left him long ago.

For those reasons, she had no intention of avoiding David. She would return his belongings only after first looking him in the face and telling him her plans to ruin him. He had caused her enough pain and humiliation for a lifetime. Now she would savor the inevitable fear and desperation that would fill his eyes when she told him about her plans to press bigamy charges against him. And once the charges were filed she would tell every tabloid news show or newspaper reporter who would listen. When she was finished, David's life as he had enjoyed it would be nothing but a memory.

Of course, that wasn't all. There were other, even more significant charges she would mention to him. She had found several boxes of secret papers among David's things. There might be enough information in those boxes, Jayne figured, to bring down at least one top political figure in California. When David realized just how much she knew about that, he would probably go crazy. She smiled to herself imagining the satisfaction of the moment.

Jayne climbed into her car and started the engine

just as her eyes fell on a pile of documents the investigator had given her detailing the research he had done on David. At that moment his words came back to her. *"Jayne, the guy's very dangerous,"* he had told her the night before when they had spoken by phone and made plans to meet Monday. *"Don't go anywhere alone with him. You've got to let the authorities deal with him now."*

Even now, with her mind made up, Jayne appreciated the investigator's concern. But he had not lived with David for the past eight months and he could not possibly know what David would or wouldn't do when confronted.

With any luck, she would see him one last time. As she pulled away from her parents' home just before noon that September day, she put the investigator's warning out of her mind.

2

There are times in the course of human decision-making when one crosses a line to a place where the mind convinces the psyche that truly anything is permissible. In this place, motives are no longer examined as selfish or wrong; they simply exist, free from the burden of self-judgment or appraisal. Free, too, from emotions that previously hindered or shaped the psyche, especially emotions directed toward or by others: love, empathy, and guilt. These become less a part of that person's motivation until they seem to disappear completely.

Medical experts describe this personality as sociopathic, or without social consciousness. This type of mind, led and directed by this type of psyche, is capable of committing acts that make headlines in cities across the country. A mother sets her three small children on fire in an effort to collect their life insurance money. A son hires a hit man to kill his father in order to inherit his classic Corvette. The stories vary only in their details. But nearly all involve a person who has walked away from standard and acceptable behavior and has instead developed an amoral motivation that gives birth to hideous actions, which in turn result in only one, dwindling, emotion.

Fear.

Once a person has abandoned society's behavioral standards and instead developed his own, fear is often the only emotion to remain. Fear of being caught, fear of being forced to adhere once again to society's standards of behavior. Quite often, the thrill of living contrary to what is acceptable is greater than the fear of being caught. In this case, fear, too, becomes something the psyche can no longer feel or be affected by. The mind is then free to plan and commit even more hideous acts—at least by the standards of those who have not yet and never will cross that line.

David Miller had such a mind, led and directed by such a psyche. Years before the moment when Jayne sped away from her parents' home plotting revenge against her husband, David had crossed that line, giving himself permission to live exactly as he pleased. Originally, this was not so much because David was without a conscience as it was that David so thoroughly enjoyed a good lie. He discovered the thrill of lying early in his life and ignored the standard parental warning that telling one lie often leads to telling two, two leads to four, and so on. David was good at lying, one of the best ever. But as the lies accumulated, he was forced to cross that line and live a life that was completely contrary to society's standards. The more lies he told, the greater the fear that he might someday be caught. And therein lay the problem.

For David had not yet learned to deal with fear.

At first, the fear was not overwhelming. David did whatever he chose, then told one lie after another in order to live the lifestyle he preferred, all the while denying the reality that he could be caught at any time. Those were happy days for David, days when he lived separate from any pangs of guilt or sorrow. Days when fear was little more than an occasional warning light on the operating panel of his mind. But those days had been cut short in February when he married Jayne.

As is typical with such people, David had needed little time to convince himself that he could manage two wives. He enjoyed his first wife and had no interest in divorcing her. And he enjoyed Jayne. Because his psyche no longer operated like those of most people, David could think of no reason to deny himself the pleasure of having them both.

But David had not first considered the implications of being caught. He had not imagined that fear of this would become an all-consuming, grotesque monster, one that would invade his mind at all hours, stealing any pleasure his selfish actions and successful lying might have brought. Because of fear, being married to two women had brought David nothing but misery.

Of course, David may have had more on his mind than being caught committing bigamy. He also must have been aware that a politician he had dealings with was under investigation for fraud.

In fact, by September 15, 1991, fear had become something of a haunting, living, breathing being in David Miller's life. It traveled beside him on airplane trips and buckled itself in next to him whenever he climbed into his car. It shared a bed with him at night and stared him in the mirror each morning. It laughed at him, jeered at him, and promised never to leave him.

That morning, after hearing Jayne's message on his answering machine, fear was threatening to destroy him.

David could not understand how things had gone so terribly wrong. By his standards he was a good husband. Kind, loving, and faithful to each wife in his own way. He was, in fact, to be applauded for making not one but two women happier than they would have been without him. Why shouldn't he have been able to continue his marriages to both women? How could either of his wives find room to complain, even if they had learned of each other? Trapped in his emotional vacuum, David had long since lost the ability to know the answers to his questions. And so, whenever fear threatened him, as it did that morning, he could only shrink away from it, puzzled and terrified by its presence.

By that morning, David had made yet another in an ongoing series of decisions that were permissible only to those who, like himself, had abandoned society's standards. He had probably decided that if fear came from the concern of being caught, he would need to eliminate the person who threatened to expose him. That person was Jayne.

David waited until that afternoon, then climbed into his car and glanced at the seat beside him. Fear was there, snickering and laughing at him with cruel eyes and a bloodthirsty, jeering smile. It was horribly real, terribly alive, and its presence permeated the car. David gazed at the narrow margin between fear and himself and saw the gun. A 9 m.m., loaded.

There was time for fear to change its mind, to leave him without being chased away by bullets. But David wasn't taking any chances. He started the car and began driving toward the storage unit.

3

David Miller was not always without a conscience. During his childhood David was much like other boys in his neighborhood, playing make-believe games of cops and robbers and participating in sandlot baseball games. But as he neared adolescence, David grew restless and began spending much of his time away from home. When Russell Miller would ask his son where he had been, his answers would be short and obviously lacking in detail. As his younger sister Diana would say, David didn't exactly lie back then, but there were a lot of things he never actually said.

Truth be known, David had nothing to hide. He was not involving himself in the sort of trouble-making teenage activities that were common in Sardis, Ohio. He did not drink or dabble in drugs and he steered clear of the rougher kids who sometimes had run-ins with local law enforcement. David was simply too busy to explain much to his parents. Whereas most kids his age might belong to one club or sports team, David had made himself an integral part of dozens of activities at the same time. He was active with the town's boys' club and he was the primary statistician and scorekeeper for several of the sports teams at River High School. Although his parents worried about when David would find time to study, he inevitably brought home brilliant grades at the end of each semester.

If his parents were confused as to what caused their son's excessive involvement, David's friends were not. He could not tolerate boredom. And in a town like Sardis, boredom was nearly an epidemic.

Sardis was and is the typical American small town. It is a tiny dot on the map along the Ohio River, where even the one stoplight does nothing more than caution passersby with a monotonous blinking yellow signal. So rural is Sardis that all of the children born to Maxine and Russell Miller were born not in Ohio but in West Virginia, because the nearest hospital was some twenty minutes away across the Ohio River and just over the West Virginia border.

When David was a teenager in the late sixties there were just 1,003 people in Sardis, and when kids complained of having nothing to do there was very little the adults could say to refute them.

Not that Sardis was without its merits. Homes along Route 7 and its handful of cross streets were spacious and nicely kept. Lush green grass and full maple trees lined the front and back yards where dogs and children were able to run free from the restriction of fences. Sprawling porches wrapped around the fronts and sides of the houses invited townsfolk to spend a great many hours passing the time sipping lemonade with their neighbors and conversing about the changes in seasons.

Though it was relaxing, the routine of quiet conversation while watching summer turn to autumn was not the stuff of interest to teenagers, especially quick-witted young men like David Miller. By the time David was fourteen, he had experienced the short-lived thrill of cruising the town's main drag—Route 7. The two-lane road ran north and south and was home to a number of houses and the town's only businesses. In fact, the Miller home was situated on Route 7 just across the street from the First United Methodist Church, which was where David's parents could often be found when they weren't conversing on their front porch. Back in the sixties people in Sardis liked to speculate about how overcrowded their town was getting and how one day Route 7 would probably be a major thoroughfare.

They were wrong. Thirty years later Route 7 is still a two-lane road with only a handful of businesses scattered on either side. There is a family-run furniture store and a trailer that houses the town sheriff's office. Townspeople have the choice of two Route 7 stores from which to purchase their weekly groceries and staple items—Able's Cheese Store or Klugs. A post office and a bank are also located on Route 7, as is an ice-cream shop where even on a busy Saturday patrons are more than likely to find the sales clerk snoozing at the cash register as she passes the time.

By all accounts, David found Sardis something of a prison. One from which there seemed no escape. David knew at an early age that once he broke free from the town, he would not return. In 1968 David graduated from River High School, but the real celebration came two months later when he turned eighteen, packed his belongings, and moved sixty miles southwest of Sardis to a small dormitory in Athens,

Ohio. There he enrolled at Ohio University. But long before he began honing his study skills, David began practicing the art of deception.

David had no trouble justifying this practice. It wasn't that he was a bad person or that he took pleasure in misleading those who crossed his path. But David seemed to find a deeply gratifying sense of freedom in being whomever he wished to be. And freedom, for someone like David coming from somewhere like Sardis, was more thrilling and more addictive than any of the drugs some of his peers had begun experimenting with. By allowing himself the freedom to create his answers, he was able to develop a myriad of fascinating backgrounds—none of which involved Sardis. Using this technique he was able to impress women, some of whom might never have given the black-haired young man another thought if it weren't for his grandiose claims. One friend remembered David as using whatever story was necessary to get whomever and whatever he wanted.

Embellishing one's past is not by itself unusual for college freshmen. David was surrounded by new students who stretched the truth a bit in order to impress their older, more mature peers. But in time most of these students no longer felt the need to lie. Under other circumstances, David Miller might also have outgrown his habit of twisting and even outright changing the truth. But there was one difference between David's lies and those of other freshmen.

David's were brilliant.

4

After leaving the confines of Sardis for Athens, David Miller discovered a world he'd only dreamed existed. He lived in a boxy college dormitory with plain walls, an uncomfortable used bed, and a single desk lamp to light the room. There were no decorative furnishings, no luxuries. But David saw past his meager surroundings. He was not concerned with whether his existence impressed those around him, because by then David was quite good at changing details.

In the university arena, David was free at last from the Sardis status quo, free from the idea that those who are born in Sardis will grow up in Sardis, have families in Sardis, and eventually die in Sardis. Now, with his college career ahead of him, David knew he had never faced so many choices. The future was his for the designing.

The problem was David's inability to make choices. Sardis, in addition to its other downfalls, had by David's standards offered no choices and therefore no experience in choosing one way of life over another. As a result, David had unwittingly become indecisive, a trait that became glaringly evident during David's first year at college.

Say, for instance, the university offered eight different freshman classes during the eight o'clock hour. David would find himself interested in five of them and agonize over his final selection. There were times when he even considered enrolling in two classes for the same hour in an effort to gain something from both. But since that was against college rules, David was forced to settle on a single class and for months afterward second-guess his decision.

The choices he was forced to make were not limited to class selection. There were hundreds of nameless girls whom David might have pursued if given the chance, and dozens of organizations, clubs, and fraternities with which to become involved. If David had truly been able to choose, he knew he would have opted for several girls and several after-school memberships. That way he would not have been forced to live within the confines of being one person with but one set of choices. And so, while David struggled to learn the art of making choices he tried to imagine ways he might be able to involve himself in a variety of often conflicting relationships and activities.

The solution was simple.

If David could lie successfully about his past, then why not lie about his campus involvements? David could see no reason why an occasional lie here or there would hurt anyone. As long as he was careful to mix in separate circles, he could not only take on different personalities and backgrounds, he could carry on conflicting relationships. David must have spent hours thinking through a scenario before he lied about it. He had to have memorized the details of every untruth he told, probably convincing himself even as he spoke that he was merely sticking to the facts.

In a very short time after David began lying in earnest, he realized he had a significant asset he'd been unaware of earlier. People trusted him, almost without question. There was a gentle, believable resonance in his voice and a sincerity in his dark hazel eyes that most people cannot fake. Even David could not explain the power he possessed to make others believe him.

By his sophomore year, David had found the perfect arena for his considerable talent of twisting the truth in a trustworthy manner—politics. By winning a low-level office in student government, David was able to have his hand in dozens of organizations at the university. Over the next few years his collegiate political career involved him in the lives of more fellow students than David had ever imagined. Athletes socialized with him, theater students liked him, girls were drawn to him, and academic wizards befriended him. David was popular beyond any of his expectations.

Years after leaving Ohio University, David would not forget that politics had given him his first taste of popularity. Politicians, in David's eyes, were larger than life. Running society and setting the standards, they could say and do whatever they pleased. In college, David knew he'd been the recipient of many favors both from campus activists and from professors vying for promotions and a positive public image.

Even more than the popularity that came from politics, David thrived on the power. For that reason, there was never any doubt in David's mind what he would do once he graduated from Ohio University. In 1973, David barely had his diploma in hand before he set out for the country's capital, Washington D.C.

During his first few weeks there, David would spend evenings walking the streets along Capitol Hill and strolling down Pennsylvania Avenue. In David's eyes, there could be no greater thrill in all of life than to be a senator or congressman—or the most prized position of all, president of the United States.

While David spent his evenings dreaming of political power, he spent his days trying to make his dreams a reality. He took a job as researcher for an influential congressman and before long had convinced dozens of people in Washington that he was next in line for the position. One of those people was a young woman with political ambitions of her own. She was impressed with David's energy and the stories of his powerful, wealthy relatives. They began dating not long after, and in 1975 the two married.

During this time in his life David developed what was thereafter known as the Wall. One wall of his modest office in Washington D.C. became a picture showcase of David standing alongside various prominent people. David managed this by taking a camera with him to every political function he attended. Once the mingling began, David would work his way toward the most influential people in the room. Then, after striking up a conversation full of any number of untruths, he would ask them if they minded having their picture taken. In this fashion David had quite an impressive number of pictures on the Wall at the end of his third year. There were framed photographs of himself with various congressmen, senators, and foreign statesmen.

But his most prized possession on the Wall was a picture of himself with President Gerald Ford. David could only imagine the stories he could create to go along with a picture of himself standing alongside the smiling president of the United States.

Not quite two years passed before David's bride grew disillusioned with him and his storytelling. The marriage crumbled, and since the two had no children and very little property to divide, the divorce was quick and simple.

In 1978, in search of a new arena in which to develop his ambitions, David moved to Los Angeles, California, and settled into the San Fernando Valley just north of the city. Although home to nearly two million people, the valley is actually a colossal suburb of Los Angeles. David knew this, and long before he made his move he researched the area's political possibilities. What he learned was that while Los Angeles was a political hotbed, complete with fierce competition and heavy scrutiny by the public eye, the valley was a less visible arena. In the valley, politicians might make a mistake or two and be easily forgiven by the public. Valley residents were also more trusting of their representatives. Perhaps their positions seemed too minor to criticize, or perhaps their lack of power in comparison with their counterparts in Los Angeles was evident to those who lived in the valley. Either way, the valley was still part of Los Angeles, making it the ideal starting ground for someone with David's ambitions. Once he determined this, he wasted no time leaving Washington D.C.

As he flew from coast to coast, David probably wondered about his new home. Somewhere across the country were people he'd never lied to, women he'd never worked to impress, and a gullible public awaiting his arrival. The thought probably sent chills of anticipation down David's spine.

5

Upon arriving in the San Fernando Valley, David found there every political opportunity he had ever desired. There were dozens of jobs he felt capable of pursuing, positions with city council representatives, congressmen, assemblymen, and senators. What troubled him at first was the fact that even in the valley's relatively insignificant arena, politicians ran in a very tight circle, one that he knew he would have to penetrate before he could truly delve into its politics.

As a solution to his problem, David began pondering the possibilities of political lobbying. The longer he thought about the idea, the better it looked. In his opinion, a lobbyist position would thrust him beyond the valley's power circle and into the realm of politicians that actually ran the state.

Not more than three months after arriving in California, in late 1978, David followed his instincts and took a job lobbying for the state's printing industry. His employer had been impressed with David's portfolio—pictures of David with senators and even former

President Gerald Ford; and projects that included the names of very influential people. David seemed too good to be true and the job was his almost as soon as the interview was over.

By his employer's standards, David took to his new position both quickly and brilliantly. In a matter of weeks the job seemed to have consumed every waking hour of David's life. Those who worked with him figured him to be a man devoted to the rules and regulations regarding the printing industry; a man dedicated to seeing the industry thrive. Those people would have been surprised to learn that David's real motive in all likelihood had very little to do with his love for printing. In fact, the reason he made himself available at every political function from Sacramento to Washington D.C. probably had more to do with his personal goal of making a name for himself.

Whatever his reasons, David soon devoted so much time to lobbying that politicians began to expect to see him at get-togethers and various meetings and sessions. Within a year, David had dozens of pictures to add to the Wall—which he had reconstructed in his new office. David with renowned senators, David with foreign ambassadors, David with the state's governor. Some were posed pictures, taken at political functions. But others were casual, pictures in which David appeared to be familiar friends with some of the most powerful people in the state.

While the printing industry moguls were pleased with his apparent devotion to his job, David was thrilled with his success. His newly made associations were exactly what he had desired when he moved to California. By David's assessment it was merely a matter of time before the connections he was making would give him the necessary influence to run for office. And once he was in office, there was no telling how far he could go.

By early 1979, while he dreamed of his own potential, David began to update his image. He purchased a flashy wardrobe replete with designer suits and handmade silk ties. He began wearing his black hair in a fashionable cut and picking up the tab for costly business lunches. He also began decorating his office with original paintings that cost as much as twenty thousand dollars. Using what seemed to be a sudden windfall of cash, David contacted various charities and offered significant donations. He pledged thousands of dollars to political fund-raisers and once gave ten thousand dollars to the California State University at Northridge for its school of education. Midway through the year, David bought a brand-new Jaguar with vanity license plates that read ADVOCAT. He became involved with the Granada Hills Chamber of Commerce in the northern San Fernando Valley and quickly became president of the organization. He chaired various valley committees and became acquainted with many powerful businessmen in the area.

Those who crossed his path at valley and state meetings or other functions believed that David was merely a successful advocate, a highly paid lobbyist who was doing his part to see that legislation favored the state's printers.

But there were those who wondered if David's apparent financial success wasn't somehow related to his connections with a certain senator, some of whose practices could at best be described as questionable.

Several times each month, when his lobbying work took him to the state's capital in Sacramento, David would work out of that senator's office. Presumably, David was performing his duties as a lobbyist, and merely using the senator's office for convenience and because he enjoyed being so close to one in power. However, when investigators indicted the senator on numerous charges including extortion and the fraudulent use of tax money, David and the senator apparently cut ties. Instead David began working from the office of yet another senator, some of whose practices also were questionable. And in the early eighties, when that senator was indicted on similar charges, David began occasionally working from the office of Senator Alan Robbins. Robbins was perhaps the most influential of the three senators David befriended. He was well-liked by the public and seemed to have a brilliant political future ahead of him. But in 1991 Robbins, too, was indicted, charged with various crimes involving the misuse of funds, and ultimately sentenced to prison.

By that time a trend seemed to have developed. It appeared that David involved himself with senators who not long afterward came under the scrutiny of investigators and eventually wound up in court. And so a theory began to circulate among a handful of people who thought they knew David. The theory had it that those senators might have needed someone to carry out certain illegal activities, someone whose trail would not easily be traced and one whom the authorities would never think to question. Someone, perhaps, in a position like David Miller. For such a job, a lobbyist might stand to make thousands or even hundreds of thousands of dollars. This theory certainly would have explained that person's ability to spend money as if it were coming from a limitless supply. While speculative theories abounded, there was never proof of any such relationship between David and the senators.

Each time a senator fell from public grace, David was apparently not questioned. Neither was he publicly suspected of any wrongdoing. Therefore, the speculation was never proven and no one ever knew whether David might have been doing more than lobbying work from those senators' offices. If the people who knew David had only known him better, he might have confided in them as to how he was able to live the life of a wealthy man while earning only a modest lobbyist's salary. But David was an enigma, a sponge of a man who made it his goal to learn all he could about a person without telling a single revealing detail about himself.

Those acquaintances who could not explain David Miller's apparent abundance of cash could also not explain his effect on women. Because, by all appearances, he was certainly not the kind of man women typically fell for. By late 1979, after a year in California, David's waistline had begun to suffer the effects of numerous buffet luncheons and dinner parties. He was still good-looking, his black hair and dark eyes still causing some women to look twice as he passed them on the street. But he had gained thirty pounds or so, giving him a well-rounded midsection. Although he made a concerted effort to hide his expanding waistline, the additional weight was beginning to take its toll on his appearance.

Still, regardless of his physical appearance David was extremely successful with the opposite sex, and people began to expect to see him with any number of beautiful, intelligent women.

On occasion one of the women he dated would turn the conversation to marriage and settling down. David would only scoff at the idea. He hadn't left Sardis for nothing and he had no intention of settling into a lifeless marriage. He had seen perfectly brilliant men and women commit themselves to each other only to become unhappy almost overnight. No, he would tell those who asked, he did not plan to marry. Not now, not ever. And certainly not as long as he could attract such a variety of willing women.

Once in a while even David was surprised at the women who accepted his offers. But David had his own understanding of women. He believed, for the most part, they were gullible creatures whose willingness to comply with his desires was in direct relation to the amount of money he was willing to spend on them and the degree of lies he was capable of telling. And so it was not uncommon for David to show up at a political function in a limousine, his date carrying a long-stemmed rose in one hand and boasting a new piece of jewelry on the other. With stars in her eyes she would gaze into his, believing him to be any number of concocted personas. This being the case, David lost respect for most of the women he dated. They did not care about the real David Miller, nor did they make any effort to know him. As long as he spent money on them, they seemed to believe anything he told them.

By then David was better than brilliant at telling believable lies. He might tell a woman that he came from a wealthy New England family whose fortune included millions of dollars in property across the country. Others might be told he was part of a royal European family who readily supplied him with money whenever he wished. Some women reacted best when he made up stories that demanded their sympathy. For those women, David would tell them he was dying of cancer, doing his best to enjoy life in the short time he had left. David could read those women like a book, and he easily told them whatever story seemed necessary to have his way with them. Worse, the lies David Miller told became an addiction that he seemed to actually like. In many ways, his lying probably made him feel larger than life and certainly larger than a simple boy from Sardis ever dreamed he would feel.

David thrived on making people believe there was more to him than flashy suits and an expensive car. But he detested the gullibility of the women who believed him. And so he developed an intolerance for women who spent more than a few nights in his presence. Women often met his physical needs and they added to the image he worked so hard to portray. Otherwise he had no use for them.

But everything David believed about marriage and women and money—if not everything he believed about telling lies—changed in 1979, the day he met Dorothy Garofalo.

6

By the time Dorothy Garofalo met David Miller she had gone far beyond her childhood dreams of becoming a cosmetologist. In 1979, at the age of thirty-one, Dorothy was not only one of the most talented beauticians in her field, she also owned Ce Chic—an expensive beauty shop in Encino, California, with a wealthy clientele.

Each day as Dorothy dressed and drove to the shop she marveled at her classy clientele, customers who would pay top dollar for one of her haircuts or permanent waves. Dorothy was certain that had she opened such a shop in Belle Vernon, Pennsylvania—the town she was born and raised in—it never would have succeeded. People in Belle Vernon usually were not concerned with having the latest European hairstyle or the expensive pampering that went along with the services at Ce Chic. But in Encino, located on the south side of the San Fernando Valley, image seemed to be everything. The moment she arrived in town after leaving Belle Vernon, Dorothy—whose quick wit and intelligence were even more of an asset than her hairstyling abilities—knew she had found a place where there were no limits on what she could do.

Years earlier, Dorothy had scarcely imagined what life might be like outside the Belle Vernon city limits. And never in her wildest dreams did she imagine a place like Encino, where people seemed to have an abundance of time and money on their hands.

Belle Vernon had been nothing like Encino. Years before Dorothy was born, the tree-covered, hilly community was the only home Lavonne and Paul Reed ever knew. The two were married on August 24, 1947, and began living in the stately old house that Paul had been born in.

Thirteen months later, Dorothy was born at Monesson Hospital, minutes outside Belle Vernon. Three years later, the couple had another daughter, Cindy.

The Reed home was a loving, deeply religious place where children were strictly taught to respect their parents and teachers. Every Sunday Lavonne dressed her girls in neatly pressed pinafores and the family spent half the day at the local Protestant church. During the week, home lessons were done immediately after school and lights were out at the same time each evening. Paul and Lavonne enforced the rule of their generation that dinner was a time for children to be seen and not heard, a time to develop the meticulous manners a young lady should learn. Lavonne also saw to it that her daughters could sew and cook, talents that in those days were vitally important if a girl was going to marry a nice man one day and be a homemaker.

When the girls were ten and seven, the Reeds had a son, Paul, and two years later, another son, Daniel.

Shortly after her brothers came along, Dorothy began to blossom from a quiet little girl with long brown hair to a beautiful young woman. By the time she was in high school, there wasn't a boy in Belle Vernon who hadn't dreamed of catching young Dorothy's attention. Her brown hair had become naturally thick and shiny, framing her pale face in a way that made her classmates stare in envy. Although she was barely five feet tall, she had curves that were perfectly proportioned to her tiny frame. But most remarkable of all were her eyes—brilliant green eyes that people remembered long after they saw her.

No one was surprised when Dorothy was chosen as the captain of the cheerleading squad at Belle Vernon High School. Outgoing one minute, Dorothy could be coyly shy the next, and the boys soon began testing the waters and inviting her out on dates. For the most part, Dorothy turned down every invitation. She enjoyed the attention and considered many of the boys to be among her best friends. But with so many suitors to choose from, Dorothy had no intention of settling for anyone but the best.

Not until she attended a dance in nearby Monesson did Dorothy meet a boy who took her breath away—as she had done to so many others. His name was Art "Archie" Garofalo and she spotted him as soon as she walked into the decorated gymnasium. He was in the center of a group of attractive and outgoing kids who were obviously the most popular and well liked at the school.

Archie was a year older than Dorothy, a football player for Monesson High with a muscular build, brown hair, and a face like an angel. When he was born, the nurses remarked that never had they seen such a beautiful face on a baby boy, and from the moment Art and Mary Garofalo brought him home from the hospital his looks often caused a stir among those who saw him.

That night at the dance, Dorothy and Archie locked eyes and Dorothy knew she had never seen a more handsome boy in her life. For his part, Archie was speechless after seeing the green-eyed beauty enter the gym. His friends teased him about his reaction, but Archie wasted no time asking Dorothy to dance. The two never left each other's side all night and by evening's end they were an item.

After that Dorothy and Archie were never apart. They spoke nightly on the telephone and dated each other exclusively long after they both had graduated. While their friends were marrying right out of high school, Dorothy and Archie had bigger plans. She dreamed of becoming a cosmetologist and he talked about working with computers. For the next few years they pursued their separate careers, finally marrying on September 28, 1968. After a brief stay in New Jersey, the couple settled down in Dorothy's hometown of Belle Vernon, where Archie sold insurance and Dorothy began living out her dream of working at a beauty salon.

But life was hardly prosperous for the young couple. Three years of scrimping and cutting corners passed while the nearby coal mines began to close down. Eventually a number of the businesses in Belle Vernon and Monesson followed suit.

By 1971, Archie's parents could no longer afford to stay in rural Pennsylvania. They sold their home and moved to southern California. Struggling to survive, Archie and Dorothy decided to do the same thing and a few months later joined his parents in Northridge, California.

Northridge was located in a wide-open section of the San Fernando Valley covered with orange groves and ripe with employment opportunities. Dorothy and Archie took an apartment adjacent to the unit his parents lived in and congratulated themselves on leaving Belle Vernon.

"There's no telling how much money we can make out here," Archie told Dorothy one evening, pulling her close to him and kissing the top of her head. "But none of it would be worth anything if it weren't for you."

Life was good for the young couple. Archie found a job selling insurance and Dorothy began to pursue her California cosmetology license. They were young and in love, with their entire lives ahead of them, and often people stared in envy when they saw them walking together in the evenings, hands intertwined and heads bent toward each other.

But after only a few months Dorothy's plans to begin working as a cosmetologist suddenly changed. Before she could take the necessary tests to earn her beautician's license, she got pregnant. Archie's insurance sales were going so well that when Brandi was born in 1972 Dorothy decided to stay home and devote her time to motherhood. At about that time, amidst changing diapers and sterilizing bottles, Dorothy began to feel unfulfilled.

The next five years brought trying times for the young couple. Dorothy got pregnant again when Brandi was a toddler and lost the baby in a miscarriage. Archie knew his wife was devastated by the loss and he watched as she began to withdraw from him. When he would ask her out for an evening, she would be too tired. When he wanted to take a drive, she was afraid of the freeways. Finally, after two years of simmering frustration, Archie began to entertain himself without her. He joined a bowling league and made numerous platonic friendships while Dorothy stayed at home, seemingly lost in her own depressed world.

Then, in 1977, Dorothy became pregnant again and suddenly seemed to become a new person. She began to buy fashionable clothes and spend time carefully styling her hair and doing her makeup. But most importantly she began to work on getting her cosmetology license. One month before giving birth to a son, Michael, Dorothy's efforts paid off and she passed the cosmetology examination on the first try. When Michael was still an infant, Dorothy began working at a local shop and barely slowed down for the birth of her second son, Tony, in 1978.

By then she had developed a considerable clientele and along with it a burning desire to open her own shop. She borrowed the money and in less than a year opened Ce Chic.

From the beginning, Ce Chic was successful. There were still relatively few high-class beauty shops in the San Fernando Valley and Dorothy calculated correctly that the people of Encino were ripe for a shop like hers. She charged more than most places and in return offered her clients a polished look that only the wealthy seemed to be able to afford. With Brandi in school and her two boys being cared for during the day, Dorothy seemed to be happy with herself for the first time in years. She was completely in her element at Ce Chic and began devoting most of her time to the shop. If she was silently growing unhappy with her marriage, no one would have known it by watching her run Ce Chic.

Archie, meanwhile, was thrilled with his wife's success. But there was a problem. She still seemed reluctant to spend time with him alone, almost as if she had gone on with her life and left him somewhere in her past. They still shared the same bed each night, but they no longer shared secrets or laughter, hopes or dreams. Their conversations had become merely a means by which to function together. Finally, Archie could no longer ignore his concerns about his marriage and one evening he sat down with Dorothy.

"We need to talk," he told her. "What's happening to us? What happened to the way we used to be?"

Dorothy hung her head, tears filling her eyes. For the next hour she told him the truth she had been dreading to tell. After eleven years of marriage, she was no longer in love with him.

"I'm tired of waking up every day unhappy about us," she told Archie, reaching out gently and taking his hand in hers. "Can you understand?"

Archie closed his eyes, unwilling to let Dorothy see the pain he was feeling. For the rest of the evening they talked about their marriage and finally agreed there was no way to salvage it. Archie felt devastated. When he went to sleep that night he knew there was nothing he could say or do to change her mind. Dorothy wanted out of the marriage and he had only one choice—to try to start his life over without her. Despite sleepless nights and feelings of utter despair, Archie agreed to a divorce and a visitation plan for their children and by early 1979 he moved out of Dorothy's life forever.

In the months that followed her divorce, Dorothy

seemed to flourish. Archie had been her first love, the only man she had ever dated. Now that he was gone she began spending time with other men for the first time in her life. For the most part, the men she met were clients at Ce Chic, successful businessmen who had the luxury of getting a manicure on their two-hour lunches. Still, the men she met seemed to bore her. They were typically predictable, wanting to take her to dinner and a movie and expecting more than a kiss in return. Dorothy wasn't interested in that kind of lifestyle and she began to wonder if she would ever find a man who would excite her as Archie once had.

Then, one day Dorothy heard a stir of commotion from the other stylists and looked up from her paperwork to see a limousine parked in front of the shop. A chauffeur opened the back door as a handsome, dark-haired man who appeared to be in his thirties stepped out. Dorothy watched as the man made his way into the shop and walked up to her.

"Hi, beautiful." The man's black eyes seemed to penetrate hers and she suddenly felt flustered. "I'm David Miller. Is there someone who could give me a manicure?"

Dorothy stammered a moment and then cleared her throat. "Uh, yes, Mr. Miller. Have a seat and someone will be ready for you in a few minutes."

As Dorothy walked away she noticed her hands were shaking and wondered how a man could have such an affect on her in so brief a time. She set him up with a manicurist who was between appointments and walked back to her desk, still thinking about the confidant way in which David Miller had entered her shop. There was a charisma about him, an almost visible aura that seemed to make him larger than life. She wondered if he was perhaps a movie star or someone from the entertainment industry. That would certainly explain the limousine, and perhaps the confidence he exuded.

The entire time that David Miller was getting his fingernails shaped and conditioned, Dorothy felt self-conscious. She constantly found herself looking in his direction, wondering who he was and what it was about him that seemed to captivate her the moment she saw him. He was handsome with dark good looks but he wasn't gorgeous like some of her clients. Still, he had taken her breath away in an instant. Suddenly Dorothy remembered the only other time that had happened— the first time she'd ever seen Archie. Quietly she chastised herself for imagining that this man might become as important to her as Archie had once been.

Look at me, acting like a love-struck teenager, she thought to herself as she tried to concentrate on the shop's accounting work. Probably married or has a girlfriend in every city.

At that moment David walked up to the counter, took out an elite credit card and set it in front of her. Dorothy looked up, thankful he couldn't read her mind, and felt her cheeks begin to blush.

"I wanted to thank you for getting me in so quickly without an appointment," he said softly, looking directly into her eyes.

Dorothy blushed even deeper and shook her head. "No problem, Mr. Miller." She looked away, silently angry with herself for allowing this man to overcome her emotions so completely. She pulled out her appointment book. "Will you be wanting another appointment?"

David continued looking at her and leaned onto the counter. For several seconds he said nothing, just continued to lock eyes with Dorothy. "Let me ask you something first," he finally said. Dorothy waited for him to continue. "Are you here every day?"

Dorothy nodded. "Every day. I own the shop; I like to be here to oversee things and take care of some of the clients myself."

"I see." David leaned closer. "Did anyone ever tell you, you have incredible eyes?"

Dorothy laughed. Normally she would not have appreciated a client, especially one she didn't know, making comments about her appearance. But for reasons Dorothy could not understand she was enjoying this man's blatant flattery.

"On occasion, Mr. Miller." She smiled coyly. "Now, did you want to make an appointment or not?"

"If you'll be here, then I'll make one for next week," he said, still staring at her.

Dorothy looked at the appointment book again and tried to concentrate. "Friday at two o'clock all right?"

"Sounds perfect. By the way, what's your name?"

"Dorothy."

David stepped back and bent into a sweeping bow. "Well then, Dorothy, nice to meet you. I look forward to Friday. Good day, now."

With the flash of a smile, David Miller left the shop and climbed into the waiting limousine. When it had pulled away from the curb and taken off, Dorothy realized that an entire hour had passed since David Miller first entered her shop. She shook her head, trying to clear her thoughts and return to the accounting she'd been doing before he came in. But for the rest of the day her thoughts kept returning to the black-haired man with the dark eyes and brilliant smile.

That evening before she went to bed she was still

thinking of him and suddenly she felt a wave of anxiety. No one had ever made the kind of impression on her that David Miller had earlier that day. It was almost frightening. As if he had placed her under a spell and as long as she was in his presence she was powerless to think for herself.

Dorothy laughed at herself for thinking such thoughts. After all, he was only a man. Harmless, at that. He was hardly capable of placing spells on people —especially bright, talented people like herself. She fell asleep dreaming of their next meeting.

7

As David Miller drove away from Ce Chic that afternoon his head was swimming with thoughts he'd never
had before. A business associate had recommended
the shop as perhaps the best place for a manicure or
haircut. But the man had never mentioned the petite
beauty who owned the shop.

For all the confidence Dorothy saw in David's eyes,
she had missed his momentary lapse in control. When
he first saw her from the tinted window of the limousine, he had been every bit as nervous as she. He had
waited until he was fully composed before entering the
shop. It was then that he first saw her eyes.

Dorothy's green eyes seemed to take in his very soul,
and as the day continued he couldn't stop thinking
about her. Her shiny brown hair, and those piercing
green eyes. He considered whether she would be after
money like so many women he dated and he decided
that she wouldn't be. She owned her own beauty shop.
She was successful, beautiful, and probably couldn't be

bothered about whether a man might have money or not.

But even then, at the very earliest hint of a future relationship with Dorothy Garofalo, David began to worry. Normally he would meet a woman, spend a few intimate evenings with her, and then cast her aside without a thought. That way he was able to see as many women as he liked and none of them ever knew anything of his political lobbying or whatever else it was he did to earn his money. Because by then his "lobbying" tended to include time spent working out of a certain high-profile senator's office in Sacramento doing things some people speculated had nothing to do with lobbying. Instead of telling them the truth, David would tell the women he dated that he was heir to royalty or that he was a brilliant attorney with money to burn hidden in foreign accounts. Or any number of concocted stories.

Until he met Dorothy, David Miller had no intention of letting a woman see him as he really was, because to do so meant she would become part of his true life. He casually lied to the women he met, saying whatever was necessary to impress them. But never did he tell them the truth about any of the details of his daily life. To do so would be to close off any possible avenue of escape. And David had been imprisoned by the confines of Sardis too long to ever want to be trapped again.

But there was another reason David did not want women to know the truth about his life. David did not feel he was average, and he believed he was entitled to more than the average man. He prided himself on being able to lie to people and use people for his own advantage. What if he met a woman at a political function—and there was never any shortage of women in attendance—and she wanted to spend the night with him? Such a pleasurable evening would be completely out of the question if his colleagues knew he was involved with another woman. Not that affairs were such troublesome occurrences. But gossip traveled quickly in political circles, and in such a scenario word would most certainly get back to the woman waiting at home, thus ending the relationship.

If David was going to get into a relationship, he didn't want to have to end it simply because of an occasional one-night stand. Other men lived by those standards. But by then, if nothing else, David was convinced that he was not like other men. And certainly not required to follow the moral codes of other merely average men.

As the afternoon progressed and David continued to worry about Dorothy and what to make of the strength of emotions he was feeling for her, he decided to resolve the issue for good. He would see Dorothy again; ask her out and take things one day at a time. If he fell in love with her—and he was open to that possibility—he would tell her whatever she wanted to know, whatever it took to keep her by his side. But he would never tell her about his true livelihood. Neither would he let anyone in the political arena know about the green-eyed beauty he'd met only hours earlier.

As David figured out the specifics of his plan regarding Dorothy, he decided that he might tell her any number of things to ward off her suspicions. But regardless of her haunting eyes he could not permit himself to tell her the truth about his life. He would never be ready to give up his options, his escape route. And he certainly was not ready to give up the possibility of living two exciting lifetimes simultaneously.

That settled, David was satisfied with himself and the plan he'd made. He could allow himself to see the woman and perhaps become deeply involved with her, while still remaining single and unattached in his working world. No one would ever have to know about Dorothy; and Dorothy would never have to know what he did when he went to work each day.

David probably applauded himself for making future plans regarding a relationship that did not yet exist. Why, he hadn't even asked her out. But, according to friends, he knew without any doubt that a relationship with Dorothy was practically a fait accompli.

Because despite his secretive ways, despite his less-than-perfect appearance, despite his lack of morals, and despite lacking a real political title, he knew from experience what Dorothy would say when he asked her out.

David smiled wryly. After all, she was a woman. How could she say no?

8

True to his prediction, Dorothy agreed to date David Miller. He courted her as he had never courted any woman before. There were exotic dinners accompanied by the finest champagne, extravagant bouquets of flowers, and what David claimed was his private limousine to take them from place to place.

For the first time in her life Dorothy felt like she had arrived. Her business was doing well, bringing in enough money to pay the bills and save a small amount for her children's future. And she looked ten years younger than most thirty-one-year-old women.

But most of all there was excitement in her life. Her friends at the shop even teased her, telling her she was acting like a lovesick schoolgirl. Dorothy did not mind their comments. She had never been happier in her life. And she attributed every bit of her happiness to David Miller.

The question of David's employment came up early in their relationship, as he suspected it might. He had already told Dorothy he was in business for himself, but after only a few dates she wanted to know everything she could about him. Having long since devised the plan for when that moment might arrive, David was more than ready when it did.

The two were returning from a lengthy evening at a romantic Italian restaurant where they had shared a bottle of wine and two hours of conversation. This time David had driven his dark-green Jaguar and Dorothy snuggled next to him as he drove.

"David," she said suddenly, looking up at him curiously. "We've talked about me all night long. I still don't even know what you do for a living. You know, besides spending time sweeping women off their feet?" She laughed softly and waited for his response.

If there had been any sign, any indication at all that what David was about to say was not the truth, Dorothy was neither looking for it nor prepared for it. She had no reason to doubt David, no reason to suspect that he was anyone but who he said he was. She knew that she had already fallen hopelessly in love with the man, and the details of what he did for a living were irrelevant. So as Dorothy looked into David's dark eyes, waiting for his answer, she did so without ever suspecting the quick-witted deceit she was about to encounter.

For his part, David's ability to lie was completely brilliant. He did not blink or swallow, he showed not a wince or hesitation as he smiled at Dorothy and answered her question.

"I do legal work," he said, in a manner that belied self-aggrandizement.

"Well, what kind of legal work?" Dorothy moved closer to David and brushed a lock of hair off his face. "I want to know everything about you."

David smiled pleasantly. "My business represents clients who have difficulty accessing certain files of communication necessary for them to be successful.''

Dorothy wrinkled her brow. ''You're an attorney.''

David laughed and tousled Dorothy's hair. ''No, silly. I employ attorneys to handle the clients and I oversee the entire process.''

Dorothy thought a minute, during which time David did not appear to be thinking about anything more than the car in front of him. If he was worried that Dorothy was not buying his story, his expression never showed it.

In truth, David's face was merely a reflection of his true feelings. He was not worried about whether Dorothy would believe him or not. He knew she would believe him. He could provide her with as many instantaneous details as she needed in order to pacify her curiosity. Besides, she was probably too busy enjoying his company to be concerned with such details.

''I see,'' she said finally. ''Amazing, the kinds of things they use attorneys for these days. Who would have thought you could make a business offering that kind of service to people?''

After that, Dorothy changed the subject, interested in whether he had any pets and whether or not he enjoyed snow-skiing or roller-skating. By the time they pulled up in front of Dorothy's apartment, she had long since forgotten about David's explanation of his work. Instead she was intent only on sharing a lengthy good-night kiss with the man who had so thoroughly swept her off her feet.

Their relationship continued on in this way for several months, David showering Dorothy with gifts and flowers and expensive nights on the town and Dorothy doing her best to understand what was happening to her heart.

Finally, less than a year after their first date, David suggested they move in together. At first, Dorothy was slightly bothered by the idea, since she had been raised to believe that living together before marriage was not only sinful but also the best way to destroy a relationship. Still, they had been spending several nights in each other's beds and David was very convincing, charming her with the idea of waking up together and sharing breakfast at the same table every morning. With little effort on his part she finally agreed, and the two rented a three-bedroom house in Granada Hills—a beautiful community on the north side of the San Fernando Valley.

What Dorothy did not know was that David had been planning to move in with her all along. Just as he had expected, Dorothy had not yet questioned his explanations about his concocted private business and was content with the sketchy details he provided on occasion. He had long since pointed out an impressive office building in Encino, on Ventura Boulevard, and told Dorothy that his office was on the top floor. He knew that she did not doubt him and that she had no idea he was telling her lies. And so he was perfectly content with the idea of living with Dorothy. His political future was looking better than ever, and after nearly a year of dating Dorothy not a single one of his peers knew of their relationship.

There was only one problem as far as David could tell. The shop Dorothy owned had been recommended to him by one of his political peers. For that reason, it was possible—however remotely—that someone might find out about his relationship with Dorothy. For that reason, he ultimately convinced her to sell the shop.

Years later Dorothy would wonder why she allowed a man she'd known only a little more than a year convince her to sell a shop she'd worked so hard to develop. But from the moment she met David Miller she became a different person, someone who no longer thought things through, someone who accepted what he said at face value and blindly allowed him to lead her into the future.

After several months of living on David's income, Dorothy opened another shop—this time in Reseda—several miles from her original shop. Once her new shop was established and David was certain that none of his political friends knew who she was, he began to relax. Life was going exactly as he had planned it.

By then David had already had several liaisons with other women, women he had no intention of seeing more than once or twice. But the very idea of living one life with Dorothy and another when he left their home each morning was for David completely exhilarating. He had more than any of the men whose positions he envied. Even the governor of the state did not have two lives.

With haughty eyes he would look at the other men at political functions, sizing up the politicians and business executives. All of them were average. Disgustingly average. He and he alone was capable of living two lives. And he alone deserved to do so.

9

In late fall of 1980, one year after moving in with Dorothy, David's political career underwent a significant change. He began to feel stuck in his position as a lobbyist for the printing industry. After all, there were only so many laws written that affected printers and as long as he worked for that industry he was limited in the number of functions he could attend and the number of people he could legitimately meet.

So that year he quit his job and opened his own lobbying office. After more than a year of telling Dorothy that he made a living operating his own business, David may have found it comically ironic that he was now doing that very thing. David's clients were made up of numerous business owners and representatives of various industries. David would meet with these people and show them his résumé and portfolio, telling them stories about politicians and making most of them sound like close personal friends. These people would then hire David for tens of thousands of dollars because of his political connections—real or contrived—

in hopes that he could make a favorable impact on future legislation that might concern them.

The work was perfect for David and the money better than he had ever hoped. Now he had reason to be involved in any number of industry-sponsored political functions, including weekend getaways, cruises, vacations to foreign countries, and other places where politicians met with lobbyists to ponder which way to vote on various upcoming pieces of legislation.

At about the same time, David became very involved in the political affairs of the San Fernando Valley. He was nominated and elected president of the Granada Hills Chamber of Commerce and he became a prominent member of the United Chambers of Commerce in the San Fernando Valley.

His office door read DAVID MILLER AND ASSOCIATES, and he hired two women to keep his business in order— one who was married and another who was considerably older than he. They were women he trusted to take care of the paperwork, appointments, and accounting end of his lobbying work. They were definitely not women he was interested in. He had no intention of getting involved with someone he would be seeing on a daily basis. He did not tell them about Dorothy and they were never given his home telephone number or any information about where he lived. If he met up with a woman at a political gathering, they never knew about it.

For their part, the women believed David to be a hard-working, very successful lobbyist. They knew of his involvements with the Granada Hills Chamber of Commerce and they knew he made a lot of money. Still, there were times when they wondered how he was able to afford the lifestyle he maintained. They frequently saw him being dropped off by a limousine and his wardrobe was made up of the finest designer suits. Even the paintings in his office were not ordinary, but rather original pieces worth thousands of dollars.

All of this caused the women who worked for David Miller to wonder. After all, they kept his books and knew that although he made a good living as a lobbyist it was not so good that he could afford his luxurious lifestyle. Despite their curiosity, they never questioned David about what other sources of income he might have had and he never talked about his financial situation with them. He paid them well and in return they did their jobs without asking questions of their boss.

But if they were uncertain about his sources of income, they were very knowledgeable about his whereabouts. By 1981, several months after opening his own office, David was completely involved in politics and had begun taking numerous trips that often lasted a week or longer. As far as the women who worked in his office were concerned, David's sudden increase in travel to Sacramento, Illinois, Florida, and foreign vacation spots was none of their business. They merely made the travel plans for their boss and took messages to relay to him each day when he called in.

It also did not interest the women who worked for him that when he worked in Sacramento he would inevitably call from the same senator's office. Neither woman knew that the senator was under investigation for mishandling public funds. And neither woman ever asked David about what he did in Sacramento or if his work there had something to do with the extravagant lifestyle he was somehow able to afford.

David was pleased with his choice in hiring the women who worked for him. They minded their own business and didn't ask any questions. Which was more than he could say for Dorothy.

Although Dorothy loved David dearly and cherished the loving time he spent with her and her children, she did not take kindly to the change in David's business situation that was suddenly taking him out of town several weeks each month.

"David, we've got to talk about all this travel you've been doing," she told him one evening. "There doesn't seem to be any time for us anymore."

David walked over to Dorothy and pulled her close.

"Sweetheart, I've told you there's nothing I can do about it. We've added a few new clients and I have to spend time with them myself or we could lose them. Now, you wouldn't want that, would you?"

Dorothy shook her head and smiled weakly. Her new shop was not bringing in the type of clients her previous shop had, and the money was not nearly as good. They paid many of their bills with David's money and because of that she didn't want to complain about his work.

"You have to trust me on this one, honey," he told her. "I don't like being away from you any more than you like being away from me. I miss you terribly when I'm gone."

In fact, his words couldn't have been any farther from the truth. In reality, he had come across more beautiful women than he cared to count in the past months since starting his own business. Each woman had her own personal agenda, her own reasons for spending an evening or a weekend with him. There were women who hoped he might have political pull on their behalf, women who were attracted to his charisma much as Dorothy had been, and women to whom he would tell anything in exchange for one night alone. He didn't mind their reasons for spending time with him so long as they were gone after a few days. He was enjoying a veritable smorgasbord of women, all the while able to keep the fire between him and Dorothy as hot as ever. Never had he imagined that his double life could be this exciting. And he had no intention of changing it even though Dorothy was becoming concerned with the time he spent traveling.

The problem was, Dorothy continued to ask questions. She was no longer content to listen to David's explanations about traveling for the good of the business and suddenly David began to worry that he was losing value in Dorothy's eyes. He knew how completely she had fallen for him when they first met and that she was still very much in love with him.

But he also believed that if he didn't think of some better story to explain his lengthy disappearances, she might wake up one day and leave him. If that happened, he would be nothing more than an average guy in an average relationship that had ended in an average way.

David apparently couldn't tolerate the idea.

At about that time he began to develop another, much better set of lies to account for his travel time. The longer he thought about it, the more convinced he became that this story would certainly pacify Dorothy. Better still, the story would raise his worth in her eyes, bringing about not only her sympathy but her high esteem as well.

He worked on the story until it was perfect and there was only one thing left to do—share it with Dorothy.

10

For the next few weeks David must have plotted and planned as he had never done before in his life. He told the story he'd created to Dorothy at a time when his travel schedule was the farthest thing from her mind. He took her by surprise and she found his explanation believable. He had no doubt that Dorothy would believe him because by then he had worked out the details of the story so well he almost believed them himself.

The Christmas holidays were approaching and David decided there would never be a better time. One evening, after the dinner dishes had been done and Dorothy was busy decorating, David walked slowly up behind her and circled his arms around her waist.

He leaned down and whispered into her ear, "I love you. Do you know what my life would be like without you?"

She turned around and wrapped her arms gently around his neck. "I don't like to think about it." She smiled, enjoying the closeness of the moment.

David looked deeply into her eyes, as if searching her soul, just as he had the first time they'd met. Dorothy was constantly amazed at the affect he had on her, even now after they had lived together for more than a year.

"Sweetheart, I have something to tell you," he said, talking in slow, measured tones, much the way an adult might talk to a child. "Something that might change our entire relationship."

Suddenly Dorothy felt a cool chill race through her and she looked up at him with fear in her eyes. She knew from the somber tone in David's voice that what he was about to tell her would not be easy to hear. For a brief moment she wondered if he might be seriously ill or whether his business had gone bad.

"I'm listening, honey," she said, forcing herself to sound calm. "What is it?"

David shook his head and tears began to fill his eyes. Dorothy leaned closer to him, panic surging again through her tense body. She had seen David upset before, especially when he was about to leave for a lengthy business trip. But she had never seen him cry. Now she watched as tears streamed down his cheeks, struggling to produce the words he wanted to say.

If David had been any other man, Dorothy might have wondered whether he was having an affair. But David was nothing like the other men she knew. When he took her to dinner or out on a date, he lavished his complete attention on her. He neither looked at other women nor commented on their appearance. Dorothy believed with all her heart that he was completely faithful to her. If he had been interested in another woman the romance between them would have fizzled long ago. Instead, their relationship was just as passionate as it had been when they first started dating. Dorothy was certain she would be able to read the warning signs if he was interested in someone else.

No, David could not be having an affair. But whatever he was about to tell her was obviously tearing him up inside. She took his hand and led him to their sofa and together they sat down.

"I'm ready, David," she said as she looked compassionately up at him and squeezed his hand. "What is it?"

"I've wanted to tell you for so long." He closed his eyes, his face twisted in agony as a loud sob escaped from his throat. Several seconds passed before he was able to continue. "But I just couldn't. You have to know that, Dorothy. They wouldn't let me tell you."

Dorothy was trying to be patient but her curiosity was beginning to get the better of her. Suddenly she wanted to know what was going on.

"Who wouldn't?"

David opened his eyes again and saw the urgency in her face. Somewhere inside the shell of his skin, an unfeeling, uncaring, completely self-absorbed person must have been laughing. Visibly he showed no signs of humor. In fact tears still poured down his face. But inside, a different David Miller thought it quite humorous that this woman beside him believed every word he was about to say. She made it easy for him. Just like she always had. He watched the growing curiosity on her face and decided he had tortured her long enough. He took a deep breath and began.

"The government."

Dorothy waited for David to continue. "What about the government?"

David released a deep sigh and ran his fingers

through his hair. "Dorothy, I don't own my own business." He paused a moment, making sure she was hanging on every word. "The whole business story was just a cover-up, a complete ruse."

If Dorothy was confused before, she was utterly bewildered now. "You lied to me, David?"

She sounded incredulous and David silently marveled at his own brilliance. He was so good at lying that the only time she doubted him was when he admitted doing so.

David nodded in response. "I had no choice, Dorothy. I've been trying to get permission from the government to tell you the truth. But they kept denying my request. Until today." He took a deep breath and looked her in the eyes.

"Dorothy, I work for the CIA, the Central Intelligence Agency." He revealed the news with a note of finality and he could tell from the shocked look on Dorothy's face that she believed him.

"I don't understand," she whispered, trying to make sense of his admission.

"I don't blame you." David stroked her soft hair. "All of this must be so difficult for you, but that's the way the CIA operates. It's too much of a risk for agents to reveal the nature of their employment."

"So you work for the CIA?" Dorothy still sounded incredulous.

"Yes, sweetheart. For nearly five years. The agency sends me on secret missions—foreign and domestic. Sometimes I'm looking for a person, sometimes privileged information. Whatever it takes to get the job done."

Dorothy nodded, squeezing his hand a bit tighter in

empathy as the impact of his revelation took hold. "Is it dangerous?"

She was afraid to ask the question, but she knew that if David's missions were top secret there was probably a considerable risk involved.

David nodded, fresh tears springing to his eyes. "I've never wanted to worry you or the kids, but believe me, I've wanted to tell you about this from the beginning. It killed me to have to lie to you all this time. There were days I hated myself for not telling you the truth."

Dorothy pulled him closer and hugged him tightly. "You didn't have any choice." She rested her head on his shoulder, still holding him close. "It's not like you wanted to lie to me."

David sighed loudly and wiped the tears from his face. "You don't know how good it feels to finally tell you the truth. All that time having to make up stories about my business dealings when they never even existed."

Dorothy thought a moment, imagining all the travel he'd been doing lately. "That explains the travel."

He nodded. "Exactly."

"But you never traveled as much as you have been lately."

David drew in a deep breath. "I think that's why they're letting me tell you the truth after all this time. The travel came after the promotion."

Dorothy looked puzzled, concern etched in her brow.

David continued. "What I mean is, they moved me to another level, gave me a raise. The missions they give me take more time now."

"Are they more dangerous than before?"

David nodded. "That's why I had to talk to you."

David took Dorothy's face in his hands and spoke directly to her. "If I'm in danger, you and the kids might be in danger."

"But why us? We don't have anything to do with your work." Dorothy was deeply frightened at the thought of her children being in jeopardy.

"The government thinks someone might be following me. There was a mission a while back that was very successful for me. But let's just say it didn't go so well for a group of terrorists overseas."

David's eyebrows were knit together with the gravity of what he was telling her. "They're very dangerous, Dorothy. The CIA thinks they're after me; they know where we live." David paused a moment and Dorothy gasped. "We need to move."

"Move? From here?"

"Yes, sweetheart. I think it's time we buy a house somewhere nearby. After that, we'll be safe. The government is taking stronger precautions so that no one will ever find out where I live again."

David watched as Dorothy closed her eyes and leaned back on the sofa. By David's standards, this was a brilliant part of the plan. The truth was that David had apparently wanted to buy a house with Dorothy for some time, and that he hoped to marry her eventually. Now they would have no choice but to move, and he knew Dorothy would agree that their money would be put to better use if they bought a home. David felt a surge of elation. He had already found a house on Aldea Street right near his office in Granada Hills. In fact, he had already discussed the purchase with a real estate agent.

"How soon?" Dorothy said, interrupting the silence.

"As soon as possible, the first week after the holidays."

Dorothy sat silent again for nearly a minute, trying to grasp all that David had told her that evening. "Will we be safe until then? Maybe we should leave today, tonight?"

David shook his head firmly. "No, the agency found out about their plan. The terrorists want to make a move sometime in February or March. As long as we're out of here by then we'll be fine."

Dorothy placed her hands over her eyes and began to cry. As she did, David leaned closer to her. "I'm so sorry, honey. I never wanted to involve you in my work like this. But I had to tell you. And at least now I won't ever have to lie to you again."

Dorothy nodded, still sobbing softly.

"Are you scared?"

She nodded again, trying to compose herself. "I know we'll be okay once we move. But what about you? Every time you leave the country I'm going to be scared to death that I'll never see you again."

"Sweetheart, please don't worry. I've lasted this long and I'll last a lot longer. It's a dangerous job, but I do it as carefully as I can," he said. "Besides, my country needs me."

Dorothy smiled weakly. Finally, for the first time, she understood why she had been so drawn to David Miller. He was a secret agent for the government, sneaking into dangerous places and performing tasks for the continued safety of the United States. No wonder he had an aura of confidence about him. He was practically a hero.

David watched as a host of emotions crossed Dorothy's face. She was reacting just as he had known she would. She wasn't angry with him; she was proud of him.

He was about to prove it.

"So where does that leave us, sweetheart?" David asked softly, the tears long since gone and only a gentleness remaining in his voice.

"What do you mean?" Dorothy looked puzzled.

"Well, I can't expect you to continue living with me. I mean, you and the kids might be in danger; and I won't be able to tell you what I'm doing, the details or even the places where I'm staying; and I'll be gone a lot. No woman should have to put up with that."

Dorothy knelt in front of David and looked intently up at him. "David, I am not like other women, and we are not like other people. I love you. With all my heart and soul. And I'll stay with you no matter where your job takes you, no matter what it means to my life personally. Do you understand?"

Point proven: Dorothy was not only proud of him, she was willing to stand behind him regardless of his whereabouts. At this point David may have been imagining the fun he would have while Dorothy sat at home and worried about him.

"You need to understand something," he said. "I can never, never tell you the details about what I'm doing. And if things ever seem strange, or if I'm acting different—there will always be an explanation for it. But in all likelihood I will never be able to share it with you."

"That's fine."

"And sometimes my cover-ups might take me to some pretty strange places," David continued. "I might even come home with a suntan. And I won't be able to tell you anything about it."

"David, listen to me," she said firmly, her voice filled with conviction. "I trust you completely. I won't ask questions, I won't wonder why you don't come home on time or where you are when you're gone longer than you said. If you can put your life on the line for this country, the least I can do is wait here until you return."

Tears filled David's eyes again. "What did I ever do to deserve you?" he asked. "You're the most wonderful woman in the world. By the way, I've got a wonderful house picked out for us. Let's look at it tomorrow."

Dorothy nodded seriously. "The sooner the better. I don't like worrying about terrorists lurking outside our home."

"Oh, one more thing. The government's sending me to Nicaragua very soon, so you might have to get the house packed up yourself."

"Nicaragua?" Dorothy cringed visibly. "Isn't there a lot of fighting going on over there?"

"That's why they're sending me." Bravery filled David's eyes as he patted Dorothy's hand and smiled. "Don't worry, I've been to Nicaragua lots of times."

11

In late January 1981, far from the deadly turmoil that plagued Nicaragua, David Miller was happily enjoying an all-expenses-paid cruise with other lobbyists and dozens of influential politicians. The trip was being sponsored by a big name computer corporation that was a money-making client for David and several other independent lobbyists.

It was the first day of the cruise and David thought briefly about the farewell scene he'd shared with Dorothy only one day earlier. By then they had purchased the house on Aldea Street and hired movers to transport their belongings to the new residence. The hard part remained, however—unpacking each box and finding a place for it in their new home.

David had no intention of spending the next few weeks undertaking such a dull and tedious task. Instead, he had long since agreed to attend the cruise where he would be paid to converse with some of the most powerful political leaders in the state.

He thought about Dorothy, taking time away from

her beauty shop to put their new home together, and he most likely found the situation amusing. She had been so sorry to see him leave. After all, this was his first trip since December when he had completely convinced her of his role as a CIA agent. He might even have been remembering the way she cried when he left their new house the day before.

"David, please be careful," she'd begged him, holding on to his jacket and pulling him to her. "I'll think about you every minute."

"Sweetheart, I'll be fine," he had whispered into her hair. "Now, come on, I have to go or I'll miss my flight."

Tears streamed down her face as she pulled away and waved one last time before David turned and climbed into a waiting limousine.

After that he had arrived at Los Angeles International Airport with only minutes to spare before his flight departed. But the plane he boarded was not destined for Nicaragua. Instead, it was headed for Miami Beach, Florida, where he would board the cruise ship the following day.

And now that day had arrived and the cruise was under way. He and the others aboard the ship were one hundred miles closer to the Bahamas. David must have congratulated himself on successfully manipulating Dorothy in such a way that he was free to do whatever he desired. He casually glanced down at his attire —a fashionable sport shirt and designer walking shorts. His plane had come in fairly early the day before and he'd had time to catch a nap in the sun. Now, boasting a healthy suntan, he was thankful he'd done so.

He felt carefree as he stood on the top deck of the

luxury liner, the sun shining in his face and a warm breeze blowing off the tropical waters of the Atlantic Ocean. He turned his back to the pale blue waters and leaned against the ship's railing. Like the other cruises he'd been on, beautiful women were everywhere. In the casinos downstairs, scattered throughout the dining room, lounging at the pool, and working out in the ship's gymnasium.

Some of the women were invited by the corporate hosts, designed to offer entertainment to the esteemed passengers aboard. Others were what David considered gold diggers and groupies. Those were the women who found out a specific cruise would be carrying numerous politicians and then booked themselves on the ship in hopes of bringing home more than a suntan.

David despised those women for thinking that he or others like him would actually be interested in a relationship with one of them. They were merely entertainment, the kind that David had enjoyed countless times in the past years without an apparent hint of concern for their feelings.

Even as he thought about the possibilities, three bikini-clad bodies passed him. One, a young woman with long blond hair and an ample bosom, winked at him. *They think I'm a politician,* he thought to himself as he winked back. David did not care what they thought so long as he spent his time with several of them during the trip.

Later that night, after dinner, the same blond-haired woman he'd seen earlier in the day approached him at his table. David had just finished successfully talking business with an elderly congressman, who now stood up and excused himself from the table. David thanked him again and looked appreciatively at the young woman.

"Hi." Her smile was warm and inviting and David pulled out a chair for her.

"Hi," he answered, standing up and pointing to the chair. "Won't you join me?"

"Why, certainly." She sat down and moved her chair close to his, bending slightly and giving David a considerable view down her low-cut evening gown.

"What's your name?" David asked, trying to keep from staring at her.

"Cassie." She purred the word provocatively and leaned slightly toward him. He could already imagine the excitement she was going to provide him. "Are you an important politician?"

David leaned back slightly, utterly confident and poised. "Now," he chuckled lightly, "who told you that?"

He was teasing her, flirting with her and forcing her to ask more questions. "Can't say," she said, turning her face downward into a mock pout. "Come on, tell me the truth. You're one of those politicians, right?"

"Okay, okay." David nodded, pretending to end the suspense. "I'm an assemblyman from California." He looked slowly down at her chest and back up at her face. "I'm here on business, but I really came on this cruise for other reasons."

Cassie leaned closer. "What other reasons?"

"Well, let's just say I was feeling a little lonely."

The young woman, whom David guessed to be in her early twenties, raised an eyebrow in surprise. "Imagine that. That's why I came too." She tilted her head and narrowed her eyes seductively. "You're not married, are you?"

"Me? Married?" David laughed and shook his head. "I'm still waiting for the right woman."

Cassie smiled and took David's hand. "Then let's get out on the dance floor and get to know each other," she whispered in his ear. "Maybe your search is over."

12

Back on Aldea Street in the middle-class suburb of Granada Hills, Dorothy worked tirelessly to put their new home in order. She had hoped to have the house neatly organized by the time David returned from his mission. Besides, there was little point in spending time at the shop while her mind was absorbed with worrying about what David might be doing and what danger he might be facing.

Though she was deeply concerned for David's safety, she was no longer worried about hers or that of her children. After they had moved, David reported back to her that the government no longer feared a terrorist attack. The house on Aldea Street had been a perfect choice, one that Dorothy agreed upon as soon as she saw it. David fronted the money for the down payment and assured her that with his raise they would have no trouble affording the payments.

The idea of buying a house with David had caused Dorothy some concern at first. She knew they needed to move for their safety, but she thought they should consider renting another house. Her feelings were not caused by any lack of trust or love for David. She loved him more deeply each day. But there seemed something so final about buying a home together. And Dorothy did not want anything to interfere with the happiness they shared.

By then, both David and Dorothy were thoroughly pleased with their decision to live together. Even though Dorothy had originally been reluctant to move in with him, she had long since realized that the situation had worked out beautifully. She was continually falling deeper in love with him, amazed that such a brilliant and brave man would be interested in a woman with three children.

Indeed, David brought more happiness to her life than she had ever dreamed. When he was home, he enjoyed spending time with Michael and Tony, wrestling with them and playing the role of their father. The boys had been merely toddlers when she and David began living together, and by 1981 both boys called him Daddy. Although they still saw their father on a regular basis, it was David who had established a presence in their home, and they loved him dearly.

Only Brandi was hesitant about David's role in their lives. She was nine years old by then, with clear blue eyes and a sensitive heart. She was the only one of Dorothy's children old enough to remember clearly ever living with her real father and she missed him desperately. Perhaps for that reason, or perhaps because he spent so much of his time with the boys, Brandi was cool toward David. Her resistance to him bothered Dorothy and on several occasions she had asked her daughter to be friendlier toward him.

"After all, Brandi," Dorothy would say, "I'm in love

with the man. The least you could do is be nice to him."

"I am nice to him," Brandi would snap back sharply. "But he's not my daddy and he never will be. Don't try to force me to love him. I didn't ask him to live with us, Mom, you did."

Dorothy would only shake her head, confused about Brandi's reaction. She felt certain that one day Brandi would come to love David. Maybe when she was old enough to understand all that he had done for them. Either way, Brandi would simply have to learn to accept the fact that David was not leaving anytime soon.

Because by then, Dorothy was beginning to consider the possibility that one day they might actually get married. In some ways she didn't care. She didn't need a marriage license to prove that David and she were in love. She'd been that route one time before and it had been painful divorcing a man she'd once loved. In light of her past, she thought she could be content to live with David the rest of her life without ever wearing a wedding ring.

Two weeks had passed and David was scheduled to return from his mission. Dorothy sat at their dining room table waiting for him to drive up. He hadn't been able to tell her exactly when his plane would be arriving, only that he should be coming in sometime that morning.

Dorothy looked around approvingly at their new home. She had unpacked everything and found a place for all their belongings. David would be pleased. She smoothed her sweater and absently checked her hair to be sure it was in place. She knew she was still as beautiful as she had been when they met. Still petite, with an alluring figure and hair now fashionably short; still aware of the effect her green eyes had on the men who noticed them. She was thankful for her looks and believed that they contributed to the way David stayed so loyal to her. She was all the woman he needed and she was proud of that fact.

She began wondering what she and David would do that evening to celebrate his homecoming. Just then she heard a car pull up and she ran to the front door.

It was David, tan and as handsome as she had ever thought him to be. His black hair was neatly trimmed and again she was struck by the aura that surrounded him. One might still have thought him to be an important celebrity or politician. Dorothy could hardly wait to have him back in her arms.

He said nothing as he turned and saw her, only grabbed his suitcase and began walking quickly up their sidewalk. Before either of them could say a word, he pulled her into a hug that swept her off her feet. For several seconds they remained in the embrace.

"I've missed you so much," he said, finally breaking the silence. He took her face in his hands and kissed her. "You don't know how good it feels to be home."

Dorothy held him back, looking him up and down as if searching for some sign that he'd been hurt. "You're okay?"

David nodded. "It was a tough one. Missions don't get a lot tougher than that," he said. "I wish I could tell you about it, but I can say this: The president can relax. The U.S. won't be sending troops to Nicaragua now."

Dorothy smiled at him and took his hand. "I'm so proud of you, David."

A thousand questions flitted through her mind, but

she had no intention of asking them. She had made a promise to David and she would keep it. Regardless of her curiosity she would never question him about his work. He had gone out of his way to seek permission to tell her about his position. After his honesty, the least she could do was cooperate by keeping her questions to herself.

"Come on," she said, leading him into their home. "See if you like our new house."

David grinned. "The house can wait." He embraced her again on the front porch and kissed her more slowly this time. "I'm with the woman I love."

Later, when they were inside and had spent much of the afternoon catching up with each other and enjoying each other's company, David stood up and walked over to his suitcase. He opened it carefully, reached into a zippered pocket, and pulled out a postcard.

"I know you have a lot of questions, sweetheart," he said, walking back to where she sat. "And I appreciate you keeping them to yourself. I really can't tell you anything about what I've been doing. But I did bring back a postcard of Nicaragua."

He handed it to her and she looked at it thoughtfully. The word NICARAGUA was printed on the top right corner and the postcard had a primitive quality about it. The picture was one of dense, green forests on either side of a rude dirt path. Two soldiers sat in a jeep in the foreground of the path, apparently keeping watch for enemy trespassers.

"Doesn't look like much of a vacation spot," she said wryly. David shook his head seriously.

"It's certainly not the Bahamas," he said, remembering the vast white beaches he had left only two days earlier and silently appreciating his own twisted humor. "They don't have many souvenir shops over there, but when I came across this, I bought it for you. Maybe that way when I have to go back again you can picture where I'll be and you'll feel closer to me."

Dorothy looked up at him, clearly disappointed. "You mean you're going back?"

David nodded sadly. "Yes, there's another mission over there. It's an entirely different matter, but it's just as important, sweetheart. The good news is, I shouldn't be gone much more than a week this time."

She sighed and smiled weakly in acceptance. "When do you leave?"

"Four days."

13

The double life of David Miller continued in that way for the next four years. Each time he needed to attend a political function, whether somewhere in the United States, aboard a cruise ship, or on some enchanted island—or even if he merely wanted some time away with one of the women he met along his travels—he simply told Dorothy he was off on another mission.

During that time he convinced her that he was involved with such grave security affairs that by 1985 she could hardly imagine how the United States would ever get along without him. As far as she knew, he was in Chile, Vietnam, Nicaragua, Iran, the Soviet Union, and Cuba. And each time, he returned with a token postcard of the place where his mission had occurred.

Not until nearly a decade later, when she was sorting through a box of old letters and cards, would Dorothy come across those postcards and realize that not one of them had been mailed to her. For that reason none of them had postmarks, making it impossible to determine where they had actually been purchased.

But at that time, their relationship was as strong as ever and Dorothy still worried terribly each time David left on a mission. She never questioned the actual source of the postcards or why David never mailed them. She was thankful only that David loved her enough to think of her, even when his life was on the line during a secret CIA mission.

For David's part, he had discovered a wonderful thing to go along with his imaginary life as a CIA agent. Many of the cruise ships he frequented had gift shops with postcards from around the world. Whenever he found such a shop, he would stock up on postcards, each representing the place of a future mission he would later concoct at Dorothy's expense.

David was fairly certain that the postcards were little more than added insurance. Despite the fact that she was a smart woman and one who typically saw through the lies of average people, he knew she believed him unconditionally. For that reason the postcards added a nice touch, but they were not necessary.

As the years slipped past, Dorothy continued to worry about David, in and out of the country on dangerous secret missions. She was never happier than when he was at home. Even then he put in many hours at what Dorothy presumed was a local CIA office. David had told her that his days were spent discussing missions with various government officials and that the location of the office was a secret.

"I'm sorry, sweetheart," he had said on numerous occasions. "I wish I could tell you where it is I go every day. That way you could come and visit me. I'd like that. But I just can't tell you. Do you understand?"

Dorothy would quickly nod. She had kept her promise not to interfere with the secrecy of his position with the CIA. In her opinion it did not matter where David spent his days so long as his nights were with her. He treated her as if she were the only woman on earth, certainly the only woman he was interested in spending time with. She felt completely relaxed in their relationship, believing with all her heart that he had never cheated on her. He loved her far too much for that.

The only thing David would tell her about his workplace was that it was approximately twenty miles from their home. Dorothy knew that Los Angeles was about that far from their home and she figured he probably worked somewhere downtown. Once in a while she might consider following David, just so she could know where he was if she ever needed to find him in an emergency. But each time the thought crossed her mind she chastised herself for even thinking of doing such a thing. David had told her the location of the office was top secret, and if David didn't want her to know its whereabouts, she wasn't going to snoop. She would have to be content knowing only that he drove twenty miles to work on the days when he was in town.

Of course, in reality, David was working less than a mile from their home, putting in enough time on his lobbying business that he had more than doubled his workload. His clientele was so significant that by 1984 he began considering hiring someone to help him.

Finally, he decided against such a move. He could still handle the clients he had, which by then included several aerospace companies, a local air-quality district, and several large printing firms. He was commanding an hourly consulting fee of more than one hundred dollars—and more than that when he spent time in Sacramento for a client.

The women he had hired to run his office, Lynne

and Cynthia, were as faithful as ever. They kept his books meticulously and never questioned his frequent travel in the years they'd worked for him.

And so David Miller was satisfied with his lives, each separate from the other in a way that proved beyond any doubt that he was anything but average. But by mid-1984 he was beginning to feel that the challenge had gone from his dual existence. At the same time, he still felt a love for Dorothy that he had never experienced with any other woman. He began to wonder what it would be like to marry her. The legality of such a move would certainly heighten the challenge of keeping her a secret. David liked the idea immensely.

But even while David considered proposing to Dorothy, he never seemed to entertain the idea of telling her the truth about what he did for a living. If he did ask her to marry him and she accepted—as he knew she would—then he would continue living a double life just as he had done before.

The longer he pondered the idea, the better it seemed. The challenge was irresistible and it wasn't as if he didn't love Dorothy. He cared deeply for her and the children and thought all of them to be very fortunate that he'd entered their lives. Where would they be without him? Dorothy would probably still be dating and her children would not have a father figure to look up to. Yes, he was definitely the best thing that had happened to them. He would make them even happier if he married Dorothy. He was sure of that much. Besides, if they got married he could set about legally adopting the children—something he'd always wanted to do.

That summer he decided to act on his desires. He took Dorothy to dinner one evening in July and when the meal was over he reached into his pocket and pulled out a tiny box from an expensive local jeweler.

Dorothy stared at the box and watched as David opened it. She could see the sparkle from the diamond ring instantly and she put her hand to her mouth to stifle a gasp.

"David!" She looked from the ring into his eyes and saw that they had filled with tears.

"I love you, Dorothy," he said softly, taking the ring from the box and slipping it on her graceful finger. "I've shared the past few years of my life with you and now I want to share my future with you."

Dorothy's eyes grew misty, listening to the man she loved declare his feelings. She waited for him to continue.

"I want to marry you, sweetheart. Be a husband to you and know that we'll be together as long as we live."

Dorothy was smiling now, tears of happiness rolling gently down her face. "Oh, David. Are you sure it's what you want?"

David nodded. "I've never been more sure of anything in my life." He took her hand in his and rubbed his thumb over the shiny diamond ring. "There will never be anyone like you for me." He paused. "So? Will you marry me?"

Dorothy knew what her answer would be every bit as much as David had. David had mentioned marriage more often recently and she wondered if he might be thinking about proposing to her. After giving the matter careful thought, she had decided that such a commitment could not possibly alter the relationship they shared, except to make it better.

"My answer is yes, David. I will marry you." She

leaned toward him and neither of them were aware of the other patrons at the restaurant.

David wiped the tears from his face and squeezed her hand. "What would you think about getting married next month?"

For the next hour they talked about their wedding plans. Neither of them wanted a big wedding, and since both of them had been married before, they wanted the ceremony to be performed by a judge.

When David suggested Las Vegas, Dorothy agreed it would be the perfect place. They could get married without the cost or fanfare that usually accompanied weddings and they would be able to begin their honeymoon as soon as the ceremony was over.

Not until they got home that evening and shared the news with the children did anything mar the happiness they were feeling. The boys, ages six and seven, didn't really understand what it meant that David was marrying their mother. Still, they were happy about the news because both David and their mother seemed so excited.

But Brandi's reaction was another thing entirely. She stared at her mother in disbelief and then stormed out of the living room and into her bedroom. David looked at his bride-to-be in confusion and Dorothy shrugged. Brandi was thirteen years old and beginning to act like a petulant teenager by Dorothy's standards.

"She'll get used to the idea," David said angrily, visibly bothered that Brandi didn't approve of their wedding plans. "I'll see to that."

As David spoke, Dorothy was struck by something she had never heard before in his voice. Something cold and unkind. For a moment she worried if she might be making a mistake and if marrying David might alienate her from her only daughter.

But she put those thoughts out of her head. David's attitude could be explained easily enough. Both of them felt they were taking a permanent step by getting married and there was bound to be some tension as a result. Dorothy assured herself that the tension would pass. Marrying David Miller would be the best move she ever made.

14

Brandi Garofalo—eyes swollen and bloodshot from hours of crying—was feeling sick to her stomach. She had done everything within her limited power to keep her mother from marrying David Miller, but now it was too late. Brandi lay on her bed hugging her knees to her chest and trying to quiet the sobs that fought to escape her. If the baby-sitter heard the sounds she might want to call her mother in Las Vegas. And then David would find out. Brandi knew too well what that would mean.

She buried her head in her pillow and wondered why she hadn't said something to her mother sooner. Maybe then the relationship between David and Dorothy never would have gone this far. If only her mother knew how David treated her. Brandi closed her eyes and remembered how it had started.

At first, David was as nice to her as he had been to the boys. He asked her about her schoolwork and how things were going with her friends. But even then she'd had a bad feeling about the man. Something about him seemed plastic, as if everything he said and did was a lie. She didn't trust him and she remembered the first time she'd said so to her mother.

"Mom, is he going to stay around forever?" she had asked Dorothy once when she was barely seven years old. "I don't like him."

Dorothy had sighed in frustration. "Yes, he's staying around, and it's obvious you don't like him," she'd said angrily. "What don't you like about him, anyway? He buys you clothes, keeps us fed, and pays the rent. And I happen to love him."

Brandi had searched for the words to describe what she was feeling. "I don't know, Mom," she'd said finally. "It's like he's phony or something."

"Brandi, the day you start trying to like David is the day you'll be a lot happier around this house, do you understand?"

Brandi had nodded and turned away. She had decided it was a mistake to try to discuss David with her mother. Brandi saw how David treated Dorothy, bringing her flowers and taking her out to dinner and constantly complimenting her on one thing or another. It was a disgusting act as far as Brandi was concerned.

As the years passed, Brandi's dislike for David grew considerably. Still, he never mistreated her until one day when she was nine years old and came home from school to find David home early from work. She had been wearing a new outfit and during recess had ripped a hole in the pants leg. David noticed the rip as soon as she walked in.

"What happened to your pants?" He stood up, anger filling his eyes.

Brandi shrugged slightly and turned away, ignoring his comment.

"Listen, young lady," David said, his voice raised a notch. "When I ask you a question, you answer me."

Brandi sighed sarcastically. "The pants got ripped at recess. Satisfied?"

David stormed across the dining room and grabbed her arm. "Don't be smart with me, Brandi." He lowered his voice and there was a seething anger in his eyes. For the first time since David had moved in with them she was frightened of him. "I might not be your father, but as long as we're living in the same house you're going to respect me. Is that clear?" David might have feared Brandi for her blatant dislike of him. In all his life he had charmed men and women alike into believing his lies. But Brandi seemed immune to the power he held over others. For that reason she threatened his very existence, possibly causing him a great deal of fear.

Despite her fear Brandi could not tolerate the idea of this man demanding her respect. She pulled loose from his grip. "Leave me alone."

"That's it." David came back toward her, yanked her arm and threw her on the floor. "You're the worst spoiled brat I've ever known." He spat the words at her. "You're ugly and you're disgusting. Get out of my sight." Then he pushed her onto her knees and watched as she scrambled to her feet and ran to her bedroom.

For the rest of the afternoon she stayed in her room crying and wondering what was happening to her life. Things had been so much happier when their father had lived with them. Brandi resolved to tell her mother about the incident, but she fell asleep and didn't wake up until her mother walked into her room several hours later.

"David told me you were rude to him," she said, clearly frustrated and tired from a long day's work.

Brandi started to speak, intent on telling her mother how David had grabbed her and threw her down, but Dorothy interrupted her. "Listen, Brandi," she said gently, sitting on the edge of her daughter's bed and gently smoothing back her long hair. "David loves us all. He has made my life wonderful ever since I met him and I'm asking you to please try and get along with him."

"But Mom, he has no right to—"

"Honey, he has the right to discipline you if you're rude to him. He told me the whole story; he feels really bad that you're in here upset with him. But sometimes parents have to show kids they're serious about discipline."

"He's not my parent," Brandi screamed, fresh tears flooding her eyes.

"That's enough, Brandi. I won't have you being rude like that." Dorothy stood up to leave the room. "When you've controlled yourself you're welcome to come out and join the rest of the family."

"He's not part of our family," she shouted again. "I hate him."

Dorothy shook her head and threw her hands in the air, then walked out of Brandi's room and shut the door. Brandi was furious, unable to believe that her mother could have taken David's side. Brandi believed David must have explained how he'd yanked her and thrown her on the floor, and her mother must have thought his actions were justifiable. Because of her youth, she did not consider the idea that David might have lied to her mother and that Dorothy might not ever have known about David's outburst.

After that, the idea that her mother would doubt her stories about David caused her to retreat into her own world. She spent more time in her bedroom and more time at her friends' houses. Perhaps because she was spending less time at home, her attitude toward David and her mother continued to deteriorate. As a result, David's anger toward Brandi increased.

At first the run-ins between David and Brandi took place only once every few months. But by the time Brandi was twelve, David seemed to be angry with Brandi more often.

But each time she felt hurt by David, Brandi would become more withdrawn. Occasionally she would complain that David was hurting her or treating her badly, but Dorothy always heard the incident from David's point of view first, and so believed that Brandi was at fault. Eventually, Brandi stopped looking to her mother for help and began to hide her feelings. That way she would not give David the satisfaction of seeing her in pain or upset.

Until August 11, 1985, the day David and Dorothy got married, Brandi had never considered the idea that her mother might not have known the truth about how David treated her. Being young and full of conflicting emotions, Brandi hadn't considered that maybe David had been lying to Dorothy about Brandi to hide the fact that he was upsetting her.

Now it was too late. Brandi tossed and turned on her bed, still sobbing into her pillow. Even if she told her mother about the harsh way she felt David treated her, Dorothy might only have thought she was grasping at straws to keep David out of their lives and prevent the marriage. Brandi cried harder, because now David's presence was a permanent thing. Gone were her dreams that one day he would leave and they could be a family again.

Fear gripped Brandi that August evening, causing her stomach to twist into knots. There was something wrong with David, something missing from his heart that Brandi couldn't quite define. She knew only that she didn't trust him and that she still believed him to be a phony. She wondered if his job working for the CIA had something to do with her doubting him. Brandi knew very little about the CIA, but she had tried to learn more about it since David told her and her brothers that he had an important and secretive job with the government agency and that he was often in danger. The job required him to keep so many details hidden, and maybe that explained why he came across as deceitful and why his eyes seemed so dark and distrustful.

For the hundredth time Brandi wondered why her mother didn't see those traits in David. And for the hundredth time she wished there was something she could do to call off their wedding.

While Brandi grieved alone in her bedroom, Dorothy and David dressed in their wedding clothes and headed down one of Las Vegas's busy, neon-lit streets to the Candlelight Wedding Chapel.

Dorothy looked like a pretty schoolgirl going to the senior prom. She was dressed in a light-pink layered chiffon dress with burgundy embroidery near the neckline and sleeves that fanned gently above the elbow. Her dress fell from the waist to just above the floor, exposing her white high-heeled shoes and delicate ankles. In her hand she held a single long-stemmed white rose resting in greenery and held together with a white ribbon.

But Dorothy's dress had little to do with her beauty that day. Her green eyes sparkled as they never had in the past and her entire face seemed to light up. Many marriages that have their beginnings in Las Vegas wedding chapels do not last. But people who took the time to watch David and Dorothy that day probably went home feeling very good about the couple's chances.

David, handsome in a fashionable suit and a light-pink tie that matched Dorothy's dress, looked lovingly at Dorothy as he promised to love her faithfully for the rest of his life. And Dorothy's eyes grew damp as she promised the same and the justice pronounced them husband and wife. A picture taken after the ceremony captured perfectly the way David and Dorothy felt about each other.

Dorothy was thrilled to be married to David. In all the time Dorothy had spent considering the merits of marrying him, she had never once thought he might be anyone but who he said he was. She loved him unconditionally and she had nothing but feelings of excitement for their impending married life together. She was sorry that Brandi did not share her excitement, but that was the way teenagers were—difficult and hard to get along with. Dorothy believed Brandi would eventually outgrow her dislike for David as she got older. But that evening, Brandi's attitude was the farthest thing from Dorothy's mind. She gazed into David's dark eyes and kissed him lovingly. At that moment, nothing else mattered but the way David Miller made her feel.

David, for all his deceitful, manipulative ways, was equally excited to be marrying Dorothy. He believed that he was entitled to marry her as long as he kept his married life separate from his single life. What harm could there possibly be in living such a double life, as long as neither one affected the other? He knew that Dorothy would never find out. And by continuing his double life he could continue to prove—if only to himself—that despite the things his father had told him years earlier, he was definitely not average.

In fact, the David Miller who held Dorothy's hand that evening had no problem at all looking at her and promising to love her exclusively. This was the David Miller who came home to Aldea Street after vacations, the David Miller who played with Michael and Tony and treated them like his own sons, the David Miller who slept with Dorothy and showered her with love and affection. This David Miller had every intention of being faithful.

What the other David Miller had planned was something else altogether.

15

In January 1988 an investigation was launched into the financial practices of California Senator Alan Robbins. Nearly three years would pass before Robbins would be indicted and plead guilty to charges of racketeering and extortion. But even as early as the first part of 1988, long before he would be sentenced to prison for misusing funds, Robbins was feeling the heat of the investigation.

At about the same time—for reasons that might have been coincidental—David Miller began spending a significant amount of time in Sacramento working out of Senator Robbins's office. In addition to the hours David spent working from the senator's office, the two were often seen jogging together and sharing quiet business lunches. For the most part, David's peers had no idea why he was spending so much time in the company of the senator. But there were those who speculated that perhaps the many days he spent in Sacramento had something to do with his apparent abundance of money.

Whatever he was doing and whoever was paying him —while spending much of his time in the office of a senator under investigation for criminal activities— David's relationship with Dorothy began to grow strained.

David seemed edgier, anxious to leave on his various missions and more tense around the children. By mid-1988 the affection he had once freely lavished on his wife had diminished. There had even been several occasions when he had snapped at her, something that would have been completely out of character for him during the years before they were married.

When Dorothy asked David about his attitude, he apologized, blaming his nervousness on the severity of the missions he was undertaking. Dorothy had figured as much and tried to be patient. She even worried that David might be in more danger than before, especially after he returned home one evening with an inexplicable bullet hole in his right pants leg and a surface wound where the projectile had scraped his skin.

None of David's political associates or peers in the lobbyist business ever claimed to know why David had been fired at. David would only say he was shot while carrying out a dangerous mission, so certainly Dorothy never knew the truth about the incident. In fact, no one would ever know what really happened to David that evening or what kind of political work he was involved with that might have included the types of shady characters who carry guns and even use them in the course of business.

"David, you could have been killed." Dorothy shuddered at the thought as she dressed his wound. "What's happening out there? You said you were safe."

David winced as she ran a gauze pad over his scraped leg.

"I know, honey. Don't worry. They don't know where we live. It seems someone's upset with me. They must have seen me leaving the office. I'll be more careful in the future." He kissed her forehead as she finished putting the bandage on his wound. "I guess things have gotten a bit more complicated lately."

The idea that his life had grown more complicated in the three years since marrying Dorothy was perhaps the truest thing David ever told his wife. Almost immediately after returning home from their honeymoon, David had begun to feel dissatisfied with his situation. The boys seemed to be always fighting, Brandi complained about everything, and he must have wondered why he had ever wanted to make Dorothy and her children a permanent part of his life. Or at least one of his lives.

Instead of leaving her, he decided to move her. He no longer felt comfortable with his wife and business—and whatever he was doing in Senator Robbins's office—coexisting in the same state.

Betraying what might have been early signs that he was not holding up well under the burden of living a double life, David decided quickly and perhaps irrationally that he wanted Dorothy as far away from California as possible.

So, in November of 1988, David came home from another mission—this time with postcards from Guam—and informed Dorothy that something terrible had happened.

"They know where we live," he said, breathless with concern, his suitcase still in his hand.

"Who does?" Dorothy asked. David was pleased to

hear the fear in her voice. As long as she was afraid, David knew she still believed him.

"The terrorists. The government wants us to leave, take everything and go to Florida."

"Florida?" Dorothy looked utterly confused. She had no friends or relatives in Florida, and leaving would mean she would have to stop working as a beautician and sell her shop. "Why Florida?"

"The CIA has an office there and they want me nearby. There are a lot of problems in Florida right now, drug problems. They need me there."

"Just like that?" Dorothy did not sound pleased with David's news. "We really have to move?"

David nodded. "By the first of December. Our lives are at stake here, Dorothy. You have to trust me on this."

Dorothy could hardly believe what her husband was telling her. This was crazy, leaving the home she'd come to love and uprooting her children because of his work. David knew she was upset.

"Sweetheart, I'm sorry about this," he said, his eyes pleading with her. "But you knew the score when we got married. We don't have any choice. You'll just have to trust me."

Dorothy looked at her husband and wondered how things had gotten so complicated. She knew he was right. She had promised him that she would do whatever was necessary not to interfere with his work. And if they were in danger, then they would have to leave. It was that simple.

"Are you sure we have to go to Florida?"

He nodded again. "They need me there. We need to pack up the house and leave as quickly as possible."

David and Dorothy spent the rest of the evening

working out the details of the move. They would drive across the country, purchase a house in the suburbs of Orlando, and hire movers to pack the house and transport their belongings. The government would take care of selling the house in Granada Hills.

Two days later, their station wagon packed to overflowing with children and toys and suitcases, the Miller family left for Florida. On December 11, 1988, they purchased a home on Jericho Drive in Casselberry, Florida, thirty minutes north of Orlando.

Five days later David left for another mission, and by early 1989 Dorothy realized that David was spending more time away from home than ever before. She was not happy about the turn their lives had taken. She had no friends and her children were angry about leaving their California schools.

That year she might have considered leaving David if it hadn't been for the friendship of Tom and Merritt Foster. The Fosters lived across the street on Jericho Drive and had been the first to welcome them after they purchased their home. That year Dorothy and Merritt became quite close, sharing lunches together and confiding in each other in a way that eased Dorothy's loneliness.

Although there were times when she wanted desperately to share the truth about David's position with the CIA, Dorothy would only say that her husband was a private businessman who was forced to travel extensively to keep up with his clientele. Merritt was empathetic, assuring Dorothy that David would certainly travel less once he became familiar with his new job.

Instead, the well-meaning neighbor couldn't have been farther from the truth. David was traveling more because his business—some three thousand miles away from his new home in Casselberry—was thriving. Therefore, most of his missions lasted more than a month and were a combination of trips back to Los Angeles, where he would spend most of his time in the Granada Hills house on Aldea Street, and trips to Sacramento.

Adding to David's stress was the fact that his busy schedule prevented him from enjoying political vacations. For that reason David was finding it more difficult to meet the women who provided the other David Miller with the excitement he felt he needed. And so David began to date women who worked in the same Granada Hills office building as his. David must have known this was a dangerous move on his part, because those women then knew where he worked. But he had grown addicted to his double life and there was no way he was going to live like a married man, unable to date other women—even if it meant being a bit careless with his secrecy.

Working was one way for David to take his mind off the increasing pressure he was feeling. So David worked day and night finding new clients and pleasing those he'd had for years. As a result, his business flourished and by 1989 he was bringing in three times as much money as he had when he'd first opened his office.

But David faced one problem. He was spending even more time in Sacramento—quite possibly living out a third life from the office of Senator Robbins. Finally, he could no longer handle the pressure and made the decision to hire an associate to share the workload.

He needed someone with connections, but someone who wouldn't ask questions regarding his whereabouts.

After a careful search and several interviews, David hired Grant Hawthorne.

Grant was a tall, debonair man with a football player's physique and many impressive connections in the political arena. He was a graduate of the University of Pennsylvania and had doctoral degrees in political science from California State University at Long Beach and the University of Southern California.

After several years of teaching political science at the collegiate level, Grant had taken a job consulting with one of the major aerospace firms. In the course of his job, Grant was also required to act as a lobbyist for the company. For that reason, he attended many political functions and by 1989 had become acquainted with David as a result.

Grant thought very highly of David Miller, being impressed that he had made a name for himself while working on his own. He thought David was an intelligent and thoughtful man who carefully couched his salesmanship so as not to come across in a distasteful manner. The result was brilliant. David used his abilities to sway even the most stringent politicians on behalf of David's clients. Then, even after falling for David's fast-talking proposals, the politicians usually had nothing but complimentary things to say about him. Grant decided that David carried with him the type of charisma that might one day make him a successful politician.

In fact, in the months before David contacted Grant —in late 1989—Grant had heard certain people discussing the idea of putting David on the city council ballot when the local elections came around again. If that had happened, Grant would not have been surprised if David won. For that matter, it would not have surprised Grant if one day David Miller wound up in Sacramento with the political elite.

Sometime before Christmas, David contacted Grant and offered him a partnership in his business. The offer did not come as a complete surprise. David had mentioned the idea months earlier after Grant had complained that he was looking to get out of the aerospace industry.

"Why don't you come and work for me," David had said casually at a dinner party that summer.

"You're kidding, right?"

"No, I'm serious." David wasn't smiling and Grant raised an eyebrow.

"It's an interesting idea," Grant had said. "Keep me in mind."

After that they had shared the specifics of such a move numerous times over a series of business lunches. Each time they met, Grant became more impressed with David. The man talked about upcoming deals with big-name clients and how much money they would bring in.

Throughout the process in which David groomed Grant for the position, Grant certainly had no reason to doubt him. David never had any shortage of money when they were together. He drove a flashy Jaguar, wore expensive clothes, and always picked up the tab for their fifty-dollar business lunches. When David talked about how the two of them could take his business into the million-dollar income bracket, Grant believed it was entirely possible.

So when David called that December day and offered Grant the job, Grant already knew his decision.

"When do I start?" he asked.

"How soon can you get here?" David answered,

chuckling at Grant's eagerness. "The clients are wait-ing."

David guaranteed Grant six months' pay, during which time he would be required to bring in clients of his own. After that, he would pay Grant ten percent of whatever money was collected from the client and David would keep the rest. David estimated that Grant would be bringing in a six-figure salary by the end of 1990.

Grant had only positive expectations about his new position working with David Miller. But after a few months strange things began to happen that Grant could not explain.

For instance, although David talked about his numerous clients, computer files indicated that many of his "sure deals" had never existed. Because of that, Grant began to calculate the amount of money actually coming in. The figure was frightfully lower than David had talked about and Grant began to wonder if David really could afford having an associate. Worse, he began to suspect David of lying to him.

Each time Grant began to wonder about David's actual financial status, David would do something that would leave Grant totally confused. One month, when the number of jobs had been so few that Grant wondered how they were able to stay in business, David provided California State University at Northridge with a ten-thousand-dollar donation for its school of education. Grant would not have believed David was capable of such a donation had he not been in the office when the school's representative came to pick up the check. Later, he answered the telephone when the woman called to thank them for their donation—so apparently the check had not bounced.

Grant tried to discuss the matter of why David's pending deals had never materialized. But David was evasive, promising that they were in the works and that he was cultivating them each time he took another trip.

"You just keep looking for new clients and work on the accounts I give you and everything will be fine," David said. "Leave the money matters to me."

"That's not good enough, David," Grant would say. "This is my livelihood you're playing with."

"Relax, Grant. I'll come through. I always do."

There were other incidents that caused Grant to grow suspicious. David had no personal pictures on his desk or anywhere in the office and he had made a point of telling Grant that his personal life was not something he discussed. He used a post office box for a mailing address and neither he nor the women who worked the front desk had access to his telephone number.

"What are you trying to hide?" Grant finally asked one afternoon.

"It's not important," David would say before changing the subject. "I'll call in every day, so there won't be any reason for you to contact me."

But one time, a client from northern California needed to speak with David immediately. Lynne, who often arranged David's travel plans as part of her office duties, knew that he was in St. Louis. After calling several of the city's major hotels, she finally located him.

David was furious.

"I don't ever want you to hunt me down again. Is that clear?" He was yelling so loudly that Lynne held the phone away from her ear.

"Yes, Mr. Miller," she said, and Grant wondered if

she was going to break down and cry. "I'm so sorry. Really, I'll never do it again. It's just that—"

"I don't care!" David shouted at her again. "I told you, I'll call in. Next time, tell them they'll have to wait."

Later, Grant asked Lynne if David had always been so particular about keeping his whereabouts a secret.

"I think he's in some kind of trouble," Grant said. "I've been catching him in one lie after another lately."

Lynne shook her head. "I can't understand what's happening to him," she conceded. "It's like he's under some sort of great strain."

Indeed. By May of 1990 David suddenly stopped taking trips to Sacramento to work from Senator Robbins's office. Perhaps the investigation into Robbins's affairs had become so evident that Robbins no longer thought it wise for David to spend so much time in Sacramento. Perhaps, since the investigating committee was now aware of Robbins's practices, there was no longer any work for David to do. Or maybe he and the senator simply had a falling out. Either way, neither man would ever discuss the break in their relationship.

As soon as David stopped spending time with Senator Robbins, an interesting thing happened to his financial situation. It fell apart.

In a matter of weeks, Grant was aware that David was in financial trouble. Grant's office was adjacent to David's and neither man worked with his door closed. For that reason, Grant knew that David was spending a great deal of time contacting banks about loans. Each time he talked to a loan officer he would tell them about various deals that were about to come through and how easily he would be able to repay the money.

They were deals that Grant did not believe existed. When Grant would try to discuss the matter, David would refuse.

Whatever money the banks had loaned David was apparently not enough to help his business. By June 1990 two of Grant's paychecks had bounced. When Grant asked David about the checks, inquiring about the financial status of the business, David suddenly became angry.

"Cash the check now," he yelled, tossing his hands in the air. "We had a little mix-up with the accounts. You got a problem with that?"

"Not as long as you pay me." Grant turned his back and walked into his office. The working relationship he had shared with David had definitely deteriorated in the past weeks.

"Don't worry, you'll get your money," David shouted. "And from now on leave the business matters to me. It's none of your business."

Grant took David at his word and cashed the checks again. Both of them cleared. But Grant no longer believed David's grandiose dreams that the business would materialize. Instead, Grant began to bring in his own clients. Because he had passed the six-month mark he was no longer receiving a paycheck from David. He did quite well by earning a percentage of the money brought in by the numerous clients he'd obtained since working with David. Grant decided he no longer needed David and had made a personal goal of starting his own business sometime during the next year.

If Grant thought David had been acting strangely up until the summer of 1990, he hadn't seen anything yet. The incident that convinced Grant he would not be working for David Miller much longer took place in July.

Apparently, David was having difficulty obtaining loans from local banks, and he contacted a business-woman he'd been dating for a few weeks named Tricia Spencer. Grant had seen her once when she had come to the office to meet David for lunch.

On July 12, 1990, Grant overheard a telephone conversation between David and Tricia during which David began to cry.

"I'm sorry to ask you this," Grant heard David say through his tears. "But I'm absolutely desperate. The chemotherapy is taking everything I have."

With the mention of chemotherapy, Grant sat up straighter at his desk and strained toward his door to hear David's conversation.

"I didn't want to tell you." David sobbed. "Yes, that's right. Cancer. I have maybe a year to live, maybe less."

There was a pause and Grant felt the color draining from his face. David Miller was dying of cancer. No wonder there had been fewer clients lately. If he was terminally ill, that explained his strange actions. Grant waited for David to finish his conversation.

"I know," David said. "You're wonderful for helping me like this." David paused a moment. "Right, don't worry, I'll pay you back as soon as I can. What would I do without you?"

As David finished the conversation, Grant understood what was happening. Because of the cost of chemotherapy, David had grown desperately low on money. Now he was going to borrow some from Tricia until the next client payment came through. But in order to do so, he'd had to be honest with her about his terminal condition.

Grant closed his door quietly. He didn't want David to know that he had heard him talking about the illness. The poor man probably was in denial. Grant decided he would say nothing about the cancer until David was ready to tell him about it himself.

The next day, David walked into the office while Lynne and Cynthia were on their lunch breaks. He was whistling an upbeat tune and carrying a check, which he placed casually on the front desk. Grant looked at him and thought he looked remarkably well for someone so deathly ill.

David walked into his office, closed the door, and picked up his telephone. Grant looked into the reception area and decided he needed to know if the check was from Tricia and how much it was for. He stood up and walked quickly toward the front desk.

Sure enough, it was from Tricia Spencer and it was for $30,500. Grant returned quietly to his desk, his eyes wide in surprise at the amount of the check. When David finished his phone call he stepped into Grant's office.

"I'll be back in a few hours," he said.

Grant nodded, looking intently at David. His black hair was as thick as ever, his eyes were clear and healthy-looking, and he seemed to have as much energy as before. Suddenly Grant wondered if David had been telling Tricia the truth about the cancer.

"How are you, David?" he asked, pronouncing each word slowly, the intensity of the question demanding an honest answer. "Everything okay?"

David shrugged indifferently. "Everything's great."

16

There were two reasons David Miller had been able to live a double life so successfully for so long. The first and most important was his ability and willingness to lie.

David could lie so well that most of the time he believed his lies himself. When he was at home with Dorothy and the children he found himself believing that he was a faithfully married man who spent much of his time on dangerous missions for the CIA.

In fact, over the years he acted as if he enjoyed the idea of working for the CIA. He told Dorothy that he would watch out the plane's window as he was flying over a war-torn country in Central America, thinking about the dangers that awaited him when they landed.

He seemed to see no harm in the idea of pretending. After all, in some ways he really was a secret agent. He actually did live a secret life and carry out transactions that no one knew anything about. In fact, David might have rationalized that he wasn't really lying to Dorothy—just doing his best not to hurt her.

Yes, David's double life was made possible in no small part by his uncanny ability to lie. But it was also possible because he could afford to live two lives. Although some of David's trips were paid for by industries who arranged the vacations for lobbyists and politicians, many of them were paid for from his own funds. Then there were the rented limousines, the double house payments, the flashy business lunches, and the extravagant gifts he lavished on the women he met during his "missions." Certainly none of that would have been possible if David had brought in a merely middle-class income. For that matter, he could not have afforded his lifestyle if he made only the money his business clients brought in.

But after David moved Dorothy to Florida it was suddenly necessary for him to fly across the country several times a month. Worse still, he had to shoulder the added travel expense at a time when his business dealings in Sacramento—whatever they were and whoever was paying him—had begun to taper off.

David probably told himself that he was not worried. Certainly the money would keep coming in and he would be able to continue the double life he thought he deserved. Still, there were moments when David must have begun to suffer the pangs of anxiety. What if the money stopped? What if he told a woman he was heir to a multimillion-dollar fortune and then he couldn't afford the dinner tab? What if someone at the chamber of commerce found out about Dorothy?

There was something else that was beginning to bother David. Since moving Dorothy and the children to Florida, he seemed to have considerably less time for fun. And by August 1989, he was losing ground quickly.

That summer, Brandi was nearly seventeen and she despised David more than ever. Each time he was home between missions he found multiple reasons to argue with her. Sometimes they fought over the clothes she wore, or the friends she spent time with. Other times it was because she came home late or because she'd given her mother a hard time. Brandi believed David hated her and that he was determined to ruin her life. She felt completely hopeless, unable to talk to her mother and afraid of what David might do to her if she did.

Sometimes Brandi would exchange hurtful words with her mother, chastising her for marrying David and ridiculing her for choosing him over her children. Inevitably, such an incident would cause Dorothy to become upset. Then, if David was in town, she would tell him what Brandi had said and David would storm into Brandi's room.

"You will stop being rude to your mother, do you hear me?" he'd shout at her.

David was disgusted by Brandi, who by then had grown into a beautiful young woman. David had ordered Brandi to be home by ten o'clock each night. But many times she ignored him, staying out with her friends until the early morning hours.

With Brandi cowering on the bed in tears, David would think of the boys she was probably sleeping with. In truth, Brandi was still a virgin. But David thought the reason she stayed out late was because she was having sex with anyone who would have her.

"You're nothing but a slut," David would shout at her. "A whore. Good for nothing. You're lucky I don't just kick you out of here for good."

If David had not had so much on his mind—trying

to remember which mission he was supposed to be returning from and wondering how he was going to keep financing his double lifestyle—he might have realized he was being unfair to the girl. But something about her rebellious teenage nature frightened David. Until Brandi, no one had ever doubted David or treated him disrespectfully. Because of that, David was terrified that Brandi might somehow learn the truth about him. She was the only woman in his life upon whom his charismatic charm had absolutely no effect.

In her room, after she had taken the brunt of David's anger, Brandi would write her feelings in her journal. Even if her mother had seen the things Brandi was writing, she probably would not have divorced David or filed charges against him. Dorothy loved Brandi deeply, but when David was home, she was too busy catering to him and enjoying his presence to realize the way her daughter was suffering.

For years David had hid from Dorothy the fact that he often acted out his aggressions on Brandi. But in late August 1989, David stayed home eight days in between missions to Central America. During that time he seemed to be going stir-crazy and he began to discipline Brandi more often than before.

Brandi thought her mother knew that David was being too harsh with her. But she also thought her mother was still very much in love with David, even if Dorothy was unhappy about the number of missions he had taken that year. There seemed always to be tension in the house if Brandi and David were home at the same time. Dorothy seemed to be getting tired of the situation.

The tension continued to build during that eight-day period. On August 31, Brandi and her mother were arguing about David when he walked into the room and exploded in anger. That night, for the first time since David had entered Dorothy's life, he acted his aggression out on his wife.

Brandi wrote about the incident later that night:

"Thursday 8/31/89. I fought with Mom earlier about the usual and David decided he heard enough and started to slap me around. Mom tried to stop him and he slapped her down. I just can't win. I'm scared."

Five days later, she made another journal entry that proved the situation between her and her stepfather was getting worse:

"Monday 9/4/89. I'm so tired. It's only 9:30 and I'm exhausted. Mom wasn't home and I got in an argument with David. As usual I got my ass kicked again. There is a huge bruise on my arm. It hurts so bad. I guess I'll be wearing a long-sleeve shirt again to hide the bruises. I wish I was dead right now. Brandi. 9:47 p.m."

Not long afterward, David returned to Los Angeles, telling Dorothy that he was on a mission to a secret destination and that he might be gone for weeks. He returned in mid-October and the arguing between him and Brandi began again immediately.

On October 18, the incident between Brandi and David was so severe, Brandi began to fear that he might kill her.

"10/18/89. I'm so confused. I think I might need real help. My grades are down (most of them). I wish I could talk to my mom and just tell her the way I really feel, how I don't care about my life anymore and how scared I am of David. She would probably turn it all around and start a fight. God, I'm so scared. I'm terrified that one time David will hurt me really bad or even kill me if he gets mad enough. This sucks. I can't even talk to my own mother. I don't know what to do. I'm so scared. I feel like my heart is stopping. I'm just dying inside. Eventually I'm going to have to talk to her. I'm just scared. I thought about writing her a letter but the same thing would happen. She doesn't understand what's happening to me and what David is doing to me. God, I'm so scared. Why, David? Brandi. 9:58 p.m."

Later that night she added this entry:

"Me and mom got in a fight and David stepped in. He beat me up once again. I hate him so much. I swear if he ever touches me again I'll kill him. Maybe Mom will listen to me then. Maybe. I can't wait to get out of here. Brandi. 11:15 p.m."

During that time, Brandi filed at least two written complaints with the State of Florida Department of Health and Rehabilitative Services charging David with child abuse. Both times, a caseworker was assigned to investigate the charges and both times the director of Florida's Protective Services System classified Brandi's complaints as unfounded, stating that there was no indication of abuse or neglect.

Dorothy was horrified that Brandi had accused

David of child abuse. She was aware of David's temper, and she had discussed it with him the evening when he had pushed her onto the floor. But David was under a lot of stress. If Brandi had been a bit more understanding and less argumentative, David would not be forced to discipline her. But even when he did, Dorothy would never believe he was actually abusing Brandi. Especially after the state investigation decided there was no evidence to support Brandi's complaints.

Distraught that no one would believe her about the way she felt David was treating her, Brandi began formulating a plan to leave Florida and return to California where she could meet up with her father, Archie, and live with him. She knew her mother would not agree to the plan, so Brandi decided to run away without telling anyone where she was going.

She began saving money from her part-time job at a Texaco gas station to pay for the flight. By the end of February 1990 she had nearly three hundred dollars and she purchased a one-way ticket to Los Angeles.

On March 1, with less than twenty dollars in her purse, Brandi left home telling Dorothy that she was going to work and wouldn't be back until later that evening. Instead, she met up with a friend who gave her a ride to the Orlando Airport. An hour later she boarded a plane headed for Los Angeles.

When Dorothy realized that Brandi had run away, she was terrified. First Brandi had accused David of child abuse, and then she had run away from home. Dorothy wondered how her only daughter had become such an unhappy teenager and why she would have run away. For one of the few times in their relationship, Dorothy lashed out at David.

"This is all your fault." Dorothy sobbed that evening

when David returned home. "I might never see her again because of you. Why couldn't you have tried to be nice to her?"

David was ready for Dorothy's outburst. He looked at her calmly and spoke in a condescending manner.

"It's not my fault any more than it's your fault, sweetheart," he said, putting a hand on her shoulder. "Brandi is a rebellious teenager, determined to do things her way. You know she's been hanging out with the wrong crowd. You've seen the way they look when they come by the house. Red eyes and long hair. For all we know she's probably into drugs, just like the rest of them."

Dorothy shook her head angrily. "That's no reason to be mean to her," she said, pleading with him through tears. "I want her back home, David. She's my daughter. Get her back here for me. Please."

Although he had no interest in retrieving Brandi from wherever she'd run to, David was willing to do it for Dorothy. Not because of his undying love for her, but because he was afraid she might always blame him for Brandi's disappearance. If she did, then their marriage would never last. If Dorothy left him, David's double life would be over. By then, the effects of living as two different David Millers were so intoxicating, he probably could not have imagined giving them up. He would have to stay married to Dorothy. And so he would have to make her happy.

"Okay, honey," he told Dorothy, pulling her close. "I'll get her back. Don't worry."

After that, David contacted Brandi's local friends and finally located her at a friend's house in Los Angeles. During the next week David flew to California intent on bringing Brandi home. But by then Brandi's father had picked her up from her friend's house and listened to Brandi's stories about David's physical anger. Through a series of telephone calls with Dorothy and David, and after receiving the evaluation of a psychiatrist, it was agreed that Brandi would be better off living with her father.

Although Dorothy knew she would miss Brandi, she eventually accepted the idea that some time apart from each other would be the best thing for all of them. Besides, with Brandi gone she and David would have a chance to renew their relationship.

After David returned home from Los Angeles, the couple shared a relaxing, romantic evening for the first time in months. The boys, now twelve and eleven, were at friends' houses and David did not show a trace of the anger and frustration he'd experienced in the time before Brandi had run away.

Demonstrating a knack for continually complicating his double life further, David asked Dorothy something that evening that he'd apparently been thinking about for some time.

"Sweetheart, what do you think about me adopting the boys legally?" He looked hopefully at Dorothy, waiting for her response.

Dorothy was amazed that the man sitting before her was the same person who had been so rough with Brandi. Yet, who could blame him for not getting along with a teenage girl who was constantly rude? After all, he was the one who had gone across the country looking for her when she disappeared.

He really was a wonderful man, she thought as she looked at him that evening. He had always been exceptionally close with the boys, especially since they had been so young when she and David began living together. David loved them like his own sons and she felt a rush of love for him now that he wanted to make his relationship with them legitimate.

"Do you really want to do that? Adopt them?" Dorothy asked kindly. "It's a big responsibility, you know. You'd be legally responsible for them just like they were your own sons."

David nodded, his eyes misty. "I know, honey. But I love those boys. And they love me. I want everyone to know that I'm their father."

That night David and Dorothy agreed to look into the process by which David could legally adopt the boys. But they were stopped short early on when Archie, who saw the boys infrequently because of the distance between them, refused to give up his rights.

Two weeks later, with David home for a few days between missions, Dorothy invited their neighbors, Tom and Merritt Foster, over for dinner. The Fosters did not know about the problems between Brandi and David, only that Brandi had left Florida to go live with her father.

After dinner, the couples were discussing the coming fall and conversation turned to the failed adoption efforts. When it did, David began to cry.

"I've taken those boys with me on our vacations, I've laughed and played with them and tucked them in at night as often as I could." David's voice cracked with emotion.

The Fosters sat in uncomfortable silence as David slouched over, his head in his hands and his shoulders shaking with every sob. "I love those boys," he cried softly. "They should be mine."

Everyone in the room was touched by the scene, sorrowful for the devastation David seemed to be feeling over not being able to adopt Michael and Tony.

Later that evening, when they were back at home, Merritt remarked to her husband about David's breakdown.

"He sure does love those boys," she said, thinking back to David's tears. "I've never seen him so upset."

Tom shook his head. "Darn shame, I say. Those children would be lucky to have David as their legal father. There aren't many guys as good as David Miller. Good provider, good husband. He's just a good guy, you know what I mean?"

Merritt nodded. "Yeah. Maybe someday they'll try the adoption thing again."

Over the next few months, David traveled more than ever, taking trips mostly to Los Angeles. By then, his business was in dire financial straits and he was doing everything he could think of to bring in extra money.

He was dating several Los Angeles women who made quite a bit of money, but he did not want to borrow from them for fear they would question his status as a businessman. But by July he had devised a plan to ask them for money without changing the way they thought of him. He decided the plan was nearly flawless.

He would tell the women and whoever else he wanted to borrow money from that he was dying of cancer. Of course, in truth he was perfectly healthy. But David decided that he could look healthy and still be dying of cancer. Especially if he was able to accompany his admission about his illness with tears. David had long since learned that people inevitably believed whatever he was saying if while saying it he could break down and cry.

During that month and the next, he borrowed money from several people, including Tricia Spencer and another woman who worked in an office near his. Her name was Tambi Mariano and she ran her own law firm in Granada Hills.

There was something about Tambi that was different from the women he typically dated and then discarded. David found Tambi more challenging, more difficult to convince. And so, ever since their first date several months earlier, he had told her even more outlandish stories than any of the other women.

For instance, he told her that he was the partial owner of a multimillion-dollar luxury housing development. Once, after a lunch date with Tambi, he even took her by the construction site and explained the progress of the construction and the plans he had for the money once the homes were sold.

Perhaps because he seemed to have plenty of money or perhaps because she had seen the construction site in person, Tambi believed him. She was only in her late twenties and determined not to become serious with anyone until her law practice became established. For that reason she dated David only once in a while, enjoying his company and pleased that he did not seem interested in a long-term relationship.

But when David asked her for money that summer and told her he was dying of cancer, her heart went out to him. She was stricken by the thought of losing him and suddenly she wondered if she had fallen in love with the man. She told David she would loan him money, confident that he could repay her once he began selling the homes he owned nearby.

Then, after giving him a significant piece of her savings account, Tambi began seeing David more regu-

larly. They shared a desperate sort of love that intensi-
fied in the shadow of his terminal illness. Finally, one
day David took her hand in his after a dinner date and
proposed to her.

"I'm falling in love with you," David started, tears
building up in the corners of his eyes. "I know I don't
have long to live, but there's always a chance a miracle
might happen. Anyway, I want to marry you, live with
you as your husband even if we only have one year
together."

He produced a stunning diamond ring and put it on
her finger. "David, I don't know what to say," Tambi
said, shaking her head and crying unashamedly. "I
love you too. I'm not afraid of your cancer. I want to
spend whatever time we can together."

They discussed the idea of getting married quickly
and quietly, perhaps somewhere like Las Vegas. That
night when he dropped her off at her condominium,
David kissed her softly. "I can't wait to make you my
wife, Tambi," he told her. "Call me in the morning."

And so, for that evening, David Miller—husband of
Dorothy Miller and a man thought by his neighbors to
be the quintessential family man—found himself en-
gaged to be married to Tambi Mariano.

At that point, David must have begun to wonder
what he had done. He was married to Dorothy. But
that was only one David Miller, he probably told himself. Wasn't the other David Miller perfectly free to do
as he pleased? Couldn't he marry this woman too?

It was at this time that David, in all his self-centered-
ness, seemed to begin to forget what it was to live by
the same moral codes as other individuals. If there is
indeed for most people a line between right and
wrong, David had long since crossed it and was begin-

ning to lose sight of it altogether. Still, with perhaps little more than a thread of a conscience left, David suddenly decided that night that he could not marry Tambi after all.

In all likelihood, his decision to call off the wedding that would have made him a bigamist was based more on the fact that by having two wives he would no longer have time to live his bachelor life. Because even a lying, conniving man like David Miller would certainly not have time to live three separate lives.

The next day he broke off the engagement with Tambi, telling her that he wanted to wait a year and see how his illness progressed. It was too selfish to marry her now, he told her, allowing her to cry on his shoulder as she took off the ring and returned it to him.

"No, you keep it," David said, placing it back in her hand. "It wouldn't be fair to marry you in my condition. But I want you to always have the ring. That way, even after I'm gone, you'll never forget me."

Four hours later he was heading back to Dorothy on a plane bound for Florida.

17

On the morning of November 16, 1990, San Fernando Valley businessman Ed Cholakian looked at his crowded calendar and sighed. That was the morning David Miller was scheduled to come in. Ed Cholakian was not a dim-witted man and he had not become one of the most well-known and highly respected community leaders by underestimating people. In fact, if ever there were someone who David felt uncomfortable lying to, it would have been Ed Cholakian.

Ed knew why David wanted to see him that November morning. The man needed cash. The same reason David had made an appointment with him four months earlier in July. That time Ed had listened to David talk about deals he was waiting to collect on and business contracts in the works. David had rambled on about his potential value until finally Ed waved him aside impatiently.

"I don't need a lot of explanations, David," Ed had said, pulling out a checkbook. "I'll loan you the money and you'll pay it back. And everything will work out just fine, understand?''

David had nodded, refraining from further assuring the man that he was capable of repaying the loan. He walked away from Ed's office with a check for $9,800 and three days later he was back for more.

Ed knew David from their involvement in the chamber of commerce, and during those appointments in July he believed David had merely run into a financial stumbling block. What he didn't know was that David had stopped spending time in Sacramento and that he had taken a significant cut in his income. So on that day, he had written David a check for $5,827.

Three weeks later, David repaid the money in full. Nevertheless, Ed had begun to wonder about David's financial status. He had been seen less often at local chamber meetings and a nervousness seemed to have replaced his cool, confident manner. Ed was beginning to wonder if David might be in worse trouble financially than he was letting on.

So on that November morning, certain that David was about to ask for more money, Ed decided ahead of time that he would most likely turn him down.

When David arrived an hour later, Ed was sitting behind his oak desk in the corner of his office, an imposing figure of local power with seventy-seven framed commendations filling the paneled walls behind him. Ed had been recognized for his community efforts by everyone from local assemblymen to President Reagan.

David gulped quickly and moved to the seat in front of Ed's desk. But before either man could say anything David began to cry.

Of all the things Ed was expecting David to say or do

that morning, he never thought he would see the man cry. Normally David was a man loaded with charisma. He had the acceptance and approval of his peers and he rubbed elbows with politicians on a regular basis. Ed could not imagine what had caused this man to enter his office during business hours and break down in tears.

When David had composed himself, he looked up at Ed through bloodshot eyes.

"I'm sorry, Ed," he mumbled. "I don't know what to say."

Ed moved slightly in his chair, uncomfortable with the scene. "What seems to be the problem?"

David wiped away the tears that continued to flow from his eyes. "I've just come from the hospital. Got some test results."

David looked away again and paused a moment. Suddenly he turned back toward Ed. "I'm dying, Ed," he said, his voice little more than a whisper. "I have cancer."

Ed was completely taken aback. It was one thing for David to burst into tears first thing in the morning during a business appointment. But Ed had never considered that the man might be dying.

A minute passed slowly while David continued to sob. Uncomfortable about what to say, Ed waited for David to talk. Finally David drew in a deep breath.

"I knew I was sick, that I had cancer," he said, shaking his head and staring vacantly ahead of him. "But now they tell me I'm actually dying." David looked up and Ed could see he was angry. "I can't believe it, Ed. This is the kind of thing that happens to other people."

Ed adjusted himself again, trying to imagine why, in

light of his illness, David had wanted to meet that morning. "How long have you known?" he asked politely.

"Three months. I've been getting chemotherapy for the past eight weeks but now they're saying it isn't working. They've given me a year."

"I'm sorry to hear that," Ed said. He was anxious to learn why David had come to see him, anxious to end the meeting so David could grieve in privacy. "Is there any way I can help?"

David sighed. "Well, actually there is." He paused a moment. "I hate even to ask you. See, the chemo has taken all my savings. I just need something to help me make it to the end of the month."

So David did want to borrow money. Ed felt his defenses disappear. If David was dying and needed help, he'd do whatever he could to assist him. But they would still need to determine a plan for David to pay back the money.

Before Ed could respond, David continued.

"I'm expecting some big money in the next few weeks, so there won't be any trouble paying you back." David sounded defeated, ashamed at having to borrow money and devastated by his disease. "If those deals fall through there are the paintings in my office. Worth thousands. You can have 'em if something happens and I can't pay you back."

Ed thought about what David had said and began to write out a loan agreement. If David was terminally ill, there might be other costs in the next few months that would take away from his ability to pay back the loan. In that case, Ed wouldn't mind taking the artwork in David's office. Carefully, he included a clause stating that the artwork was to be his if David defaulted. He would collect the paintings only as a last resort, but Ed knew from past business dealings that unless something was in writing it would be nearly impossible to prove.

"How much do you need?" Ed looked up, his checkbook open, poised to fill in the amount.

"Well, I really need about ten thousand." Concern crossed David's face as he watched Ed's reaction.

"That much?" Ed wondered if it was only chemotherapy that had placed David in such a financial bind.

David nodded and explained to Ed how he planned to spend the money and how badly he needed it. Occasionally, during his explanation, David would pause a moment and wipe the tears that continued to slide down his face.

Ed thought the whole scene rather pathetic. Suddenly he cut David short.

"Okay, okay," Ed said, filling in the amount on the check and handing it to David. "Give me a call when you get the money." Ed thought of something else. "Hey, David, do me a favor."

Ed had recently acquired a travel agency, which he was running out of his office. "You still do a lot of traveling?"

David nodded. "I'm going to keep working as long as I can," he said, managing a smile on his tear-swollen face. "When I work, I travel."

"That's what I thought. Hey, why don't you make your travel plans through me next time."

Some people might not be willing to ask such a question of a grief-stricken man. But Ed had not built his baseball cap-making business into a national success by missing opportunities. He could see no reason to miss this one.

"Sure thing." David nodded quickly. "Definitely."

Ed smiled. "Thanks. Oh, and mention the agency to the other lobbyists, will you?"

"You bet, Ed." He stood up and shook Ed's hand. "Thanks again for the loan. I'll get it back to you soon as I can."

Ed nodded somberly. "Hey, I'm real sorry about your health."

David gazed down at the floor, fresh tears springing to his eyes. "Well, there's always that one-in-a-million miracle. Can't give up hope."

After that, David left Ed's office and headed out to his Jaguar. He looked at his watch and realized he was running late. He had to collect several more loans before the day was through.

The next day, nearly fifty thousand dollars richer, David picked up the telephone and booked a flight for the Bahamas. His plans were made through his usual agency, his promise to Ed Cholakian long since forgotten.

The trip would give him a chance to collect his thoughts and straighten out the compartments of his two lives. There must have been times when David had trouble remembering who thought he was dying of cancer and who thought he was in perfect health. He must have wondered sometimes if his lives were perhaps beginning to get too complicated. But everything was going to be just fine, David probably told himself. A vacation in the Bahamas would be just what he needed.

He thought about Dorothy and congratulated himself for lying successfully to her all these years. A lesser man, a more average man, might have broken down under the pressure of such falsehoods and told her the truth. But David had not once lost sleep over the lies he told Dorothy. She would never find out, and if she did, what reason would she have for being angry with him? Hadn't he been kind to her, loved her and her children and paid their expenses? Who could blame him for telling a few lies? David knew there was no other way to live two lives at once. After all he did for Dorothy, he believed he deserved his life outside the home they shared.

Three weeks later, David arrived back in Casselberry suntanned and full of presents for Dorothy and the boys. There were T-shirts and hats and assorted trinkets that he'd found along the beaches of the Bahamas. As he sorted through the souvenirs David must have remembered the days he'd spent with a beautiful island girl and how she'd helped him forget the troubling details of his double life.

"But I thought you were in Kuwait," Dorothy said absently, too thrilled that her husband was home safely for the holidays to really care where he had been.

"I was. But I've been a few places lately, honey," David said proudly. "I wish I could tell you the things I've been doing for the government."

"Is it still dangerous?" Dorothy looked up from her stack of presents, worry clouding her face.

David nodded. "I wish I could tell you more, but you'll just have to trust me. It's a matter of life and death."

Dorothy understood. After all, they'd been living this way for such a long time that she had almost grown used to the idea of worrying about her husband's safety. His dangerous job was a part of their lives.

As they prepared for Christmas that week, Dorothy and David had their neighbors, the Fosters, over for dinner and homemade cookies. Tom and Merritt stayed late into the evening laughing and sharing warm eggnog with the Millers.

Merritt was privately very happy for Dorothy that her husband would be home for the holidays. Poor Dorothy was lonely so much of the time, waiting for her husband to return from his business trips.

That evening Merritt watched the way David doted on Dorothy, waiting on her and holding her hand as if they were newlyweds. Merritt's heart was warmed by the scene. David loved Dorothy the way a husband was supposed to love his wife.

Over the next few days, David and Dorothy seemed to be happier than ever. They bought presents for the boys and each other and seemed to have caught the Christmas spirit completely. Merritt decided that whatever the New Year brought, whatever amount of travel David would be involved in, nothing would erase the happy memories the couple would have of that Christmas of 1990.

18

Early in the morning of New Year's Day, 1991, David Miller drove to the airport in Orlando and boarded a plane back to Los Angeles. He had shared a wonderful Christmas with Dorothy and the boys and he felt refreshed, ready to take on the financial challenges that awaited him in Los Angeles.

Because of the numerous loans he'd received from Ed Cholakian and the others, he'd been able to be generous with his gift-giving and still manage to save more than ten thousand dollars. He knew it was time to drum up new contracts by putting more time into his lobbying business. But in the meantime he did not see why he should have to change his style of living. So what if he'd had to borrow a few thousand dollars? He would repay the money. Now that he wasn't spending nearly as much time in Sacramento, and no time at all in Senator Robbins's office, David believed that getting his business to be lucrative once again was merely a matter of devoting time to it.

As he boarded the plane that morning he may have

been thinking about how well he and Dorothy had gotten along during the holidays and how much fun they'd shared. She was a wonderful woman, and he must have been deeply pleased that he had continued the relationship despite the time months earlier when his double life had seemed too complicated.

Now that he had seen how easily he could borrow money from the gullible people around him, David was no longer worried about the financial trouble he faced. Without the pressure of worrying about money, he was once again excited about having a secret wife in Florida. She did not know about his life as a lobbyist and his political peers did not know about her. The thrill of his situation probably made him smile. A lesser man could never pull off the double life he'd been living these past eleven years.

He found his seat and stretched out his legs. He hoped the new year held as many exciting challenges as the previous one. As in years past, he had no intention of telling Dorothy the truth. She thought he was headed for the Middle East to carry out secret missions regarding Operation Desert Storm.

Only a few months earlier, the United States had given Iraq a deadline to pull out of neighboring Kuwait. Operation Desert Shield was something that David immediately used to his advantage.

For the past year he'd been telling Dorothy that his increased travel was the result of additional secret CIA missions needed by the government.

"Dorothy, something big is going on, but you're just going to have to trust me," he'd tell her each time the subject of his travel came up.

When Desert Storm became a reality, David's talk of

something big happening with the government appeared to be true.

"See, honey," David told her once President George Bush had sent troops overseas. "I've been working on this a long time, but there was no way I could tell you."

Before he left home that New Year's morning, he kissed her softly on the lips.

"Sweetheart, you know the situation," he said somberly. "It's a dangerous place."

Dorothy nodded, tears in her eyes. "Please stay safe, David," she whispered. "I'll miss you so much." She hugged him tightly. "Do you think the war will last much longer?"

David smiled bravely. "Not if I can help it. I'll be in touch as soon as I can."

Now, hours later, his wedding ring packed away in one of his suitcases, David leaned back in his airline seat and closed his eyes. Among the many things he may have been thinking about were the clients he would be contacting upon arriving in Los Angeles, and his broken relationship with Tambi.

Suddenly his thoughts were interrupted by a woman's voice.

"Excuse me, I think you're in my seat," the woman said softly, tapping David on the shoulder. She was afraid that he might have been sleeping.

David jumped and glanced at the ticket in his pocket. The woman was right. He slipped into the seat closest to the window and moved his briefcase so the woman could sit down.

As he moved, he caught a whiff of the woman's perfume and suddenly caught himself staring at her. She appeared to be in her late twenties or early thirties, a little over five feet tall with a well-proportioned figure.

David looked appreciatively at her, noticing her deep brown eyes, tanned skin, and bleached blond hair. The woman was a knockout and David was completely taken in by her as she arranged her belongings and tried to get comfortable before the plane took off.

When she was finally situated, she turned to David. "Hi, I'm Jayne." She flashed her warm smile again and David felt his heart melting inside him. He noticed her designer tweed slacks and fashionable suede and silk blouse. She was obviously a businesswoman and David wondered if she worked in Florida or Los Angeles.

He cleared his throat, and using his most dignified and confidant tone of voice, introduced himself.

"I'm David Miller," he said. "Looks like we're about to spend New Year's Day together." David hoped to learn something more about the woman beside him, but he felt like a schoolboy experiencing his first crush.

When she didn't say anything, he broke the silence again. "I have to get back to my law practice, what's your excuse?"

"Same as yours," she admitted. "Back to work, I'm afraid."

David raised an eyebrow casually. "You work in Los Angeles?"

Jayne nodded. "I'm a purchaser. Just came back home for the holidays. You know, visiting Mom and Dad and all."

"I will say this for Florida, it's not a bad place to spend the holidays," David said. "I was out visiting my sister; she owns a dress shop in Orlando. Even in L.A. you don't have sunshine and temperatures in the eighties."

"Of course, you don't have humidity in Los Angeles, either," she said, and again David found himself drawn to her. "I think I'll stay in L.A.," she said, a mischievous look in her eyes. "You can have Florida with its thunderstorms and insects."

Only Dorothy had ever had the kind of instantaneous hold over him as this woman now had. He seemed to be completely taken with her. She was beautiful, but so were most of the women he spent time with. There was something different about this woman and it no doubt had something to do with the way she dressed and the self-assuredness she obviously possessed.

Dorothy had looked this way that first afternoon behind the desk of her beauty salon. She'd had the same air of challenge about her, as if she were not waiting for just any man. Dorothy had been different, special. And now Jayne seemed the same way.

David watched as she took out a magazine from her carry-on bag and began casually flipping through the pages.

Maybe Jayne was trying to give him a hint. She probably had better things to do than talk with him the entire distance between Orlando and Los Angeles. He racked his brain to think of something else to say. But just then she looked up from her magazine.

"What kind of work do you do in Los Angeles?" she asked.

David guessed that she was probably just trying to be polite by asking. Desperate to capture her attention and admiration, David searched frantically through the recesses of his mind to think of something to tell her.

"Well." He chuckled lightly. "I'm an attorney, but it's kind of a long story." He glanced at Jayne, hoping she was interested enough to keep listening and trying to create a story that she would believe.

She shrugged her slender shoulders in a way that David found completely irresistible. "Well, I'm not going anywhere, so I just might have the time to listen," she said, closing her magazine and turning slightly so as to give her full attention to David. He was nice-looking, although she didn't really think he was handsome. Certainly not the type of man who usually turned her head. But there was something about this man that made her want to know more about him. He seemed very intelligent and he handled himself like someone who had lived his life among the socially elite.

David took a deep breath before beginning. In less than a minute he had contrived a plausible story that was bound to get the woman's interest.

"See, it started about four years ago," he said, pausing to be sure he had her attention. "I was an attorney, had been for years. Then in 1986 I found out about the inheritance."

"The inheritance?"

David nodded, feigning embarrassment. "Seems my father had made much more money in his business than I ever knew about. He passed on suddenly about four years ago and his attorneys informed me I was heir to fourteen million dollars."

Jayne's brown eyes widened considerably. David may have silently found it humorous that she was now caught between wanting to comment on the fourteen million dollars and feeling sorry that David's father had died. Best of all, though, he could tell she was believing his story.

"Anyway, about the time I found out about the money, I started having these sharp pains in my side. I went to the doctor and found out I had a cancerous tumor in my pancreas," David said.

"That's terrible."

David paused a moment for effect. "The doctors told me I had only a year or so to live," he said. "So what do I do? Quit my job, travel the world, and blow my inheritance."

"You spent fourteen million dollars in one year?" Jayne sounded incredulous.

"No, I spent ten million," he said somberly. "I'm not proud of that fact, but I wasn't thinking like myself. I never dreamed I would die in the prime of my life and when they told me I had no chance to survive I just took the money and went crazy."

David paused and closed his eyes a moment. When he opened them again they were filled with tears. Impulsively, Jayne reached out her hand and set it on his knee.

"Are you okay?" She looked worried about him.

David nodded. "Sorry," he said, wiping his tears and shaking his head in embarrassment. "It's just, I've never shared this with anyone else."

Jayne nodded in understanding as David continued. "Anyway, after a year, doctors began telling me I was showing signs of remission. The cancer was disappearing from my body. They asked me to participate in this experimental program, and last year I got word that the cancer was gone for good." David smiled proudly, new tears spilling from his eyes. "That was the happiest moment of my life."

"I can imagine," Jayne said softly, her hand still on his knee.

"So, when I found out I was going to live, I invested the remaining four million dollars and returned to my job as an attorney. I've been doing that for the past six months."

Jayne was amazed by the man's story. "The cancer is completely gone?" she asked in as sensitive a voice as she could manage.

David nodded. "The doctors say I've never been healthier."

"That's an incredible story, David. You've really been given a second chance at life."

"That's how I feel. I have friends who can't understand why I would want to go back to work as an attorney if I've got four million in the bank," he said. "But I know how quickly that money can disappear. I'm saving it for something special."

Suddenly Jayne realized she hadn't even asked the man if he was single or not. She glanced at his left hand and saw that he did not wear a wedding ring. Still, Jayne thought she was better off presuming he was married.

"What did your wife think of all this?" she asked.

"I haven't been married for years now. Way back when I was still a very young man I married my college sweetheart. We were divorced a few years after I finished law school," David said. "I'm forty and I've been single for nearly fifteen years."

Jayne looked puzzled. The man was kind and sensitive, if not stunning-looking. And he was, after all, a millionaire. She figured David must have intended to stay single or he would have long since settled down.

David looked intently at her, trying to read her thoughts. "It's not that I don't want to be married; I do," he said softly, wanting to dispel any thoughts she might be developing about his inability to settle down. "I just haven't found the right person."

Jayne nodded thoughtfully and withdrew her hand from his knee. "I know what you mean. I've been married twice, and neither man was the right person. Sometimes I tell myself that there's something wrong with me, that maybe there isn't a 'right person' out there for me.''

"Oh, come on," David said. "Don't be so hard on yourself. A beautiful girl like you? You must have men dropping at your feet all the time. How old are you, anyway?''

"Thirty-three."

"See, you have plenty of time," he said while looking meaningfully into her eyes. "Besides, you never know when you'll meet the right person. Sometimes that kind of thing happens when you least expect it.''

Jayne blushed. She could read between the lines of David's comments and she had been thinking the same thing. They were both single, they worked near each other, and they were getting along as if they'd been friends for years. But more importantly, there was a chemistry between them, something that made her wonder what it would be like to dance in his arms or share a romantic dinner with him near the beach somewhere.

Jayne wondered if she might be losing her mind. Never had she been so taken with a man in such a short amount of time. But one idea kept replaying in her mind. *Sometimes two people find each other when they least expect it.* As the plane took them closer to Los Angeles, she and David kept talking and Jayne wondered if this might perhaps be the luckiest day of her life.

Five hours flew by and suddenly they were only fifteen minutes away from Los Angeles International Airport. David shook his head in amazement.

"I feel like I've known you all my life, Jayne," he said quietly, taking her hand in his. "I've shared things with you I haven't shared with anyone. It's like you can see right into my soul."

Jayne nodded, not doubting any aspect of the man she'd shared the past five hours with.

"Go to dinner with me tonight?" David's eyes pleaded with hers, terrified that she would say no and that he'd never see her again. He didn't even know her last name or the company she worked for.

But he need not have worried. Jayne was thrilled with his invitation and giggled impulsively upon his request. "I was hoping you'd ask," she said. "Where should we go?"

19

By the time she met David Miller, Jayne Leebrick had experienced a considerable amount of heartbreak in her adult years.

Born on March 4, 1958, in Fort Bellworth, Virginia, Jayne had had a happy childhood. She and her sisters and brother were raised by parents who doted on them, and Jayne grew up feeling good about herself.

But in 1975, when Jayne was merely seventeen years old, she became involved with a boy named Jake who she'd met at school. The relationship worried her parents, who knew that Jayne's head was filled with romantic notions and that she thought of her boyfriend as something of a Prince Charming. Several times they suggested she spend more time at home and not be so serious with Jake.

But Jayne was a beautiful girl with honey-blond hair and soft, deerlike brown eyes who had been warding off boys since she'd turned thirteen. Now, at seventeen, she felt old enough to make her own decisions.

She was in love with Jake and she would see to it that no one got in their way.

For his part, Jake was every bit as in love with Jayne. He was tall and athletically built with wavy brown hair and clear blue eyes and could easily have dated any girl at Central High. But he wanted only to be with Jayne, and the two of them began spending many of their evenings at his house watching movies and making out.

Sometimes at night, after coming home from his house, she would confide in her parents how deeply she loved him and how they had their futures planned out. They would graduate from high school, get married, and go to college together before starting a family. Jayne began looking at bridal magazines and dreaming of her wedding gown.

Despite their feelings for each other and the fact that their relationship had gotten very physical, both of them were shocked when Jayne became pregnant. Later that year, after graduating from high school, Jayne gave birth to a son, Dillon. Jayne loved the tiny child and never considered giving him up for adoption. She and Jake married, but the plans they had for their future seemed to slowly slip through their fingers.

Over the next eight years Jayne divorced Jake, married again, and was once again divorced. She began new relationships full of hope for the future. But each time, the men she had married would let her down.

The lesson she seemed to be learning was that men could not be counted on. But Jayne was not like some women who after a series of bad relationships grow bitter and disillusioned with the idea of love. She continued to hope, with the thought that one day she would meet a man who would bare his soul the way she had done in the past with Jake. When she finally met that man, Jayne believed, he would be the kind of man she would feel as if she'd known all her life.

By 1984 Jayne was twenty-six, had earned her bachelor's degree from the University of Florida, and was once again single. She decided it was time to begin her career and she left her family—which by then had settled in Sanford, near Orlando—and moved to Los Angeles to take a job as a purchaser. Her son was nine years old by then and wanted to live with his father. Jayne decided the timing was right and that Dillon needed to spend some time with Jake for a while. So she packed his things and after a tearful good-bye sent him to his father's house in Orange Park.

Compared with Sanford, Jayne found Los Angeles both impersonal and overcrowded. She was homesick for her parents and her son and she spent many evenings wondering how she would get through another day of loneliness.

But her outlook changed almost as soon as she met Jodee Bowen. Like Jayne, Jodee was outgoing and willing to share her feelings. From the first few times they spoke together at work Jayne and Jodee knew they had found a special friend in each other.

Not long afterward, Jayne and Jodee rented an apartment together and Jayne felt as if her new best friend was her family away from home. They laughed together and cried together and often stayed up late into the night dreaming of their futures and what exciting things they might hold. That summer Dillon came to Los Angeles and spent his entire three-month vacation with her. Before he returned to Florida, he promised that as long as she lived there he would spend his summers with her. Jayne was pleased to see that he was enjoying living with his father and the influence Jake was having on him.

As the next six years slipped away, Jayne grew successful by every one of her measurable standards, save one. She had advanced in her career and was respected by her peers, and she was earning $65,000 a year before bonuses. But the man she still dreamed of, the man who would see straight into her heart and sweep her off her feet, had not yet materialized.

Jayne had grown into a beautiful woman, her brown eyes lively and filled with warmth and her skin boasting a rich tan through most of the year. In the course of her purchasing work she had the opportunity to meet dozens of men each week and she never had any shortage of invitations.

But each time Jayne agreed to a date, she inevitably came home disappointed. Sometimes the men she dated did little more than sit across from her and listen to her talk. Other times they spent the entire evening talking about themselves and seemed uninterested in who she was. She began to wonder if there existed a man who could open up to her and be himself on a first date. Finally, she grew disillusioned with such dates and began avoiding all but the most interesting opportunities.

Jodee, meanwhile, had been dating a wonderful man and the two were talking of marriage. Jayne was happy for her friend, but there were times in the privacy of her own room when she wondered why a happy relationship had so often eluded her.

In 1990, just before the Christmas holidays, Jayne began to wonder if perhaps her life needed a drastic change. As with any time when her heart was heavy with emotion, she talked over her feelings with Jodee.

"I'm going home for Christmas," Jayne said as she came home from work one afternoon in November of that year. She was dressed in a fashionable business suit and her hair had just been styled in a way that accentuated her cheekbones.

Jodee looked up from their sofa, where she had been reading a magazine. "So? Why so serious about it?"

"I don't know." Jayne flopped down beside her friend. "Maybe L.A. isn't the place for me."

"Oh, I get it." Jodee had heard Jayne talk this way before. Whenever she seemed discouraged with her love life Jayne talked about leaving Los Angeles. "You're tired of the men in southern California and you're ready for a change. Just like last week."

"This time I'm serious," Jayne said, then sighed loudly. "Maybe if I moved back to Sanford I'd meet someone with good old-fashioned values, someone real. These guys out here are all the same. Besides, I miss Dillon."

Jodee smiled at her friend. "Well, then, you go ahead and go back to Florida for Christmas and see if you meet Mr. Wonderful."

"I will." Jayne sounded defiant and Jodee laughed.

"You'll be back as quick as you can get a flight, as soon as the humidity and all those Florida bugs start to get to you."

"I don't know, Jodee. I feel like my life is passing me by and I still haven't found the right man for me."

"Like you always say, he's got to be out there somewhere, right?"

Jayne nodded, her mind racing ahead to the vacation she was preparing to take. She was looking forward to seeing her parents and Dillon for the holidays, but she meant what she'd said. This time she might decide to move back home.

The next few weeks passed slowly, until finally the day arrived for Jayne to leave. Jodee drove her to the airport and hugged her good-bye.

"Be careful and have a great time," she said. "I'll miss you."

Jayne smiled in return. "It's really weird, Jodee, but I have a good feeling about this trip," she said.

"Of course," Jodee said, responding lightly to Jayne's serious tone of voice. "Remember? You're going off to meet Mr. Wonderful."

20

In the early morning hours after his first date with Jayne, David Miller found it difficult to sleep. He could not stop reliving their time that night, the meal they'd shared and the romantic kisses afterward. Jayne was wonderful, the kind of woman Dorothy had been when he'd met her more than ten years earlier.

David switched gears and began thinking of Dorothy. She had always been the love of his life. She still was. And he had every intention of keeping her in his life. After almost six years of marriage, their relationship had entered a comfortable stage that brought with it an easy friendship that hadn't been there in the beginning.

But as the friendship stage with Dorothy had begun, so had the passionate stage fizzled. Although David liked the comfortable way he and Dorothy had between them, he also missed the excitement they once shared.

For hours he lay in bed staring at the ceiling in his Granada Hills home and wondering why he had been so vulnerable to Jayne's beauty, what possibilities she might bring to his life. Would she be like so many others he had used and let go? David did not think so. He imagined that Jayne might become a very important part of his life. But why? Why, when his lives were already so complicated?

As the sun began to rise, sometime around six o'clock that morning, David realized the answers to his questions. His life had become boring and predictable, if only by his standards. He needed Jayne because he needed more excitement.

He had worked so hard to live his double life that it had become easy. It no longer offered him the challenge it once had. After a lifetime of using the people in his life to his advantage, David did not appear to have even a remnant of remorse for the lies he had told. He saw things only from his perspective, and so after hours of analyzing his double life he truly believed he was suffering from a lack of excitement.

Jayne represented everything that Dorothy had once been. She was new and so she had not heard any of his lies. She was beautiful and so she would make for a very satisfying means of excitement.

David knew that he had already allowed himself to fall in love with Jayne. He also knew that his feelings for her had less to do with her beauty than her willingness to believe him. She believed everything he had told her about his status as a cancer-cured millionaire. At one time David would have been disgusted by her gullibility, thinking her greedy for believing him so easily. But now he needed her to validate his ability to live beyond the moral codes of average men. In Jayne's adoring eyes was proof that David was someone special. As long as she stayed in his life, he would always be better than those men whose lives were centered around one woman.

The longer David thought about Jayne and what she represented to him, the deeper his need for her grew. Dorothy lived in Orlando; Jayne in Los Angeles. He spent a great deal of time in both cities. David began to imagine that having both women in his life might be the perfect solution to his lack of excitement.

And Jayne was better than any of the other women he'd dated in Los Angeles, because she did not know about his political life. Therefore, Jayne represented perhaps the ultimate challenge, one unlike that of any woman he'd met since Dorothy.

By dating Jayne, he could actually live three separate lives. He would be the CIA agent married to Dorothy and carrying out dangerous missions across the world. At the same time he would be the millionaire attorney with a new lease on life and a clean bill of health from his oncologist. And finally he would be the playboy lobbyist and respected chamber of commerce president, vacationing with politicians and spending whatever time he desired in the company of numerous beautiful women.

That, David decided, would definitely be exciting. Of course, David had grown so addicted to the wrong kinds of excitement that in the course of his musings he did not once consider how he would fund such a triple lifestyle. After all, his relationship with Senator Alan Robbins had been all but severed and his lobbying business was already nearing financial ruin.

But none of those thoughts entered David's mind. He had more than ten thousand dollars left from the money he'd borrowed before the holidays and he did not believe it would be difficult to get more if he needed it.

Psychiatrists would later agree that at this point in David's life he actually turned a corner and began traveling down a dark and deadly road of destruction. His decisions—at one time merely self-centered—were now irrational and self-destructive. But since David answered to no one and told none of the people in his life the truth, he was able to go on making such decisions with blatant disregard for their consequences.

So it was that by ten o'clock that morning, less than eight hours after leaving her side, David picked up his telephone and dialed Jayne's number.

"Baby, it's me," he whispered into the phone. "I can't stop thinking about you."

"Me too. This is the craziest thing that's ever happened to me."

David broke into a smile. "Get dressed. I'll be there at noon to take you to lunch."

After he'd hung up the phone, his plans for the afternoon set, David called the limousine company he used and booked one for the rest of the day. He could hardly wait to see Jayne's reaction when he picked her up in a stretch limousine complete with champagne on ice and a television in the back. He got dressed quickly and smoothed his hair into place.

Just before he walked out the door he picked up the telephone again.

"Hello?"

"Hi, sweetheart. It's me. I'm in Washington D.C. meeting with some officials at the Pentagon."

"It's so good to hear your voice," Dorothy said. "I thought you were in Kuwait."

"I will be. I'm leaving in an hour, but I wanted to call you and tell you how much I love you."

Dorothy closed her eyes, thankful to be married to such a devoted man. "Please be careful, honey."

"Don't worry, you'll be on my mind everywhere I go. Oh, and I found out this might be a long mission. Could last a month or longer."

A frown crossed Dorothy's face. "That long?"

"Honey, trust me, if I get this thing done any sooner you'll be the first to know."

Dorothy sighed. "Okay. I'll miss you."

"Me too. Give the boys a kiss for me."

And with that he hung up the phone, glanced one final time at the mirror, and set out to meet Jayne for lunch.

21

Jayne was not sure what to make of her whirlwind emotions. She had never been one to fall for a man instantly, but there was no denying her feelings in the hours after her first date with David. She was falling in love with the man.

Even when she'd been in love with Jake she had tried to take their relationship slowly. But there was something different about David. Somehow, he seemed to have known her all his life even though she'd just met him the day before. Jodee, too, knew something special had happened.

In all the years they'd been friends she had never seen Jayne look as happy as she did that morning after meeting David.

"He's wonderful, Jodee, absolutely wonderful," Jayne said. "He's sensitive and warm and kind. He's not like any other man I've ever met."

Jodee looked hesitant. "You just met him yesterday, Jayne," she said. "Be careful. Sometimes those smooth-talkers are the worst of all."

Jayne shook her head and explained to her friend that David was not like other men she'd met. He had opened up to her and bared his soul on their first meeting.

"There's something else," Jayne said, lowering her voice in contained excitement.

"I'm listening." Jodee sounded slightly bored, afraid to show excitement for her friend over a man she'd known less than twenty-four hours.

"He's a millionaire." Jayne said the words slowly so Jodee would grasp the truth of what she was saying.

Suddenly Jodee wrinkled her eyebrows skeptically. "A millionaire? What'd he do, show you his bankbook?"

Jayne sighed. "Don't you believe anyone, Jodee? We sat next to each other for five hours and he told me his life story. He inherited fourteen million dollars from his father's business and then he was diagnosed with cancer."

"Cancer? You're falling for a guy who's dying?"

Jayne shook her head quickly. "No, he's completely better. The doctors can't explain it, but the cancer is gone."

"So now he's got fourteen million, huh?"

"No. When he found out about the cancer he took a year and traveled the world. He spent ten million. But he still has the rest in bank accounts and investments."

Jodee raised an eyebrow. "So is he really all that wonderful or does four million dollars make him a whole lot more interesting?"

She didn't want Jayne falling for a man because of his money. If he didn't love her, she would never be happy no matter how many things he might buy her.

"Well, I've been thinking about that this morning.

The money is nice, very nice. But I think I'm falling in love with the man, not the money. I mean, he can just look at me and it feels like he's known me his entire life. Jodee, I think this is it. Really.''

"It's awfully quick, Jayne. But you thought this would be a great trip, remember?'' Jodee smiled at her friend. "So maybe he is Mr. Wonderful. Time will tell.''

Jodee knew that for some people love really did happen during their first meeting. Her own parents were married forty-five days after meeting on a blind date and they'd been married thirty years.

Jayne looked so happy that morning as she got ready for her lunch date with David. And when he picked her up in a limousine, even Jodee was impressed.

For the next three weeks David courted Jayne much the same way he had courted Dorothy over a decade before. He took her to expensive restaurants, bought her a gold bracelet and matching necklace, had bouquets of roses delivered to her work, and used the limousine service on a regular basis for their dates.

They saw each other every day and Jayne had never been happier in her life. He shared his feelings and his escapades from the past. She was especially impressed to learn that he had worked for former President Richard Nixon as a Spanish interpreter for foreign relations. David was multitalented, a brilliant man who seemed to be everything she had ever dreamed of.

David, meanwhile, was falling in love with Jayne in a way that was both desperate and dangerous. He had not had time for his business and he was quickly running out of money. In the past those two facts might have brought him to his senses, but suddenly he was no longer interested in finances as a priority. He figured he could borrow more money if necessary and if the loans were no longer possible he could always use his credit.

In the days when he'd had more money than he knew what to do with, David had established a sophisticated line of credit that would have enabled him to have as much as fifty thousand dollars instantly. So far he hadn't had to touch his credit cards. For that reason, and because he was so quickly becoming obsessed with Jayne, money worries were the last thing on his mind.

Still, by the end of the third week he must have decided that he might have to make some changes in his original plan of living a triple life. Even if he quit going into his office completely he would not have time to live that many lives. So he began working out a plan that would enable him to keep Jayne in his life, perhaps permanently, while remaining married to Dorothy. Apparently he couldn't work out the details of the plan while he was in Los Angeles. Jayne would be too near, her presence too intoxicating. He would be too tempted to call her or drive to her house and visit her.

He definitely needed some time away from her to work things out. After all, he was going to have to do a great deal of traveling back and forth from Florida in order to keep Dorothy from growing suspicious. And so far he had given Jayne no reason to explain why an attorney would have to spend so much time away from his office.

One day while they were at lunch he told her that he needed to take a business trip to Illinois.

"The law office needs me to take care of some business in Chicago," David told Jayne, taking her hands in his and looking intently into her eyes. "I'll miss you."

"How long will you be gone?" she asked. She hoped

the trip wouldn't take long. Their relationship was moving along so quickly that Jayne even wondered if David might be thinking of marrying her. He had mentioned marriage once or twice and neither of them seemed frightened by the idea.

"Not long, sweetheart," David said softly. "Maybe a week at the most."

"I'll miss you."

"I know. But I'll be back soon. We'll talk every day, I promise."

When their lunch date ended and David dropped Jayne off at home, he drove to his Granada Hills house, packed his bags, and left for the airport. His plane bound for Florida left one hour later.

When David walked up to the front door of his Casselberry home late that evening Dorothy was thrilled to see him.

"What a surprise!" she said as she wrapped her arms around his waist and smiled up at him. David bent down and kissed her. "I didn't expect you home for another week at least."

"Things went well, honey," David said proudly. "I don't think Operation Desert Storm will last much longer after that mission."

Dorothy could only imagine the kind of danger David must have been in during the past three weeks. The war in the Middle East had begun with horrifying images of deadly air raids and Scud missile attacks happening around the clock. She had been so worried about her husband's safety that she had barely been able to tear herself away from the news reports that were being given hourly on the television.

Each time the camera showed camps of men waiting to start the ground attack, Dorothy would scan the scene searching for David. For the first time since she'd learned about his position with the CIA, Dorothy found herself desperate to know where he was and what he was doing. She hadn't worried so much in the past because his missions had never involved an actual war. And now that David was back home in her arms, Dorothy could not have been happier.

"Have you eaten? Can I get you anything?" Dorothy took David's jacket and looked eagerly at him, wanting to help him feel relaxed after his harrowing mission.

But David shook his head. "I'm not hungry, honey. Think I'll just turn in early tonight."

Dorothy looked hurt, but only for a moment. She knew he must have been tired after more than a dozen hours on an airplane and all the debriefing he'd probably had to go through when he landed.

"Okay," she said. "Let me know if you change your mind."

David nodded and walked down the hallway to their bedroom. He needed to call Jayne. Had to call Jayne. The reunion with Dorothy would come later. But if he didn't call Jayne soon she might think he didn't care. And if she thought that, then she might lose interest and start seeing someone else while he was gone.

He waited until he was certain Dorothy was watching television, then he quietly picked up the telephone.

"Hi, sweetheart, how are you?" he said softly.

"David? I can hardly understand you. Where are you?"

"In Chicago. I've gotten a little case of laryngitis, though. Can't talk long."

"Oh, that's too bad." Jayne sounded worried. She was not losing interest. "Well, I'm glad you made it there safely. Take it easy, love."

"I will. I'll be thinking about you," David said. "I love you, baby."

As he hung up, Dorothy walked into the room.

"Who was on the phone?" she asked casually.

David felt a rush of adrenaline. Dorothy was supposed to be watching television. What had she heard? What did she suspect? He quickly thought up an answer. "One of the agents."

Dorothy looked puzzled. "At this hour? It's almost midnight."

Suddenly David stood up and looked at his wife angrily. "Listen, you're going to have to stop snooping around and asking all these questions if this marriage is going to work, do you understand?" He moved toward her menacingly as he shouted the words. "I'm sick of all your questions."

Dorothy's eyes grew wide in disbelief. She had meant nothing by her question, only asking out of curiosity. And now David's outburst had caught her completely by surprise.

Instantly David knew he'd made a mistake by lashing out. He sighed loudly and let go of his anger as he walked toward Dorothy and pulled her into his arms. "I'm sorry, honey. I'm just under a lot of pressure, that's all. Can you forgive me?"

Dorothy wiped a tear from her cheek and nodded. "I wasn't trying to check up on you, David. Really."

"I know, I know. It's my fault. Everything will be okay in a few days. It just takes a while to forget about all the death and destruction over there. I wish I could tell you what I've been through."

"Me too, honey."

"Well, let's forget about this and start over." David

kissed Dorothy softly and ran his hands down her sides. "I love you. Do you know that?"

Dorothy nodded, and later that night, as she lay in his arms, David knew she was no longer upset with him for his outburst.

The next day David left the house early, telling Dorothy that he had several days of debriefing ahead of him. Normally, since they'd moved to Florida, David spent his days at home. The debriefing sessions that had taken him away from home in Los Angeles were now conducted immediately at the end of a mission. But he told Dorothy that because there was still fighting going on in the Middle East and because he might be needed back in Kuwait, he would be spending quite a bit of time at the local CIA office.

Instead, David spent the day sorting out his lives.

By that afternoon, David must have decided that he would need to tell Jayne the truth about what he did for a living. That way he could introduce her to his politician friends and formally end his single lifestyle. Jayne had bewitched him so thoroughly that he was ready to give up that lifestyle. After all, he was 39 years old and spending time with women he neither knew nor loved was no longer as thrilling as it had once been.

By allowing Jayne to see his lobbyist business and his political friends, he would be able to work at his office while he was in Los Angeles. David was certain that the money would begin to flow again soon afterward. Also, by telling Jayne about his lobbying, he would have a reason to travel and therefore an explanation for his twice monthly visits with Dorothy in Orlando.

What David did not consider was that his business actually did require quite a bit of travel. Oftentimes in the course of lobbying for representatives of the printing industry or other corporations, David would need to meet with influential politicians in cities such as Washington D.C., St. Louis, and Chicago. If he told Jayne he was traveling for business when in reality he was traveling to see Dorothy, he would have no spare time to actually get his work done. But David apparently never considered this nor thought about the ramifications of the plans he was devising.

Instead, his thoughts rushed ahead to the place in his life he was creating for Jayne. When he returned to Los Angeles, he would tell Jayne that he hadn't wanted to brag about his political ties early in their relationship. That would explain why he had told her he was merely an attorney. But once she knew the truth, he would take her to political functions and introduce her to powerful people so that she could see him in action. David could hardly wait.

Then, after a few weeks of seeing how he really lived, he was certain she'd be even more in love with him and he with her. He considered asking her to move in with him in the Granada Hills home. But he didn't want to just live with Jayne, he wanted to marry her.

As he sat on the park bench that afternoon, the warm Florida sunshine belying the fact that it was still January, he thought the idea over and decided he was no longer afraid of being married to two women at once. He would love each of them faithfully, being sure that the David Miller married to Dorothy never interfered with the David Miller married to Jayne. What harm could possibly come from such a lifestyle? After all, a man of his stature, a man of his intelligence, could certainly not be expected to live his entire life married to only one woman.

David knew that he would have to be away from Dorothy even more than before. But the war in the Middle East gave him the perfect excuse for that. After such a war, there could potentially be cleanup missions that might continue for the next few years. Even when the war was long over, he would never run out of ideas as long as the United States was involved in any type of foreign relations.

David smiled to himself and pulled a tiny jewelry box from his pants pocket. He had bought the ring the day before, just after his plane landed in Orlando. And when he got back to Los Angeles, he was going to present it to Jayne along with a proposal.

The idea that marrying Jayne would make David a bigamist apparently did not affect him. Perhaps in his mind a man was a bigamist only if people found out he had two wives. And David did not intend for that ever to happen.

22

As his week in Casselberry passed, David found several opportunities to call Jayne. Dorothy had no idea, of course, that David had met a woman in Los Angeles and fallen in love with her. But he was quieter than usual and more evasive about his future missions. Finally, Dorothy suspected that something was wrong with her husband, but she decided not to ask him in light of his outburst earlier in the week. She trusted him and she did not want him to think otherwise.

At week's end David told Dorothy he had to return to Kuwait. Although she was worried, she believed what he told her about the significant danger having passed.

"Don't worry about me, sweetheart," David told her as he left that afternoon in late January. "I'll be home in a month and then we can spend some real time together. Okay?"

Dorothy nodded, too choked up with emotion to respond. These long missions left her so lonely, she only hoped the war would end soon so that David could spend more time at home.

So while the war raged on in Kuwait and Iraq, David boarded a plane for Los Angeles. The moment he returned to the house in Granada Hills, David phoned Jayne and invited her to dinner.

"I've missed you so much, honey," he told her. "Wear your best, because tonight's going to be a celebration."

Jayne could hardly wait to see David after he'd been gone a week. During that time she'd had a chance to consider the new relationship she'd developed with David and decide whether she was acting in her best interest to continue it. After very little thought, she came to the conclusion that David was not only good for her but that he was the best thing that had happened to her in years.

David had told her that he loved children and had always wanted his own. She knew that as soon as he met her son the two of them would get along wonderfully. Dillon was nearly fifteen by then and becoming a handsome young man. Jayne knew that he would approve of her relationship with David because for the past few years he'd been encouraging her to settle down with the right man.

"You need someone who will love you like you deserve, Mom," he'd told her several times.

Well, now she'd found that someone. Jayne appreciated everything about David and began searching through her things for a black sequin-covered cocktail dress that would be perfect for the evening. She wanted to welcome David home the right way.

That night at the restaurant while they waited for their meals to be brought to them, David cleared his throat and moved closer to Jayne.

"Jayne, darling, I have something to tell you," he said.

Suddenly she wondered if David was going to propose. "Yes?" Her voice was shrill with excitement.

"Well, it's about my employment, something I haven't shared with you before."

Jayne looked confused. She had believed David to be so honest and now he was admitting there was something he hadn't told her. She didn't like the idea and she waited for him to continue.

"I am an attorney, just like I told you. But I'm not practicing law right now." He paused for effect, guessing correctly that she was hanging on every word. He continued.

"Actually, I'm a political lobbyist," he said softly, speaking to her carefully like a teacher conveying a new idea to his grade-school children. "I spend a great deal of time in the company of very powerful politicians. And someday I might even run for office myself."

Jayne was more confused than ever. "Why didn't you tell me sooner?"

"I didn't want you to think I was boasting." He looked bashfully down at his hands and then smiled meekly at her. "I mean, we've only known each other a few weeks and already you know about my money and my personal background. If I'd told you about the lobbying business you might have thought I was just handing you a line."

Jayne considered David's excuse. She didn't like the idea that he had lied to her. But then, he really hadn't lied, he had just omitted the fact that he was a lobbyist.

"Do you understand, honey?" David looked beseechingly at Jayne, trying to read her emotions.

She shrugged. "Is there anything else you haven't told me?"

"Of course not," he said, and it occurred to Jayne that he had never looked more dashing than he did that night. "I should have told you the truth about my job from the beginning. But try and understand. I wanted you to love me for who I am inside, not my position."

Jayne decided that she couldn't blame David for wanting her love to be for who he was, not what he was. Wasn't that what she liked most of all about David? His ability to share his feelings and relate to her without the pretenses so many other men had?

Jayne smiled. "I understand." As she said the words she realized that she meant them. At least David was honest enough to tell her the truth now, even at the risk of upsetting her.

As the evening progressed, Jayne and David finished their dinner and went dancing at a local nightclub until well after midnight. As they sat in the back of his limousine at two o'clock that morning, David pulled the ring from his pocket. With tears in his eyes he looked at Jayne and smiled.

"I know this is fast, I know we haven't known each other very long," he said. "But, Jayne, will you marry me?"

Jayne was thrilled. David had taken her by surprise proposing to her at the end of the evening. She looked at the large diamond ring David held in his hand and she blinked back tears. "Oh, David, I don't know what to say."

David leaned close to her and kissed her on the mouth. "Say you're in love with me and you can't live without me," he whispered in her hair. "Say you'll marry me, Jayne."

"I will," she said, her voice cracking with emotion. "I will marry you, David Miller. And this wonderful love between us will keep growing forever."

Until that point, when Jayne agreed to marry David, there had still been time for David to change his mind about becoming a bigamist. But at that moment, when Jayne looked lovingly at her future husband and agreed to marry him, David finally lost sight completely of the line that separated right from wrong.

He knew that he would not change his mind about marrying Jayne, as he had with Tambi. This time he must have convinced himself that not only would it work having two wives, it would restore the excitement to his life.

During the next two weeks, David spent a great deal of time introducing his fiancée to his business and political associates. He took her to his office and pointed proudly to the sign on the door that read DAVID MILLER AND ASSOCIATES. He introduced her to his secretaries, Lynne and Cynthia, and to his business partner, Grant Hawthorne.

Grant remembered later that Jayne was a pretty girl who was completely enamored with David.

"She just stood at his side and took in every word he said," he would say later. "He could have told her he owned the moon and she would have believed him. She was that in love with him."

On Super Bowl Sunday that month, David had a party for several of his business associates who hadn't yet met Jayne. He had decided by then that if he was going to include her in his working life, he wanted everyone to know her.

Ed Cholakian was among those invited that day. He decided to go because David had not yet paid back the money he'd borrowed and Ed was beginning to get a bit nervous. An afternoon at David's house would give him a chance to survey David's health situation first-hand and talk to him about when the money would be paid back.

Ed had been surprised when David said he had met a woman and wanted to introduce her to everyone at the party. David was supposed to be dying of cancer, stricken by the effects of chemotherapy. How, then, had he been able to meet a woman and begin dating her? Ed wanted to see David in person before he drew any conclusions.

When he arrived at David's home—which by then had no pictures or indications that Dorothy had ever lived there—Ed was shocked to see David looking trim and handsome in an expensive cardigan sweater and trousers.

"If it isn't my good friend, Ed Cholakian," David said, rushing to the door to greet Ed and whisking Jayne along beside him. "This is Jayne, my fiancée."

Ed looked at the young woman beside David and was struck by her pretty features and honest brown eyes. Ed wondered why a woman like this would want to marry a dying man like David Miller. Ed looked narrowly at David and began to wonder whether he was actually sick.

In fact, by the end of the afternoon Ed had spent a great deal of time watching David and he had decided that David could not possibly be sick. No one had mentioned his illness and Jayne did not seem to know anything about it. The only explanation was that David had lied. He had wanted to borrow money badly enough that he had made the entire story up.

Before he left David's house, Ed pulled him aside.

"Listen, David," he said softly, not wanting to make a scene in front of David's fiancée. "I'm still waiting for the payback. What's going on?"

"Oh, right, I'm glad you mentioned it," David said, looking sincere as he spoke. "I'm just about ready to pay you back. All kinds of contracts coming in and I'll have the money in your hands as soon as I get it."

Ed opened his mouth to ask David about the cancer, but before he could say anything David leaned closer.

"Hey, Ed, I have a favor to ask," David said. "Would you mind being my best man next month when I get married? You're the closest thing to a best friend I have. Whaddya say, pal?"

Ed was taken aback. He had been thinking terrible thoughts about David, believing him to be a liar and a cheat and nothing more than a con man. And here the man considered him his best friend. Ed smiled weakly at David and nodded. "Uh, sure, David," he said. "I'd be honored. When's the wedding?"

"February sixteenth, right after Valentine's Day," David said. "We'll all be flying up to Vegas."

Ed resisted the urge to ask David how he could afford to fly a wedding party to Las Vegas when he hadn't paid back the money he'd borrowed. Ed put the thoughts out of his mind. David was probably planning on using the money he'd be getting any day from the contracts he'd spoken about.

Later, when Ed realized he had a business conflict and would be unable to attend David and Jayne's wedding, he decided it was just as well. There was something about David that Ed no longer trusted. Something that suggested he was perhaps just a con man. Ed felt guilty thinking such thoughts about a man who thought of him as a friend. But Ed was a man who trusted his instincts and everything inside him told him to beware of David Miller.

Jayne, meanwhile, had no such thoughts. And on February 16, 1991, with her best friend Jodee standing by her side, she became David's second wife in the We've Only Just Begun Wedding Chapel in Las Vegas.

David looked lovingly into Jayne's eyes and promised that only death would separate them. As he spoke his vows, Jayne's eyes filled with tears. After a lifetime of broken relationships, she felt that David was the man she had been looking for. Her parents had not yet met him, but they would soon. And he had spoken with her parents on the phone, asking for permission to marry their daughter. Jayne was thrilled with David's old-fashioned morals and his desire to include her family in their new life together.

Standing beside her that evening, Jodee no longer had reservations about David Miller. Although she had only known David a short while, it was obvious even to Jodee that David was humble and gentle and clearly in love with Jayne. Jodee was impressed with his sophistication and the list of politicians he knew on a first-name basis.

Besides, he was a millionaire. Jayne would not have to worry about money ever again. Jodee looked on as Jayne promised to love David regardless of their circumstances, and she realized how happy she was for her friend. Jayne, so trusting and kind to others, deserved this, and Jodee only hoped their marriage would be as happy as these past six weeks had been for them.

While David Miller exchanged wedding vows with Jayne that evening, Dorothy sat at home enjoying a cup of tea and flipping through the pages of a women's magazine. She missed David terribly and wondered how much longer this mission would last. He had never been gone this long and she was more worried about him than ever before. If only he would call or write or find some way to let her know he was okay. Her thoughts began to drift and she began thinking about the places she and David might go when he returned.

Her husband, meanwhile, was doing quite well and in no danger whatsoever. While Dorothy cleaned house and waited patiently for David's return, he was spending that weekend with his new bride. Worse, the newlyweds were staying in a romantic suite at the same hotel where he and Dorothy had spent their first married night together six years earlier.

The morning after their first night together as husband and wife, David left Jayne and went for a walk down to the hotel lobby.

"I'm going to get some coffee," he told Jayne as he left. "Catch a little extra sleep and I'll be back in a half hour or so."

As David walked toward the hotel's coffee shop, he spotted a pay phone. Dorothy. He hadn't called Dorothy in two weeks and she would certainly be worried about him. The fact that he might make such a call while his new bride waited for him in their honeymoon suite did not strike David as twisted or even a bit strange. Dorothy needed to know he was okay and he needed to call her. There could be no harm in handling the situation with a phone call.

He picked up the telephone and dialed his Florida number. "Hi, honey, it's me," he said happily.

"David, where are you?" Dorothy sounded thrilled to hear from him.

"The mission is over, honey," he said. "It was a huge success. I can't tell you where I am, but I'm fine and I wanted to hear your voice."

"Oh, David, I've missed you so much."

David smiled. "Me too."

"When will you be home?"

"I'm not sure, sweetheart," David said, mentally calculating the amount of time he would need to spend with Jayne to properly celebrate their wedding. "Probably two or three days. Hey, I miss you, honey."

"I miss you too. Hurry home, David."

"I will, love. You know I will."

And with that, David hung up the phone, bought a cup of coffee, and returned to his waiting bride.

23

Toward the end of February, after he and Jayne had been married for one week, David began to realize a few of the flaws in what he'd done by taking on a second wife. He had been back to visit Dorothy for a two-day trip and had spent the entire time worrying that he was running out of both time and money. By telling Jayne he was traveling for business when in fact he was traveling to see Dorothy, he was leaving himself no time for any real business travel.

As a result, his business was crumbling. Even long-time clients who had trusted his lobbying efforts for years were beginning to cancel their deals with David. For even though he was living two separate lives, he was still only one man and he simply did not have time for everything he was trying to accomplish.

Because of his failing business, David was in worse financial trouble than he'd ever been in. He had tried to borrow money from some friends who still believed he was dying of cancer. But they had been unable to loan him the amount he needed. He knew there were still a few sources he hadn't tried, but his situation was becoming quite desperate. David had told associates that he planned never to resort to using the credit he'd established. Once he started using the credit cards, he said, he was afraid there would be no way to stop. And if he then had no way to pay off the debt, he could face financial ruin. Of course, David probably could not imagine that happening, since it would also mean confessing the truth about his finances to both Jayne and Dorothy. David publicly vowed never to let his situation get so bad that he would pull out his credit cards. Instead, he would find a way to generate more money.

David had given the matter some thought and decided there was no reason to panic. The answer was simple. He would tell Jayne that they needed to move to Florida. Once Dorothy and Jayne were living in the same city, he could see both of them whenever he spent time in Florida. And when he traveled, he could really be traveling for his business, thereby bringing in money and contracts. Getting Jayne to move to Florida was a brilliant plan, he decided. She could hardly disagree, since her son lived there, as did her parents.

David continued to work on the plan. He would tell Jayne that he was tired of politics and had accepted an offer from Orlando's Disney Studios to work for them as an in-house attorney. Then, if she had questions about his career change he would tell her he'd been waiting for such an opportunity for years. No, he didn't need the money, but he had always wanted the challenge of representing a big corporation like Disney. It was a chance of a lifetime, he would tell her, and one he could not possibly pass up.

The move would coincide with a trip to Orlando that he and Jayne had been planning to take in March, when he would meet her family. The more he thought about his newest plan, the more David must have realized he would need some other measure to pacify Jayne in case she was not thrilled with the idea of quitting her job and moving.

He decided to arrange a vacation to Europe for himself and Jayne, her parents, her son, and her sister. He would tell the family that the Kuwaiti government was picking up the tab because of some political dealings he'd had with the country. The longer he thought about it the more convinced he became that treating her family to such a trip would make up for the fact that he wanted to move her to Orlando.

He went home that evening and broke the news to Jayne.

"Sweetheart, we need to talk about something," he said, pulling her close and kissing her gently.

"Okay, what's up," Jayne said, returning his kiss and looking forward to spending time with him. Their physical relationship was very exciting and neither of them felt like they ever got enough of each other. They'd only been married a week and already he had spent two days in Washington D.C. She hoped he would be able to spend more time with her now.

"Maybe we should sit down," he said, directing her to a nearby chair and kneeling in front of her.

"David, what is it?" Jayne was suddenly worried. Maybe his cancer had returned and he'd just found out about it. Maybe the doctors had told him they were wrong and he really was going to die in a year after all. "Are you sick?"

"No, no, nothing like that," he said quickly. "It's about my career."

Jayne leaned back, relief flooding her face. "You had

me worried, David. What about your career?" She remembered when he had told her the truth about what he did for a living. Maybe there was more to it, something he still hadn't told her.

"I've been offered a job in Florida," he said, watching for her reaction. There was none. "Disney wants me out there to act as their in-house attorney. It's a fantastic job offer that would make our investments very secure."

Jayne looked confused. "But, David, you have four million dollars," she said. "What does it matter how much you make?"

"*We* have four million dollars," he corrected her gently. "But that money will disappear awfully fast if I don't find a way to make money in the meantime. Besides, this doesn't really have anything to do with the money."

Jayne listened patiently, hiding her frustration. She did not like the direction the conversation was heading in.

"Actually, I've wanted to work for a big company like Disney for years. It's been my dream, sweetheart," he said, imploring her to understand.

"What are you trying to say, David?" Jayne asked stiffly. "You want me to quit my job so we can move to Florida?"

David nodded somberly. "Yes. Disney wants me to start working for them by the middle of March. I told them I had to talk it over with you and I'd let them know by tomorrow."

Jayne thought about David's proposal. She knew when she married David that she would no longer need to work. But she hadn't wanted to quit her job because of the friends she had there and because it was such a challenge to her. Still, she had married David and now she needed to be willing to compromise. He obviously had his heart set on the job in Florida.

She drew a deep breath and looked up at the ceiling. Moving to Florida could be a good thing. She would see Dillon more often and she would be closer to her parents and family. And there were probably other purchasing jobs in Florida she could apply for eventually. Besides, maybe it would be good to take some time off work to just be David's wife. She looked at David again and smiled. There really wasn't any reason she should spoil David's job offer by complaining about the move.

"I would need to give two weeks' notice," she said softly. "They deserve at least that."

David threw his arms around her neck. "Oh, sweetheart," he said. "I knew I could count on you. Believe me, we'll be so happy in Florida you'll never once be sorry we moved."

But Jayne knew it would be a difficult transition. She would have to leave Jodee, who after so many years as her best friend had become more of a sister. And she would have to be completely dependent on David for her finances until she got a job in Florida.

"I know what you're thinking," David said as he watched Jayne withdraw into her own thoughts. "You don't want to be a burden to me. Sweetheart, you know our situation. You don't have to work another day in your life if you don't want to."

Jayne nodded. "But I want to, David. After we're settled, I'll look around until I find something. I need a life outside our home."

"Okay, don't worry. I'm sure there are plenty of positions you could fill once we get moved in. I just want you to know that you don't need to work if you don't want to."

Jayne began considering the benefits of David's job in Florida. For one, he would certainly spend more time at home once he was no longer required to travel for political reasons. She looked curiously at her husband. "Will you have to travel much with Disney?"

David shrugged as he searched for the perfect answer to her question. He would have to spend at least two weeks out of each month in Los Angeles. But if he told Jayne that now, she might not agree to the move. For now he needed to get her to agree, then once they purchased a home in Florida and began their life together he would suddenly realize that his new position required more travel than he'd thought. He cleared his throat.

"Not much travel, honey," he said, taking her hands in his. "From what they say, there'll be a few trips to the Los Angeles studios but probably only a few times each quarter."

She was silent for a few moments and David knew she was trying to absorb the significance of what was about to happen to their lives in the next few weeks. He decided to tell her about the trip to Europe.

"I have some more exciting news," he said hopefully, desperate to convince her they were doing the right thing by moving. "The government of Kuwait wants to treat me and my family to a trip to Europe in June. We would have plenty of time to move to Florida and get settled in before the trip. Then when I get some vacation time in June, we'll spend two weeks overseas, and when we return to Florida I can start my new job."

Jayne held up her hand and shook her head.

"Wait." She looked confused. "What do you mean, the government of Kuwait?"

David smiled. "Well, it's a long story but I did a few favors for them before the war broke out and they want to make it up to me," he said. "I was thinking we could take your parents and your sister, maybe even Dillon."

Jayne's mind was racing in several different directions. Was this how David had lived before she met him? Impulsively accepting job offers and traveling to foreign countries compliments of Middle Eastern governments? She had never seen this side of him and she wondered if he had thought out these options before presenting them to her.

"Shouldn't we wait and take a trip like that later, like a year from now after we're settled in?"

"Honey, there's plenty of time to get ready for the trip," he said. "By then I will have been working for more than two months and I'll be ready for a break. Besides, your family might really enjoy it. What do you think?"

Jayne's parents were semi-retired and would not have trouble taking two weeks away from home in June. But she wasn't sure about her sister or Dillon. What would they think of this impulsive invitation? She shrugged. Maybe she needed to loosen up a bit. Her family probably would be thrilled with the invitation.

"Let's start packing," she said, allowing herself to become excited with all the changes that awaited them in the next few weeks. Besides, she had never been to Europe before.

If Jayne had had any doubts about David's job offer in Florida or his explanation about the government of Kuwait wanting to treat them to a trip to Europe, she did not voice them. She believed David to be a millionaire with an impulsive past. He had spent a great deal of time touring the world when he'd been sick with cancer. Perhaps he had developed habits during that time that were difficult to break. Anyway, David was better than the men who Jayne had dated in the past who were predictable and therefore boring. David was exciting—even if he had caught her by surprise with his announcement.

David leaned toward his blond-haired wife and kissed her firmly on the lips. "You're the best wife any man ever had," he said. "I can't wait to meet your family."

24

Richard and Janice Leebrick were not thrilled about their daughter's decision to marry a man she'd known only six weeks. They had no reason to dislike David; after all, they had never even met the man. But after she'd been involved with two failed marriages in less than ten years, Jayne's parents thought their daughter should spend at least a year getting to know a man before she married him.

When they had separately voiced their concerns to Jayne, she chastised them for doubting her taste in men. "I know I've made some bad choices in the past," she said. "But this time is different. David doesn't keep anything from me and he's already like my closest friend. I'm in love with him."

When Richard and Janice still weren't convinced, Jayne told them to be patient. "You'll meet him soon enough and then you'll see what I mean. He's a wonderful man, really."

But when Jayne called to tell her parents about David's offer to take the family to Europe in June,

Richard began to grow suspicious. He and his wife agreed to the trip, as did his daughter Sandra. Jayne's son, Dillon, would go too. But Richard was less interested in the sights of Europe than he was in getting to know his new son-in-law. And that would happen in a matter of weeks when the newlyweds moved to Orlando.

Before Jayne and David were scheduled to arrive in Florida and begin house-hunting, Richard put in a call to another of his daughters, Virginia. She had worked for an attorney in the past and had access to information regarding Florida's bar association. David said he'd graduated from Georgetown University Law School. That was something that could be verified.

He called Virginia a few minutes after accepting David's invitation to Europe.

"Hi, honey," he said when he heard his daughter on the other line. "I have a favor to ask."

"Sure, Dad. What do you need?"

"You know this David Miller that Jayne's married?" he asked.

"I don't know him any better than any of us do, but she's told me about him," Virginia said. "Why? What's up?"

"Well, I want you to check him out with the bar association," Richard said. "Find out if he's able to practice law in the state of Florida or for that matter in the state of California. And then check with Georgetown University Law School. See if he really graduated from there."

Virginia was surprised by her father's request. Normally he did not meddle in the affairs of his children. "No problem, Dad," she said. "What's wrong, don't you trust the guy?"

Richard paused a moment, wrestling with his feelings and the vague reasons that had caused him to grow doubtful of David. "I can't put my finger on it, but something about the man makes me worry about him," he said. "Now he's invited the family to Europe. Says the government of Kuwait is going to pay for the whole trip. Now, why would the government of Kuwait be interested in some two-bit lobbyist like David Miller?"

"That's strange, all right," Virginia said. "Well, I'll check him out for you and get back to you as soon as I find out anything."

After that, Richard was satisfied. If David Miller was a fraud he'd find out soon enough. And then he could share the information with Jayne and she could break things off with him before she invested any more of her time in the relationship. Richard hoped he was wrong, but his instincts told him David was a liar. And over the years Richard had learned to trust his instincts.

Jayne and David arrived in Florida the first week of March. They had dinner with Jayne's parents their first night in town and in Jayne's opinion the meeting went well. Richard, however, spent the evening analyzing David. His new son-in-law held Jayne's hand and doted on her every need. He certainly appeared to be in love with her. But there was something in his dark hazel eyes that made Richard reluctant to welcome him into the family. For Jayne's sake, however, Richard kept his feelings to himself.

When the couple had been in Florida less than forty-eight hours Jayne called to tell her parents they'd found a house.

"Oh, Daddy," Jayne said, and Richard could tell she

was more excited than she'd ever been before. "We found a beautiful house. You have to come and see it."

Richard agreed to meet them at the property and took down directions from Jayne over the telephone. As he realized the location of the house Richard wondered if perhaps David really was a millionaire.

The new house was in Heathrow, an upper-class area with very expensive houses placed on several acres each. Indeed, when Richard arrived at the house he was very impressed. The house was brand-new and still vacant. From the outside it appeared to be at least three thousand square feet and the grounds were beautiful. Richard got out of the car and shook hands with David.

"Nice house, David, nice house," Richard said, narrowing his eyes and looking at the two-story structure. "How much they asking?"

"Hardly anything," David said. "They want two-eighteen. It's a steal, really."

Richard raised an eyebrow. Two hundred and eighteen thousand dollars in Orlando was a lot of money. David would have to put down quite a bit of cash on a house like this. "You have access to a down payment for the house?" Richard asked. He didn't want to pry. But there was still something about David that rubbed Richard the wrong way and made him doubt the man's sincerity.

"Down payment?" David asked, and he laughed softly. "Mr. Leebrick, I'm not interested in a mortgage. I'm paying cash for the house. That way we'll always have this property in case anything happens to me or my investments. Jayne needs to feel safe and secure, and buying the house outright will give her that feeling."

Richard stayed and watched warily as David worked out the details of the purchase with the real estate agent. Finally, David promised to transfer the necessary funds into a newly opened checking account in Florida. After that he would get a cashier's check for the purchase price and the title to the house would be transferred to his name.

"See, Dad," Jayne whispered to her father while David finished up the paperwork on the house. "He's wonderful. He'd do anything for me."

Richard had to admit that David did seem to be a man of his word. So far he had given no reason for any of them to doubt him. Still, Richard was not convinced. He wondered what Virginia was finding out about David's legal background.

The next day, Jayne called her father and said that there had been a glitch in the paperwork involving their new home. They would have to rent an apartment for a month until the details could be worked out. But in the meantime they were going to buy furniture. Jayne could hardly wait.

During the next few days, with David scheduled to begin work at Disney the following week, Jayne and David spent many hours purchasing furniture for their new home. At one store, Jayne was awestruck by the beautiful furnishings and David encouraged her to buy whatever she wanted.

"Money is no object, sweetheart," David said, believing the words as he said them. "Pick out whatever you want."

By then Jayne had spent several hours going over the inside of their new home and she had a very good idea of what they needed to furnish it. At David's prodding, she began picking out the tables and sofas and bedroom pieces she thought they would need.

When she was finished, Jayne was more than satisfied. She had picked out everything except for the window fashions and some accessories. Otherwise, she had chosen enough furniture to make their home comfortable.

The tab that day was eleven thousand dollars, including a considerable fee for the delivery and assembly of the furniture at the new home in Heathrow.

"How would you like to pay for the furniture, sir?" The salesman was clearly salivating over the commission he had made in one afternoon.

David pulled out his wallet and for a moment he hesitated. He had dreaded and feared this moment, knowing when it came there would be no turning back. Slowly he took out a piece of plastic. "Credit card," he said.

As the words rolled off his tongue, David began a desperate plunge into debt that left him drowning in despair. But he was no longer able to see beyond the moment. And at that moment he needed to impress Jayne, needed to live like a millionaire if she was going to believe he really was one. He was very happy with his double life and his two wives and he was willing to do whatever was necessary to keep them from doubting the lies he constantly told.

One week later, while David was supposedly spending his first full day at Disney Studios and Jayne was at the apartment going over a list of the furniture they had purchased, Virginia called her father with news about her research.

"You were right, Dad," she said sadly. "He isn't a

lawyer. Not here and not in California. They've never heard of him.''

Richard felt a seething anger begin to build in his veins. "What about Georgetown University?" he asked.

"No record of him there either," she said. "Does Jayne suspect him?"

"Not at all. He has loads of money, just bought a house over in Heathrow for her. Why should she doubt him?"

Virginia knew her father was angry. She wondered why Jayne's husband would lie to her if he had so much money. Jayne wouldn't have cared what he did for a living.

After their conversation, Richard called his daughter and told her the news.

"Listen, Jayne, he's a fraud, a liar," Richard told her. "You've gotta get away from the guy."

Jayne did not like what she was hearing, but she wanted to give her husband the benefit of explaining himself before she came to any conclusions about him.

"Thanks for calling, Dad," she said. Richard could tell she was angry with him for checking out David's story. "I'm sure David will be able to explain the entire thing."

Still, the longer she sat in their apartment waiting to hear from David the worse she began to feel about him. What if he had lied to her? After all, he'd lied to her before when he hadn't told her about his job as a lobbyist. Maybe he wasn't even a millionaire. She'd never really seen proof of his money; she'd just taken his word for everything and trusted him.

At just after noon that day the phone rang and Jayne answered it immediately. "Hello?"

"Hi, sweetheart." David sounded cheerful and Jayne

wondered how he could be so happy when he had knowingly lied to her about his position as an attorney.

"How's the job going?" she asked, hoping he would tell her the truth himself.

"It's just great. I got an employment package and the benefits are even better than I thought. And guess what they're going to pay me?"

Jayne said nothing, waiting for David to continue. If he was going to lie to her she didn't want to stop him until she'd caught him at it.

David was confused by Jayne's silence. "Okay, if you won't guess, I'll tell you," he said, still sounding up-beat. "Eighty-nine thousand dollars a year. Isn't that great?"

"David? Where are you calling me from?"

A momentary flash of concern may have raced through David's mind. But Jayne could not possibly know that he was lying about the Disney job or that he was calling from the bedroom of the home he shared with Dorothy.

"From the studios, darling," he said casually. "Where else would I be calling from?"

"I don't know," she said. "Honey, I want to see your office. When can I get the tour?"

David swallowed hard but not loud enough for Jayne to hear him. "Is tomorrow okay? We could meet at the studios and I'll show you my office. Then we could go to dinner with my boss. How would that be?"

Jayne felt herself relax. David couldn't be lying or he wouldn't make such an offer. Still, she wanted to see the office for herself. "That's fine, sweetheart. Will you be home late tonight?"

"Not too late," he said. "See you in a while."

For the next several hours, in addition to taking Dorothy to lunch and explaining to her that he had some lengthy missions in Saudi Arabia coming up, David spent some time on the telephone with Disney Studios.

The next day, David drove to the apartment at four o'clock and picked up Jayne. As they made their way to the studios he handed Jayne his employment package. There was no denying that the material was from Disney Studios in Orlando and that it contained the paperwork the company gave to its new employees.

"I've been reading about the benefits and they're really great, sweetheart," he said. "Why don't you take a look at it."

Thirty minutes later they arrived at the studios and parked in the employee section. David took Jayne's hand and walked her into the offices and down a carpeted hallway.

"This is it," he said proudly, ushering her into a spacious office. Inside was a walnut desk with a high-backed leather chair. On the desk was a sign that read DAVID R. MILLER, DISNEY ATTORNEY and alongside it was a framed picture of Jayne.

Jayne smiled at her husband and circled her arms around his neck. Her father had been wrong after all. She should have known she could trust David. He had always been honest with her. Now, just because her sister hadn't been able to find him listed with the state bar, she had begun to doubt him. She was disgusted with herself for doubting David.

"Honey, it's a beautiful office," she said. "I'm so excited for you."

"Well, are you hungry?"

"Sure, but what about the tour?"

"Oh, we can do that later, honey," he said. "I say we go get dinner now. I'm famished."

"Okay, where do we meet your boss?"

David paused but not long enough to cause Jayne to grow suspicious. "He called at the last minute," David said. "He won't be able to make it."

Dorothy and David's wedding photo taken at the Candlelight Wedding Chapel in Las Vegas, where they were married on August 11, 1985.
(Photo courtesy Brandi Garofalo)

February 14, 1991. Jayne and David on their wedding night in Las Vegas.
(Photo courtesy Richard Leebrick)

Sardis, Ohio. David's hometown was very small and David bided his time until graduation, when he was finally able to escape the confines of Sardis.

(Photo by Mary Russell)

The home David grew up in was on Route 7, the main street in Sardis. David's hometown was so small, there was only one stoplight and it was merely a yellow warning signal advising passersby to slow down.

(Photo by Mary Russell)

David graduated from River High School, where he was busy with a number of activities and, according to family members, first became secretive about his personal life. "It wasn't that David lied," one relative said, "it was just that he wouldn't tell the whole story."

(Photo by Mary Russell)

David used photos like this one to illustrate his work with the CIA. He might use such a photo to prove to Dorothy that he was on an airplane and about to embark on a secret mission.

(Photo courtesy Brandi Garofalo)

June 1991. Jayne and her sixteen-year-old son in the limousine on their way to the airport, where they'd meet David and leave for Rome, Italy.

(Photo courtesy Richard Leebrick)

June 1991. David and Jayne on vacation in Rome, Italy.
(Photo courtesy Richard Leebrick)

One of the final photographs taken of Jayne Leebrick.

(Photo courtesy of Richard Leebrick)

Jayne Marie Leebrick. March 4, 1958–September 15, 1991.

(Photos courtesy Richard Leebrick)

25

While David continued to spend money he did not have and his wife Jayne continued to believe him to be a millionaire recently hired by Disney, his wife Dorothy began to grow disillusioned.

David was rarely home anymore and when he was he seemed constantly distracted. Finally, Dorothy had begun to wonder why David was allowing the CIA to so thoroughly dominate his time.

"Don't they know you're married?" she asked him once in early March. He had been home less than twenty-four hours and he was already planning to leave the next day.

"Yes, sweetheart," David said calmly, patting her hand and looking lovingly into her eyes. "They know I'd rather be home. But the country is still wrapping up the war and there are a lot of stressful situations right now involving our government. Believe me, they could keep me busy around the clock if I were willing. But I'm not. They know I have to see you and spend time with you."

"David, this is crazy," Dorothy complained. "You don't spend time here. You're in one day and out the next and then I don't see you for weeks at a time. That isn't a marriage. It's barely even an existence."

David took his wife in his arms and stroked her still-beautiful brown hair. She had cut it short years before and ever since had taken on the look of a young college student. David marveled that she was still as pretty as she had been when he'd first met her.

"Try to understand," he whispered softly. "I love you and you're just going to have to trust me. I want to be with you more than you know."

But similar conversations had taken place too many times and now Dorothy was no longer easily pacified. "I'm tired of understanding, David," she said angrily. "This has got to stop. This is no marriage, seeing each other a few days each month. I need you home."

Then it was David's turn to be angry. "Listen, Dorothy," he said. "Haven't I done everything I can for you and your kids? I've provided for you and loved you and done everything in my power to be with you." He continued to raise his voice. "If you're going to start making demands now, then maybe I'll leave tonight."

"Fine. Leave," she said. For the first time she was not interested in making peace with her husband. His schedule was completely unreasonable and she wanted him to make some changes.

After their argument David had packed his things and returned to the apartment he shared with Jayne. She thought he had left immediately after work for a business trip to Los Angeles, but when he came home at eight o'clock that evening he simply told her the trip had been canceled. Jayne was happy to have him home and did not question the peculiar way in which his plans could change from one hour to the next.

But back in Casselberry, Dorothy wondered what was happening to their marriage. Because she had no choice, Dorothy had begun to make a life for herself outside of her relationship with David. She'd met a new set of friends in Casselberry and she still spent a great deal of time with her neighbors, Tom and Merritt Foster. She was still young—only forty-two—and men seemed just as interested in her as ever.

The more she began to enjoy the distant attention of strangers, the less she thought about David's dangerous missions. In fact, there were days when she did not even think about her husband's whereabouts, let alone worry about his safety. Sometimes she wondered why they had stayed married so long when they spent so little time together.

In the past when she would become frustrated by his traveling, she would think of the element of danger he faced each day and have pity on him. But the idea of feeling sorry for her husband was beginning to grow old. He did not seem to miss her the way he once had and he telephoned less frequently than before.

Now, in the wake of their fight, she decided that whenever she saw her husband again they would need to have a long talk. If they didn't work things out between them soon, there would be no reason to bother trying.

But while Dorothy considered their angry words and the reasons her marriage seemed to be falling apart, David apparently had completely forgotten about the earlier argument. He was looking forward to the cruise with Jayne in the Bahamas. They hadn't had a proper honeymoon, he told her, and it was time they took such a vacation by themselves.

"But, David, what about your job?" Jayne asked, shocked that her husband could arrive home one evening and expect her to be ready to take a cruise by the next.

"They gave me a week off because of all the travel I've been doing," David said, smiling at Jayne and running his fingers through her blond hair. "You don't have any choice in the matter, my love. I've booked the cruise and we leave tomorrow night."

Jayne was secretly thrilled by the idea of a vacation. Their new house would still not be ready for several weeks and even though she'd been able to visit her son and her parents, they had their own lives to tend to and she found herself spending most days alone in the apartment.

"But I don't have anything to wear," she said, the excitement showing in her eyes.

"We can solve that problem," David said. "We'll go shopping in the morning and then drive to Miami. The boat leaves from there and then we'll be aboard one of the finest ocean liners in the world for one perfect week."

"Oh, David," Jayne said, throwing her arms around his neck and kissing him squarely on the mouth. "What did I ever do to deserve you?"

After charging several hundred dollars in clothes for the cruise, David and Jayne arrived at the ship's boarding area the next day an hour before departure. While Jayne waited nearby, David paid for their tickets.

"I have a surprise for you, sweetheart," he said, walking up to her and taking her hand in his. "Follow me."

David led her onto the ship and took her up two

flights of stairs to the ship's luxurious resident deck. He led her down a corridor toward the stateside suites and used a key he'd been given at the boarding area to open one of the rooms. The suite had a king-size bed, a spacious bathroom, and a private balcony with a small table and two chairs.

"David," Jayne gasped as she looked around the room. "This must have cost a fortune."

David smiled modestly. "We were going to stay in a standard room—but then I remembered, this is our honeymoon," he said, looking suggestively into her eyes. "We're going to be spending most of our time in our room, so we might as well enjoy it. Right?"

Jayne felt like a princess in a fairy tale. She had seen pictures of beautiful cruise ships with suites that had private balconies. But she never dreamed she'd be vacationing in one.

For the next week, she and David rarely left their room. When they did, they were deeply affectionate with each other, holding hands and kissing during their meals and on the ship's ballroom dance floor. Jayne called her parents once from one of the ship's ports and told them where they were.

"Mom, we're in the Bahamas," she said. "Can you believe it? David wanted to take me on a honeymoon, so we just dropped everything and left."

Janice was puzzled. "Without making any plans or telling anyone where you were going?"

"Mom, I'm a big girl," she said patiently. "I can take care of myself. You should be happy for me. I'm having the time of my life."

Janice sighed. She didn't want to burst her daughter's happiness by voicing her doubts. But she did not understand how David could act so impulsively and still be a responsible husband to her daughter. The man was trouble, Janice was certain, and she knew Richard felt the same way. But they wouldn't say anything now. Jayne was too happy.

"Well, honey," she said finally. "Have a good time. Tell us about it when you get back."

When the cruise ended, Jayne and David were driving home to their apartment when they pulled up at a stoplight next to a car very much like the one he'd bought for Dorothy. Although it was not actually her car, David's face turned white and he pressed his foot on the gas pedal, sending the car lurching through the intersection against the red light.

"David, what's wrong?" Jayne looked terrified. They had narrowly missed hitting two cars.

A fine layer of sweat had broken out on David's forehead. "I don't know. I'm not sure," he said, stumbling over his words.

"Are you okay? I mean, do you want me to drive?"

"No, I'm fine," he said, sitting straighter in his seat and wiping off his forehead with a handkerchief. "I must have been daydreaming."

But David apparently knew what had happened. For a brief instant he seemed to think Dorothy was in the car beside them. After all, she lived in the same city. Until that moment, David had apparently never considered the possibility that his wives might accidentally run into each other. But now that he must have realized how easily such an incident could happen, he was probably terrified. If they found out about each other he would be ruined. His political chances would be finished, he would lose his lobbying clients, and he would have to let go of the lives he'd worked so hard to build.

David needed to work out a plan that would prevent his wives from ever finding out about each other. He would have to wait. A plan like that would require his full attention and as long as he was with Jayne he could not allow himself to think of anything but being her husband—a task that required him to remember which lies he'd told her and which lies she knew nothing about.

They had been home less than an hour when David pretended to call into the office.

"Well, it's a good thing we took the cruise when we did," he said sadly.

"Why? What's up?"

"I have to go to L.A. again," he said. "Looks like they're having more problems with their legal department and they need my help working them out." He paused a moment. "Are you mad?"

"Mad? How could I be mad?" she said. "I'm married to the best man in the world. Of course I'm not mad." She sidled up next to him so that he could see down her silk blouse past the tan lines from her new bathing suit. "I'll miss you, though," she said.

As David looked at her he could feel his excitement building. "I'm not leaving yet," he said, and his voice was husky as he moved her gently toward their bed. "The plane doesn't leave for two hours."

An hour later, David said good-bye to Jayne and headed toward a local restaurant. He needed an oasis, a place where he would not have to be anyone's husband. A place where he could sort through the crashing pieces of his life.

He had wanted Jayne and Dorothy to be in the same

city so that he would be able to spend more time on his business. But the plan had not worked. When he needed to spend time with Dorothy—even though she lived less than fifteen minutes away from Jayne—he found himself telling Jayne he was traveling to L.A. There was no other way to explain the nights he spent away.

As a result, he still had no time to travel for his business. And now he faced another problem, one he hadn't considered until earlier that day when for a moment he thought Dorothy was in the car beside them. What if his wives found out about each other? As long as they lived in the same city there was always a chance that could happen. It was something David couldn't bear to imagine.

He needed to get one of them out of Florida. But which one? Certainly Jayne would not be open to moving. She thought he was working at Disney Studios and after convincing her that he did indeed have an office there she would never understand another move so quickly. Besides, she was already near her parents and her son. That way she had something to occupy her time when he was out of town.

He would have to move Dorothy. David thought quickly and remembered that her parents lived in Pennsylvania near the small town where Dorothy had grown up. That was it. He'd move her back to Pennsylvania to be near her parents. As a host of paranoid thoughts slammed about inside his head, he decided he would have to move Dorothy immediately. Perhaps in the next few days.

He would tell her that their lives were once again in danger. That would explain why he'd been so upset lately and why he'd fought with her the last time he'd seen her. Yes, he would have to move Dorothy right away if he could ever get rid of the fear that had been consuming him since the scare earlier that day. His wives needed to be far away from each other.

Once David had worked out the details and how he would present them to Dorothy, he got in his car and drove to Casselberry. Before he walked up the sidewalk, he must have purposely tousled his hair. He wanted Dorothy to believe he was in a desperate hurry to get them to safety. That way Dorothy would not argue with him about the inconvenience of moving.

Waiting inside their home, Dorothy had not come any closer to feeling sympathetic for her husband in the week since he'd stormed out of the house. She did not know where he was or what type of mission he was on, but she knew that whenever he returned she would have to talk with him about their marriage.

But when David walked into their home that afternoon, a terrified look on his face and his eyes wide with concern, her plans to talk with him disappeared.

As soon as he saw her, he burst into tears and wrapped her tightly in his arms. "You're okay," he sobbed. "Oh, honey, I'm so glad you're okay."

Dorothy felt her heart skip a beat as the adrenaline surged through her body. "David, what is it? What's happened?"

"Death threats," he said, tears streaming down his face. "They told me it might be too late."

"What do you mean? What might be too late?"

"Dorothy, sweetheart, we're all in terrible, terrible danger," he said, and Dorothy was struck by the urgency in his voice. "The CIA told me that a group of terrorists knows where we live. They're planning to kill us all sometime this week. And I thought it might already be too late.''

"Oh, my God.'' Dorothy gasped. "The boys! They're outside playing with their friends.''

She ran outside and several houses down Jericho Drive until she saw Michael and Tony playing baseball with a few of the neighborhood boys. Her sons were thirteen and fourteen now and old enough to come and go as they pleased. But suddenly Dorothy feared for their safety. Terrorists could be lurking behind any house on the block waiting for a chance to kill them.

"Get home,'' she yelled at them frantically. "Right now. Get home immediately.''

The boys did not want to leave what they were doing, but they could tell something terrible had happened. They put down their baseballs and followed their mother.

Once Dorothy had gathered her sons and was safely back in the house, David asked them all to sit at the dining room table. He carefully explained to them that their lives were in danger because of a mission he'd undertaken recently. The children had known that David's job could be dangerous ever since he'd told them about it years earlier. But they never thought the danger would affect their lives also. They listened nervously as David continued.

"We really have just one choice,'' he said finally. "We have to move.''

Dorothy knew from the moment she'd seen the terror on David's face that afternoon that they would have to move. She would be sad to leave because of the friends she'd made, but clearly there were more important things to think about now. Her safety and the safety of her children and her husband was more important than leaving their friends. Besides, perhaps one day they would return to Casselberry.

As David outlined the plan he had for moving them to Pennsylvania, Dorothy was reminded of the time he'd moved them to Florida to escape danger in Los Angeles. But that had been less intense than this situation. This time it seemed their lives were in imminent danger, as if terrorists might break into their home at any moment.

"Will we have time to pack?" she asked, drying her damp eyes and trying to still her racing heart.

"Get as many things together as you can," he said. "There will be Secret Service men watching our home tonight and tomorrow. Tomorrow morning they'll follow us to the airport and we'll all leave for Pennsylvania."

Dorothy nodded. "What about our belongings?"

"Just like before," he said, and Dorothy could see the sorrow etched in his face. "Professional movers will pack everything and it will be sent along to our new place in Pennsylvania. We'll rent out this house and decide later if we want to sell it or not." He paused again. "I'm so sorry to put you all through this."

Dorothy nodded, completely understanding the agony in her husband's voice. "Why Pennsylvania, David?"

"My choice, sweetheart," he said. "I wanted you and the boys to be near your family, in case."

Dorothy's eyes widened in horror. "In case of what?"

David looked down at the floor and up again into Dorothy's honest green eyes. "In case something happens to me. This is a very dangerous time for me, honey."

A silence passed between David and Dorothy. Finally she walked over to her husband and took him in her arms. "I'm sorry, David," she said, her voice cracking with emotion. "Can you ever forgive me?"

"You don't have anything to be sorry for," he said. "I'm the one who's sorry. I'm sorry I ever got you involved in this mess."

Dorothy shook her head quickly, fresh tears filling her eyes. "It was my choice. I loved you and I wanted to be part of your life," she said. "I knew the risks when I married you."

"Yes, but you're right. I haven't been home and I haven't been the kind of husband you need."

Dorothy laughed bitterly. "Yes, but I should have known you were in danger. I was so busy feeling sorry for myself I forgot to think about you and what you're going through."

"Well, we don't have time to worry about the past," he said. "We have to get out of here and make sure nothing happens to any of us."

"How long will we be in Pennsylvania?"

"I hope not too long," he answered, gently wiping the tears from her cheeks. "Maybe a year at the most. Just until this series of missions is over and the danger passes."

Dorothy nodded. "I'm so scared, David," she whispered.

"I know, sweetheart. But we have the top security forces in the nation watching out for us. We'll be okay. And anyway, at least now you know why I've been gone so much. I was beginning to worry that you didn't believe me, that you might even leave me."

"I was thinking about it," she said, shaking her head sadly, regretting her past thoughts. "But now, because of this, I can see clearly again. My priorities were in the wrong place. But I could never live without you, David. Never."

The next day, with only a few suitcases filled with their clothing, Dorothy, David, and her sons left for Pennsylvania. When Dorothy asked David why the Secret Service men hadn't followed them to the airport after all, he assured her that they had.

"That's why they're Secret Service men, honey." He smiled at her. "Even I don't know when they're following me."

Dorothy felt thankful to have gotten her family away from the Casselberry home without any of them being hurt. She only hoped that no one would find them at their new home in Pennsylvania. When they arrived at their new home, David spent the next two days setting Dorothy and her sons up in a small apartment and spending some time with Dorothy's parents.

"Take care of her while I'm gone," he said. David had sensed a certain wisdom in Dorothy's parents and had never explained his concocted CIA job to them. "I can't explain what's happening in my life right now except to say that it's very secretive and it has to do with the security of our country. But please believe me that I'm doing this because I love your daughter. She's going to need your support."

Two days later he left for Los Angeles, where he planned to get his business accounts in order and finally spend some time drumming up new clients. Before he left for L.A. he decided to purchase several new suits. He would need to look good if he was going to rebuild his clientele.

He charged the purchases on his credit card.

26

Ed Cholakian was losing his patience. He considered himself a reasonable man, and when David had asked to borrow money back in November he had seen no reason why he should refuse him. But it was April now and he hadn't heard from David in nearly a month. The promises that David had made about the contracts had not come through and he hadn't even mentioned his cancer in weeks.

Finally, Ed decided he'd had enough. He picked up his office phone and called David.

"David Miller, please." Ed's voice was curt and David's secretary could tell the caller was unhappy about something.

"I'm afraid David's out of town on business," Cynthia said.

"That's impossible," Ed said. "David promised he'd use my travel agency and I haven't had any business from him in months."

Cynthia wondered if perhaps the caller was a prankster. David never used any travel agency. She made all his travel plans. "I'm sorry, sir, but I book all David's travel. He doesn't use any agency for his plans."

"I see," Ed said as he worked to control his anger. "And where is Mr. Miller now?"

"He's in Washington D.C., sir," Cynthia said, instantly wondering if she should have revealed David's whereabouts. In truth she hadn't made many travel plans for David either lately. He was spending much of his time away from the office but until the Washington D.C. trip she hadn't booked a flight for him in nearly two months. Everyone at the office was beginning to wonder where David was spending his time and rumors were circulating that he was suffering from a fatal illness.

"Will he be calling for his messages?"

"Yes, sir."

"Then tell him that Ed Cholakian called. I want my money now."

Two hours later, David called his office and was livid with anger when he learned that Cynthia had told Ed he was in Washington D.C.

"I'm sorry, Mr. Miller. It won't happen again," Cynthia said. Secretly, though, she wondered what was happening to her boss. The books showed that they were still bringing in some money, but not nearly as much as they once had. And there had been several calls lately from people who had loaned money to him. She and Lynne had discussed the problems and decided they should probably start looking for other jobs. If the business was suffering, their positions could no longer be considered stable.

As soon as David got the message from Cynthia he put in a call to Ed's office. "Hey, Ed, it's David Miller returning your call." As usual David did a convincing job of sounding cheerful, and Ed seethed at the other end.

"Listen, Miller," Ed said, skipping the niceties. "You said you'd use my travel agency. What are you doing in Washington D.C. without calling me about your plans?"

"I'm not in D.C.," David said. "I needed to get away from the office for a few days, so I told them I was in D.C. I cancelled the plans as soon as my secretary made them. I'm here. In L.A."

Ed raised his voice a notch. "I don't know what kind of game you're playing, Miller, but I'm sick of it. If you're here, then get over to my office in an hour. I want to talk about your loan."

"Sure, Ed, no problem," David said calmly. "I'll be there in fifteen minutes."

True to his word, David arrived at Ed's office in Sunland fifteen minutes later. For the next hour he produced paperwork and contracts proving that he would be able to pay the loan back in one week. Ed decided he would have to be satisfied with the arrangement.

"Don't forget," David said, referring to the loan papers he had signed, "those paintings in my office are yours if these don't come through."

Ed nodded angrily. He would never again loan money to David Miller, regardless of his health conditions.

"By the way, how's your health?" Ed asked sarcastically, already convinced that David had never been sick.

"Good news," David said. "The cancer's in remission. Didn't I tell you?"

"No, David, you didn't," Ed said, his voice sounding dry. "That's good news. Now that you're not sick you'll have no trouble getting all those contracts to come in, right?"

"You bet," he said as he stood to leave. "Hey, thanks for your patience, Ed. Talk to you later."

David knew Ed was angry with him, but he could do nothing about it. He had been flying to Los Angeles for three and four days at a time every two weeks or so and he truly was trying to bring in more business. But he no longer seemed able to concentrate on his lobbying efforts.

His plan of having Dorothy and Jayne live in the same city so that he could have more time to travel on lobbying trips had backfired. He still had to spend time in Los Angeles to keep the business going and he had been forced to turn down one trip after another. Valuable connections he'd spent years developing were disappearing and David knew his financial situation had gone beyond desperate. In one month's time he had run up what he estimated were credit card accounts of fifteen or twenty thousand dollars.

He had no idea how he was going to pay the bills when they began to come in. But by then David apparently no longer cared how he was going to deal with his money troubles.

His only concern was that he keep his recent credit purchases from Dorothy. He had hoped that she would not receive the statements because of their sudden move to Pennsylvania. But after the move she had contacted the credit card companies and notified them of her changed mailing address.

David would have to intercept the statements before they wound up in Dorothy's hands. He must have telephoned the credit card companies and asked the exact date they intended to mail their statements. That way, he must have learned when the first bills might arrive at Dorothy's new apartment in Pennsylvania and he made plans to be with her at that time. He would have to dispose of the bills as soon as they arrived so that Dorothy would not know what was happening to their finances.

Some of the purchases might be easy to justify. But there would be no way to explain why he had spent eleven thousand dollars on furniture during the month of March. David must have cringed if he thought about what Dorothy would think if she ever saw that statement. But even as the anxiety began to build, he forcibly calmed himself down. She would never find out the truth. Never. He would do whatever was necessary to keep it from her.

Once he had convinced himself of that, he telephoned the airlines and booked a flight back to Orlando. Jayne needed to spend some time with him or she would inevitably begin to wonder where he was spending his time. He waited patiently for the operator to make his flight plans.

"How will you pay for that, sir?" the operator asked him.

"Credit card," David said.

27

Jayne and David had planned to move into their new house in Heathrow by mid-April. The furniture—costing eleven thousand dollars—had been placed in storage and David had lined up movers to transfer their new belongings into the home as soon as escrow closed.

Of course, David apparently never intended to purchase the home with cash. He would keep the real estate agent at bay promising to pay the purchase price as soon as he could clear the funds from his investment accounts. In the meantime he would continue to work on bringing in new clients and more money.

That way, he could eventually put down several thousand dollars to hold the house and then get a mortgage loan from a local bank. He would pay the Casselberry house payments with money from the renters and he would pay for the new home with the money he planned to start making as soon as his business got rolling again.

But things were not working out the way David had

hoped they would. With Dorothy safely moved to Pennsylvania he no longer worried that his wives might bump into each other at the supermarket. And he had actually spent several days recently at his Los Angeles office. But instead of building his clientele, he found himself fending off loan collectors. Everyone he had borrowed money from was worried about getting paid back. The calls from those people represented a constant distraction and David had been unable to slip back into the mode of lobbyist.

At the same time, he had learned that investigators were closing in on Senator Alan Robbins. Although it was never clear what amount of stress that might have added to David's list of problems, it was something to consider. And perhaps combined with the fact that his friends had now become merely loan collectors, David must have begun to dread spending time in L.A.

During the early part of April, David was notified by the real estate agent working with him on purchasing the Heathrow house that a new offer had come in. The people wanted to put money down right away and buy the home. David was not surprised, but the news forced him to create a story to explain to Jayne why they would not be moving to Heathrow.

"Honey," he said as he walked into their apartment one evening that week. "I just heard from the real estate agent about the house."

Jayne's eyes lit up. She couldn't wait to move into the new house and they'd been waiting to hear from the real estate agent for several days. She had long since grown frustrated with living in the small apartment and once in a while she even wondered if she'd made a mistake by marrying David. After all, she rarely saw him and she had only known him a few months. She had begun to wonder if perhaps her father was right and she'd acted too quickly in marrying him. But before her doubts about David could crystalize, she convinced herself that once they moved into their new house everything would work out fine. Now, as David stood before her with news from the real estate agent, Jayne figured the deal had finally gone through.

"When can we move in?" she asked, clasping her hands and waiting excitedly for his answer.

David shook his head and grimaced at Jayne's obvious disappointment. "I'm sorry, honey, the deal's off. And it's a good thing too."

"What do you mean, David? We're not moving in?"

David shook his head. "It seems the broker has been doing some checking on the house and the foundation is built over dried-up swampland."

"What?"

"Swampland. It's a big thing here in Florida, you know. Developers come along and fill in a dried-up swamp and build houses on it. Sometimes it's okay, but other times there's a danger the swamp could fill up again during the rains. If that happens, the entire house could cave in. It could be very dangerous."

"I can't believe it," Jayne said, shocked by the news. "How come we're just finding out now?"

"I guess the city's been out making some checks on the property and they've condemned it until the foundation can be reinforced."

"This is incredible. One day it's our dream house and the next day it's condemned?"

David nodded. "I know, honey," he said. "I'm disappointed too."

"Isn't there any way we can wait until they fix the

foundation and still buy it,'' she said hopefully. ''We have all the furniture picked out and everything.''

''The furniture will be good wherever we move,'' he answered. ''Let's not worry about it. We can spend the whole weekend looking at houses.''

Jayne was frustrated by the news. She had spent more than a month cramped in the tiny apartment and she had been desperately ready to move into their new house. Now they would have to start all over again searching for property.

She knew the problems weren't David's fault and she tried not to be angry with him. ''I suppose we should be glad they found all this out before we bought the house,'' Jayne said.

''That's right, sweetheart.'' David walked behind her and began to massage her shoulders. ''I'm so glad you have a good attitude about this thing. I was worried you'd be upset.''

That weekend David and Jayne found a different real estate agent who showed them several beautiful homes including one that was even larger than the house in Heathrow. The house was thirty years old and had ten acres of property situated along a peaceful pond in the Lake Mary Woods area.

As he had done before, David began working out a deal with the agent, assuring him that he would pay for the house in cash. But by Sunday night he had changed his mind and allowed another offer to replace his. Jayne still thought he was a millionaire, but in fact he did not have enough money to buy a house, let alone an expensive luxury home on a lake. He wondered how long he could keep making offers on homes and allowing the deals to fall through.

''It's too old, Jayne,'' he said, referring to the house

they'd made an offer on just one day before. "I want something new, something we can retire in and spend the next thirty years enjoying."

This time Jayne did not try to hide her disappointment.

"The house was wonderful, David," she said. "I can't believe you let it go. What are we going to do now?"

"Don't take it so hard, honey," he said calmly. "We don't want to rush into something and then be stuck with it. We can start looking again next weekend."

"That's easy for you to say," she said, and for the first time since they'd gotten married two months earlier she allowed herself to be angry with her husband. "I'm the one who has to be stuck in this small, cramped apartment."

David thought quickly. He didn't like the idea of Jayne being angry with him. "Listen, maybe it's time you started looking for a job. You wouldn't mind it here if you got out more."

The movers David had hired when they left Los Angeles had brought Jayne's red Hyundai and David's sports car with them. So David knew Jayne had the transportation if she wanted a job. In fact, they could really use the money she might bring in, although there was no way he could tell her that. She had no idea that he had run out of money.

"I can't start a new job now," she complained. "I'll be too busy trying to put the new house together."

"Well, suit yourself," he said, shrugging his shoulders. "We won't be looking at any new houses until next weekend."

"And how much time will you be spending in Los Angeles this week?" She sounded bitter and almost hateful as she asked the question. The doubts she'd begun to feel in the past weeks were making themselves known.

David raised an eyebrow. This was not the Jayne he knew and loved, questioning him and suggesting by her tone of voice that David was doing something wrong. "What?" he asked.

"I said, how much time will you be spending in Los Angeles this week?" she said again. "You seem to spend an awful lot of time there, you know."

"Listen, didn't we just get home from taking a cruise?"

"So what?" Jayne said, her voice rising. "That was wonderful but it wasn't real. This is our real life and I need to know why you're gone so much of the time."

"I thought you were worried about buying a house," David said, his voice rising to match hers. "Now you change your mind and your biggest concern is the time I spend traveling. Well, it's none of your business."

David wanted to take the words back as soon as he'd said them. His secretive business trips were a part of his life with Dorothy, not Jayne. He always told Jayne the concocted details of his trips to Los Angeles.

"None of my business?" Jayne stood up and moved closer to David, her face red with emotion. "I sit here while you gallivant back and forth to Los Angeles and it's none of my business? You're the one who moved me out here so we could have this happy life together, remember?"

David held up his hands. "Wait a minute, wait a minute," he said, his voice once again calm. "Why are we doing this to each other? I love you, Jayne. I don't want to fight with you like this."

Jayne narrowed her eyes. "Then spend more time at home."

"Sweetheart, you know I want to. I just have to work out the wrinkles of this new job, that's all. I promise I'll make it up to you."

"Okay, then answer my question," she said evenly, looking directly into his dark eyes and searching for the man she thought she loved. "How much time will you be spending in Los Angeles this week?"

David's mind raced. He needed to see Dorothy in Pennsylvania to intercept the credit card bills before they arrived at her apartment. But if he left Jayne she would only get more angry.

Suddenly David must have known that he had underestimated Jayne. She would not sit idly by while he spent more than half his time traveling to Los Angeles. He would have to work out a new plan, but for now he knew he would have to spend the rest of the week in Orlando with Jayne, pretending to go to Disney Studios each morning. He still needed to get back to Dorothy before the credit card bills started arriving. He cleared his throat and stared at his wife.

"I'm not going anywhere this week," he said firmly. "I'll be right here in Florida with you. I promise."

Jayne smiled slowly and the tension in her shoulders visibly disappeared. She needed to trust David more. He truly did love her and Jayne worried that she was beginning to expect him to let her down like the other men in her life had done. "That's better," she said. "I'm not trying to run your life, David, but I just can't live in this apartment by myself. You're my husband and I need you here."

David nodded. "I know, honey," he said. "I need you too."

For the next week, David spent his days working with a lobbying client he'd once had in Florida. Whatever business they had formerly done was quickly reinstated that week and by the weekend David had somehow earned $25,000. He mailed receipt of the payment to his secretaries and told them that more money would be coming in shortly.

Both Lynne and Cynthia were relieved. In light of the loans David had been unable to repay, they had begun to wonder if David might be considering closing down his business. Now he had apparently established a connection in Florida and was already collecting payments for his efforts.

However, in his excitement over the profitable week he'd enjoyed in Orlando, David forgot about the credit card bills making their way to Dorothy in Pennsylvania.

By mid-April, on a rainy afternoon when Dorothy thought David was back in Kuwait on a dangerous mission, she walked from her apartment to the community mail board and used her key to retrieve her mail. At first glance she did not notice anything unusual about the mail that afternoon. The credit card companies sent statements on a regular basis even though they owed nothing on any of the accounts.

She brought the mail inside, took off her raincoat, and began opening the bills. The first bill included two pages of charges and an account balance of more than ten thousand dollars. Dorothy gasped out loud, scanning the charges in confusion. There were clothing charges, restaurant charges, and a charge to a cruise-liner company in Florida for several thousand dollars.

Dorothy looked the bill over for several minutes and then put it aside. She decided there must have been some kind of mistake or perhaps someone had stolen one of their credit cards. David carried a duplicate set of the cards with him and it was possible he'd lost his wallet during one of his missions.

Slowly, Dorothy picked up the next bill in the stack and opened it. Again the statement included several pages of charges and showed a balance of more than seventeen thousand dollars. Included on the statement was an eleven thousand dollar charge for furniture and several cash advances. Dorothy shook her head as she tried to understand what had happened to their credit. When she opened two more bills and saw that the accounts for those cards equalled more than ten thousand dollars, Dorothy decided she must have been right. Someone had stolen David's cards. That was the only possible explanation.

Not once did Dorothy consider that David had actually spent the thousands of dollars itemized on the statements. Whereas some woman might have analyzed the purchases and come to the conclusion that their husband was having an affair, the thought never crossed Dorothy's mind. David could not possibly have been having an affair, taking cruises behind her back and buying furniture for another woman's home. He was in Kuwait on a dangerous mission. And for that reason, she did not for one moment believe the purchases had actually been David's.

Back in Orlando, David spent the weekend house-hunting with Jayne and on Monday morning he flew to Pennsylvania. Jayne had not been happy about his travel plans, but David finally convinced her that as the new man on staff he had no choice but to cooperate.

He took a cash advance from one of his credit cards and purchased a ticket to Pennsylvania. He devised a plan during the trip. He knew that by then Dorothy would know about the credit cards, but he had been very careful about what he charged. He had only charged a few airline tickets and otherwise he always took a cash advance to pay for his flights. That way no one could track his whereabouts by looking at the credit card statements.

He decided he would tell Dorothy his cards had been stolen. He would promise to call the companies immediately to report the loss and get the charges removed from their account. That way he would have another month's time before the next statement arrived. One month, David must have calculated, would certainly be enough time to make more money and pay off the accounts before Dorothy could grow suspicious.

Dorothy met him at the door of their apartment when he arrived in town that evening. "Honey, I have something very serious to show you," she said, holding the credit card bills in her hand.

"Wait, before you tell me I need to know if I left my credit cards here," David said quickly, walking past Dorothy and setting his luggage down. "I've been looking everywhere for them and I can't find them anywhere."

Dorothy held up the statements. "Looks to me like you lost them, all right," she said, letting out a deep sigh. "And someone else has found them."

David feigned anger over the idea that someone had run up their credit cards with stolen purchases. He vowed to take care of the problem first thing in the morning and then, with the credit card dilemma successfully behind him, he hugged Dorothy tightly.

"I'm so glad to see you, honey," he said. "You don't

know how much easier it was to be away from you this time knowing that you and the boys were safe in Pennsylvania.''

Dorothy smiled weakly at him. "Yes, but what about you?"

"The mission went well," he said, pulling out a postcard from Saudi Arabia and handing it to her. "I think most of the danger has passed."

He bent down and kissed his wife more passionately than he'd done in weeks. "Now, what do you say we celebrate my return?"

28

April 15, 1991, was the beginning of the end for David Miller and Associates.

The day began normally enough, with Grant Hawthorne reporting to work and David's secretaries busy taking care of the front office. But sometime around one o'clock that afternoon, when Lynne and Cynthia had come back from lunch, Ed Cholakian walked into the office.

"I'm looking for David Miller," he said curtly. "Where is he?"

Cynthia looked at the man standing before her and knew instinctively that he would not be satisfied with the standard answer that Mr. Miller was out for the day. "Well," she said slowly. "He's out of town. Can I take a message for him?"

Ed shook his head, clearly angry at the situation. "No, I've tried that before. I talked to David last week and he said he'd pay back the money he borrowed from me within the week. The week's up and I still haven't gotten my money."

Ed took a piece of paper from his pocket and unfolded it. "It says here that if David doesn't pay back the money by the end of December 1990, I am entitled to the artwork in his office."

Grant had been listening to the conversation from his office and he stood up to talk to Ed in person. They knew each other vaguely from business gatherings in the valley, but Ed was much better friends with David. Grant reached out and shook Ed's hand.

"Can I see that?" Grant asked, and Ed handed him the loan paper.

Grant shook his head. "I don't know what's going on with David these days," he said. "You heard he'd been sick?"

Ed nodded. "He's in remission right now, at least that's what he tells me," he said sarcastically. "Anyway, I'm beyond worrying about whether he has cancer or not. I want my money. He borrowed ten thousand dollars from me and he hasn't paid me back."

"I understand."

Grant had long since stopped worrying about David's affairs and the degree to which they were falling apart. He had his own clientele and he had lived up to his deal by paying David a percentage of the money he made. But lately he had been seriously considering breaking off and starting his own business. The overhead would cost less than the commission money he was paying David. And he was beginning to wonder whether he still wanted to be associated with David Miller. The man seemed to have made enemies out of even his closest friends. Since February it seemed that whenever he made an appointment he didn't keep it. Many times Grant had done the business for the client because David had simply never shown up for a meeting or function. When that happened, the client would then become Grant's responsibility.

"As you know, he's not here, Ed," Grant said, handing the paper back to him. "I don't know what to tell you."

"I didn't expect to find him here," Ed said. "But if he doesn't have my money, it's time to collect my paintings."

Ed opened the door and grabbed a large cardboard box.

"Do me a favor, Grant, and watch what I take," he said. "I don't need David accusing me of taking more than what's already mine."

Grant nodded his approval. The artwork had been the collateral and Ed was entitled to take what he wanted since David hadn't paid him back. He wondered what David would do when he found out Ed had been by the office. Grant suddenly hoped he wouldn't be around when it happened.

For the next twenty minutes Ed moved about David's office collecting artwork. The first thing he took was an oil painting of dueling eagles in flight. David had said he'd paid eight thousand dollars for the piece but that it was worth twenty-five thousand. Next he took three Marty Bell paintings that were likely worth another thousand dollars. He looked around and discovered David's personal wall filled with framed pictures of him with various politicians.

He began taking the pictures off the wall and placing them in the box. Finally, he glanced over David's desk and saw a 1984 Olympic pin set and a 1988 framed Olympic flag. He picked up both items and looked around the office one final time.

"I guess that'll do it," he said. Then he nodded to Lynne and Cynthia and thanked them for their time. "Give David my best," he said as he left the office. "And tell him I'd be happy to sell him this stuff for ten thousand dollars if he's interested."

David learned about Ed's visit later that day when he called in from Orlando for his messages. For reasons his associates and peers in the business world may never understand, the idea that Ed had taken the art-work from his office represented a final straw to David Miller.

He operated the rest of the day in little more than a trance, canceling a business meeting with his client in Florida and coming home to Jayne earlier than usual. He calmly told her that he would need to go to Los Angeles the next day and when she began to complain about his being gone he turned to her and snapped.

"Shut up," he shouted. "I'm sick of your complaining."

Jayne was so taken aback by his response that she did not continue the fight. Instead, she locked herself in her bedroom and called her friend Jodee.

"He's not the same man I married, Jodee," she cried that night. "He yells at me and he's gone all the time. What happened to our wonderful life we were supposed to be having out here?"

Jodee didn't know what to tell her friend. She had doubted Jayne's wisdom in marrying David so quickly. But he had seemed so kind and loving when they were in Los Angeles.

"I don't know, Jayne," she responded. "Maybe he's just under a lot of stress right now."

Jayne decided that Jodee was probably right, and even though she didn't talk to David the rest of the night, she tried not to be angry with him for the trip he was about to take. Things were bound to settle down eventually and until then she would have to make the best of it.

David meanwhile seemed unconcerned with Jayne's reaction. The time had come for him to end his business dealings. He owned money to too many people and he could no longer afford to travel to Los Angeles every week or so.

He left the next morning, and when he arrived at Los Angeles International Airport he rented a car—as he always did when he was in L.A.—and drove to his office.

He walked into the office at just after three o'clock and stood in the entryway looking at his secretaries.

"It's over," he said somberly. "I'm closing out. There's no more money."

Cynthia moved closer to Lynne as the two women stared in shock at their boss.

"What do you mean, Mr. Miller?" Lynne asked as Grant came out into the hallway. He had heard David's voice but not the content of what was being said.

"It's over," he said, sounding like a man who had given up on life. "There will be no more work after today. No more money, no more business. It's over."

David looked toward Grant. "I'm willing to sell you my office equipment for a flat fee and you can take over renting this office if you like," he said slowly.

"David, are you sure about this?" Grant thought David looked gaunt and haggard, like a man trapped with no alternative but to give in to despair.

David nodded. "There's nothing to think about. It's over."

Grant reached out and shook David's hand. "Well, it's been a pleasure working with you, David. I don't know what's been going on lately, but I wish you the best in the future. I'm sure you'll wind up back on your feet eventually."

David did not smile. Instead he watched as Grant drew up an agreement stating that from that day on the money Grant received from his clients would belong solely to him. The document also stated that Grant would pay a flat fee for David's furniture, facsimile machine, and computer.

While Grant worked on the agreement, David sat nearby, pale and distracted. Grant wondered if he was perhaps sick again or whether he and Jayne had broken up. Whatever had happened, it had devastated him and completely robbed him of the charisma and charm he was once known for.

After David and Grant had signed the agreement, he wrote out business checks for Lynne and Cynthia, paying them all he owed them. There had been times in the past few months when he had been late with their paychecks, but they had always believed David would come through with their money. Now they were suddenly without jobs and unsure where to turn. They hugged David as he turned to leave.

"Good-bye," he said, and Grant noticed that his voice was little more than a monotone. "Thank you for everything. It's all over now."

When he was finished at his office, he drove to the chamber of commerce and handed in his resignation. Afterward, he drove to the house in Granada Hills and packed up the few belongings he had left there. When he was finished, he drove to the airport and purchased a ticket back to Florida.

It was the last time anyone in Los Angeles ever saw David Miller.

29

After closing up his business, David began to operate like a child on a spending spree with no concept of what will happen when his money runs out. He was unable to imagine what the future held and so he concentrated completely on the present. He boarded a plane and returned to Orlando—where he had at least one client who was still paying him very well for his political connections.

Perhaps he met with this client upon arriving in Florida or perhaps he spent some time by himself trying to figure out how he had gotten so desperately broke. Either way, he did not show up at the apartment he and Jayne shared until four days after pulling up stakes in Los Angeles.

Jayne had not heard from her husband during the four-day period she assumed he'd been in L.A., and with each passing day she had grown angrier at him. How dare he leave her alone in a tiny apartment without calling her once during his travels? And the nerve of him yelling at her for complaining when he had gone back on his promise and was spending more time on the road than at home.

She had talked her troubles over with Jodee and her best friend agreed that David needed to be more considerate if their marriage stood a chance of surviving.

"I mean, he may be under stress but this is ridiculous," Jodee said when Jayne called her a few hours before David got home. "You need to sit down and have a serious talk with him, Jayne."

Jayne was so disappointed she didn't know if she could talk rationally with her husband. She had placed so many hopes on this relationship and now he was turning out to be no different from the other men she knew. His business came before her and there didn't seem to be anything she could do to change that fact.

The only hope Jayne had was that things would change when they bought a house. Perhaps owning a home would remind David that he needed to spend less time on the road. Jayne imagined how after they bought a house David might come home from work by five o'clock and help her decorate. Then they could spend the weekends hanging wallpaper or curtains or planting a flower garden around the front porch. If only they could find a house they liked and buy it before the plans fell through.

She planned to talk to David as soon as he got home about continuing their house-hunting. But she forgot her plans when he walked into their apartment later that day and swept her up into his arms.

"I have a surprise for you," he said, his eyes sparkling with adventure.

Jayne struggled back onto her feet. "David!" she said, taken aback by his sudden arrival. "What's all this about?"

"You know that trip I told you about, the trip to Europe that the government of Kuwait wants to treat me and my family to?"

David had not mentioned the trip in so long that Jayne had almost forgotten about it. She nodded now, remembering the details and how her parents and sister and son had agreed to come along. "What about it?"

"Well, we're going sooner than we thought," he said.

"Why?"

David's face fell. He had expected a different reaction from his wife. "Because the officials in Kuwait want to meet us there and they want us to leave this Wednesday. I thought you'd be happy about it."

Jayne sighed. "David, that's only four days away. How are we going to be ready for a trip to Europe in just four days?"

"What do we have to do to get ready?"

"Minor details like getting our passports and packing and buying clothes for the trip," she said sarcastically.

"Listen, Jayne." David was losing patience with her. "If you don't want to go, just say so."

He would forget about his money troubles with a trip to Europe. The credit cards still had plenty of room to charge the vacation and by telling Jayne and her family that Kuwait was paying for the trip he would become even more prestigious and important in their eyes.

By then, David apparently had convinced himself that he could erase reality by creating whatever scenario he desired. The worse off his financial situation grew, the worse he thought of himself and the more necessary it became to convince his wives of his worth.

But now Jayne wasn't even acting interested. Again David was struck by the notion that he had underestimated Jayne. She was no longer swayed by his importance or the money he spent. In fact, she did not seem interested at all in his worth. Instead, she seemed focused only on developing a domestic existence—something David found repulsively boring.

"Of course I want to go, David," Jayne said, breaking the uncomfortable silence between them. "It's just that I want to do things in the right order. We need to look for a house and get settled in before I can get all excited over a trip to Europe. Do you understand?"

"We'll only be gone two weeks, Jayne. We can buy a house when we get back. What's the rush?"

"What's the rush?" She raised her voice again and David could feel his frustration growing. He loved Jayne, but he was beginning to dislike her personality. She was never satisfied, never happy with what he was trying to offer her. Didn't she understand that he was an important man? She should be thankful that he was willing to take her and her family to Europe.

Jayne began pacing the narrow floor of the apartment's living room. "You don't spend your days cooped up in this place like I do," she shouted. "This is no way to live, David. I had much more space in L.A." She stopped pacing and stared at him. "I want to start looking for houses tomorrow."

David sighed and tried to think of a solution. He was tired of working so hard to please Jayne while worrying at the same time how he was going to pay off the credit card accounts he was running up. "Okay," he said softly. "We'll look for a house tomorrow and the next day and the day after that. But then we're leaving for

Europe. I've already told the officials of Kuwait that we'll go and now we don't have a choice."

Jayne nodded her understanding. "All right," she said. Her voice had returned to a normal level as she forced herself to be agreeable. "If you're willing to spend some time house-hunting during the next few days, then I'll make an effort to get ready for Europe."

She contacted her parents, her sister, and her son, and told them of the change in plans. As it turned out, they were all able to go despite the short notice. That Monday morning they made arrangements to get passports and that afternoon she and David contacted their broker and resumed their search for a house.

This time the broker showed them a tract of sprawling houses in the countryside, several minutes outside the city of Orlando. These homes were nestled amid acres of weeping willow trees and had a quiet sophistication about them. Jayne fell in love with them instantly. The homes were new and had all been sold but one, located on Red Bug Road.

The broker took them inside and Jayne was immediately impressed. The home was a single story and seemed to have an endless amount of hallways and adjoining rooms. There was a screened-in patio with a built-in pool and barbecue area and acres of green rolling grassland behind the house.

"I love it," Jayne said when they'd seen the entire layout. "When can we move in?"

The broker laughed lightly. "Don't you want to talk about it awhile?"

Jayne looked at David, who shrugged casually. "It seems fine to me. How long has it been on the market?"

"These homes were built a year ago and this one was

finished last. It's been for sale for a month or so," he said.

David nodded his approval. The asking price was $253,000 and with the housing market still very active David knew better than to offer much less.

"Let's offer two-fifty," he said, looking at Jayne. She nodded quickly.

They spent the next hour filling out paperwork and by the next afternoon they got word that their offer had been accepted. They would need to put five thousand dollars down to hold the house until David could clear the funds from his investment account to pay the remaining price.

David could not cancel the deal too quickly or Jayne might begin to suspect the truth—that he wasn't a millionaire at all. He was going to need a mortgage, but there was a problem. He would have to lie to get one.

He would tell them he had his own business and show them whatever real or created documents were necessary to get the loan. After all, he planned to reopen his business in Florida and eventually he would have more than enough money to make the payments.

With these thoughts stumbling over each other David drove to the bank and used his credit card to take out a five thousand dollar cash advance. He asked for the money in the form of a cashier's check, which he then took to the broker as proof that he was serious about buying the home. Then he returned to Jayne, back at the apartment, where she was busy packing for Europe.

"See, honey," he said as he walked in. "I knew we could find a house quickly if we looked in the right place."

Jayne smiled. She had begun to wonder whether

David's interest in buying a house was sincere. Especially after he had already canceled deals involving what were in Jayne's opinion two perfectly good houses. "Let's see the receipt," she said, walking anxiously toward her husband.

David held up a slip of paper. Jayne looked it over and felt a sense of peace wash over her. According to the receipt, they had successfully secured the house by putting down five thousand dollars until the remaining funds could be obtained.

"Oh, David," she said, throwing her arms around his neck. "We're going to be so happy in our new home. I can't wait to move in."

David nodded proudly. "I had every intention of buying you your dream house, sweetheart," he said. "We just had to wait for the perfect place. Now, we better get to packing or we won't be ready for the trip."

"When do we move in?" she said, ignoring his comment about Europe. She almost wished they could skip the trip and focus completely on moving into their new home.

"It should take about two weeks to get the funds, so by the time we get back from Europe everything should have fallen into place. We can probably have the furniture delivered as soon as we get home."

Jayne jumped up and down like a child at Christmas. "I can't wait."

"In the meantime, we'll have a wonderful time in Europe," he said. "Is your family ready?"

"Yes. I talked to Mom earlier today and they're all packed and ready to go."

"Sounds great. Now, I'll be gone all day tomorrow on business but I'll be home early the next morning. I was thinking that your father could bring you and the others and meet me at the airport.''

For once, Jayne did not complain about David's travel plans. He would be gone only one day and then they'd be off to spend two weeks in Europe. And when they got home they would finally be able to move into their new home. "I'm sure my dad won't mind," she said. "Why don't you call him and work out the details.''

David turned toward the telephone and then paused a moment and looked back at Jayne. "You are happy, aren't you, Jayne?"

Jayne tilted her head compassionately. David looked suddenly pitiful and hurt and she was sorry for having complained so much in recent weeks. "Yes, love. Things have been rough lately, but everything's coming together. I'm happier than you know.''

David left the next morning before Jayne got up and by noon he was in Dorothy's arms, hugging and kissing her and telling her how much he'd missed her.

After they'd enjoyed each other's company and caught up on what was happening with the boys, Dorothy remembered about the credit cards. "Did you call the credit card companies and tell them you lost your cards?''

"Oh, that," he said. "Sure. I took care of it the day after you told me about it. They said they'd take all the charges off. Should be cleared up by the next billing statement.''

But two days after David left—telling Dorothy he was bound for a mission in Saudi Arabia while in fact flying back to Orlando to meet Jayne and her family and begin a two-week vacation in Europe—the credit card statements arrived. This time they had the words PAST

DUE stamped across them and each statement included even more charges than before.

Dorothy picked up the statements angrily and marched toward the telephone. It was just like those credit card companies not to make the necessary adjustments even after David had wasted his precious time reporting the cards stolen. She picked up the phone and dialed one of the companies.

"Yes, this is Dorothy Miller and I'm calling about my account," she said, giving the operator her credit card number and waiting while her account was pulled up.

"Did you want to make payment arrangements, Mrs. Miller?" the woman asked sweetly.

"No, of course not," Dorothy said, the frustration obvious in her voice. "My husband already called and reported that his cards were stolen. He was told that these charges would be taken off our account. I want to know when that's going to happen."

"Just a minute, Mrs. Miller, and I'll pull up the list of charges to verify the signatures."

Dorothy waited patiently. She was certain the woman would see a note somewhere on the account that David had called. Someone had probably forgotten to take care of the charges before and now Dorothy expected this woman to clear up the problem as soon as possible.

"Ok, I've checked the signatures, Mrs. Miller," the woman said. "Everything seems to match up just fine."

Dorothy paused a moment, confused by the woman's statement. "What do you mean? The cards were stolen."

"I don't know about that, but I do know that the signature on the charges matches the one we have on file."

"Whose signature?" Dorothy was beginning to get angry. The charges had not been made by her or David and there was no way their signatures could have been on the charges. "Who signed the charges?"

"David Miller, ma'am," she said. "We matched his signature card with the charges just to be sure. It's a perfect match on every one of them."

30

If Richard Leebrick doubted David's sincerity upon meeting him the first time, he was completely skeptical after talking to him about their upcoming trip to Europe. At Jayne's request, David had called Richard, told him about his business trip, and asked him to bring Jayne and the others to the airport Wednesday morning where they would meet and then together board a plane bound for Europe.

"Nassir should have our tickets waiting for us at the airline check-in counter," David said.

"Who's Nassir?" Richard asked.

Jayne had mentioned months ago that the government of Kuwait was paying for the trip. But when they had been unable to find any proof that David was in fact an attorney, Richard decided that the idea of government officials in Kuwait paying for the trip had probably fallen through. David was probably paying for the trip out of his own money. After all, the man was a millionaire and he could spend his money whatever way he wished.

"Oh, didn't Jayne tell ~~you~~ about Nassir?" David asked, laughing modestly. "Nassir is one of the top officials in the government of Kuwait. He'll be arranging for our tickets and then we'll meet him as soon as we arrive in France."

"David, I've got a question for you," Richard said. "Might be none of my business but I'm going to ask it anyway."

"Sure, Dad, go ahead." Lately he'd taken to calling Jayne's father Dad. It was a habit that Richard detested.

"Now, I understand that you're working for Disney as an attorney. Jayne saw your desk and the name plaque, so apparently the job's for real. But why in the world would the government of Kuwait want to treat you and a bunch of your family members to a vacation in Europe?"

David laughed. "It does sound a bit farfetched, doesn't it?" he said. When Richard didn't respond, David cleared his throat and continued. "Well, Dad, you see, back in Los Angeles I was involved in some very important political deals. One of them involved the government of Kuwait. I worked with this man, Nassir, and helped him with legal advice regarding the deal. It's kind of complicated, but in the end Nassir was very thankful for my help. So was the rest of the government over there.

"Anyway, they wanted to find some way to thank me and I absolutely refused a monetary gift because I didn't want it to seem like a payoff. So they suggested this trip to Europe."

Richard was silent for a moment. "Isn't that the same thing?" he asked. "A trip to Europe is every bit as much a payoff as plain cold cash, don't you think?"

"No, no." David scoffed at the idea. "Gifts are commonplace in the political realm," he said. "But payoffs are something else altogether. This is definitely not a payoff."

"And so this Nassir is going to pay for the whole trip?"

"That's right. See, Dad, Kuwait is a very, very wealthy little country. The people there don't have any military might and so they're vulnerable," David explained. "But they have plenty of money. And they know how to take care of the people who help them out."

After that, Richard changed the subject. The entire story sounded ridiculous to him, but if Jayne believed him, then maybe it was true. There was no point in worrying about whether David was lying or not. If David wanted to take him and his family to Europe, then why should he care who paid for the trip? What did he know, anyway? The man was Jayne's husband and she knew him a great deal better than Richard did.

When Wednesday finally arrived, Richard, Janice, Sandra, Jayne, and Jayne's son, Dillon, waited for two hours at the airport for David. As the minutes slipped by, Richard began to stare at his watch and then to pace the airport terminal. Their plane would be leaving for Europe in less than thirty minutes and so far there had been no sign of David.

"His business meetings probably ran a little late," Jayne said nervously, trying to defend her husband for being two hours late to meet them.

Richard looked at his daughter warily but said nothing. He should have known the trip was too good to be true. Just like everything about David. "We wait another thirty minutes and then we leave," he said flatly. "I won't have David Miller make a fool of me."

David, meanwhile, had decided to take Dorothy to

breakfast before leaving Pennsylvania. He knew that the credit card statements were bound to arrive sometime after he left and he had not yet devised a way to explain the truth about the charges to Dorothy.

He would have to savor the time they had together, since it was becoming distinctly possible that their relationship would become strained when she realized that the charges were actually his. The breakfast would be something of a last meal together before the storm hit.

As he and Dorothy sipped their coffee and commented on the beautiful spring weather in Pennsylvania, David knew he was going to be late arriving in Orlando. But he had already called the airlines and booked a later flight to Europe. He would find some way to explain the delay once he saw Jayne and her family in person.

When David finally arrived in Orlando, it was after one o'clock in the afternoon and there was no sign of Jayne or her family. He walked to a pay phone and dialed the apartment. No answer. David slipped in two more dimes and dialed Jayne's parents' home. Jayne answered it on the first ring.

"David, where are you?" she said, sounding very upset. David couldn't tell if she was angry or worried. He decided to catch her off guard.

"Sweetheart, I was worried about you," he said breathlessly. "Thank goodness you're okay."

"Of course I'm okay," she said. "David, we waited for you for over two hours. You never showed up. Where are you?"

"I've been at the airport all morning waiting for you," he said, sounding confused. "I arrived on an earlier flight and I went to the restaurant to wait for you. I kept waiting and waiting and waiting. And finally

I had you and your family paged. But there was no sign of you anywhere and no one ever answered the page."

"That's impossible, sweetheart," Jayne said, baffled by her husband's statement. "We were waiting at the terminal from ten o'clock this morning until after noon. By then the plane had left for Europe so we turned around and came home."

"You waited at the terminal? You were supposed to meet me at the restaurant."

"Oh, no!" Jayne rolled her eyes. Here her father had been upset with David and it was all his fault for getting the meeting place wrong. She decided she would have to have a word with her father after she got off the phone.

"Well, none of that matters now," she said anxiously. "What are we going to do about Europe? Is the trip canceled?"

"No, not at all," he said. "Nassir left the tickets for me and I worked something out with the airlines so we can catch the later flight. It leaves at four o'clock. Can you all be back here by then?"

"Sure," she said. "We were all just sitting around waiting to hear from you. We'll be back there by two and that way we can have something to eat before we board the plane."

When Jayne got off the phone, she lectured her father about his forgetfulness. "We were supposed to meet him at the restaurant," she said, shaking her head in frustration. "How could you forget a simple detail like that?"

"It wasn't my mistake," Richard said gruffly. He did not want to argue with his daughter, but he knew David had not planned to meet them at the restaurant. He had specifically said they should meet at the terminal. He did not know what David had really been doing or why he was late, but he decided it would be best to drop the subject and enjoy the vacation.

When they met David an hour later, he handed each of them a boarding pass stamped with the round-trip ticket price for them to fly to France, Spain, Italy, and back to Orlando. The price was marked on the bottom of each ticket: $1,652.

After a smooth flight they arrived in France, where David set Jayne and her family up in a fashionable hotel near the Eiffel Tower. For three days the group stayed in France and each day David continued to talk about Nassir and his plans to meet the man. But every time they went to a restaurant or tourist attraction to meet Nassir, he would never show up.

Finally, David walked into their adjoining hotel room one afternoon and announced that Nassir had made a change in their plans. The government of Kuwait had needed him these past few days. But he would be free to meet them in two days in Rome. David and his family could spend the next two days in France and then they would be off to Rome where Nassir would meet them at the airport.

When the time came, the group left for Rome and once there booked three rooms at the Excelsior Hotel.

"So, where's Nassir?" Jayne asked suspiciously. She was beginning to wonder if her father was right about David being untrustworthy. The whole notion of Nassir standing them up while they were in France was starting to sound farfetched.

"He'll be here," David insisted.

David had promised Jayne and her family that Nassir would be treating them to lavish meals and expensive tours through the city. When he hadn't shown up in

France, David had paid for the group's expenses, assuring them that Nassir would reimburse him when he met up with them. But now that they were in Rome and Nassir still had not arrived, Jayne's family was beginning to make secret jokes about the mysterious Nassir and whether or not he actually existed.

Finally, after four days of waiting for Nassir to meet them in Rome, David decided they would have to go on to Spain. They arrived on a Thursday in Barcelona and stayed in the town of Sitges at another luxury hotel.

"I just can't understand what's happened to Nassir," David said when the Kuwaiti official failed to meet them at the airport in Barcelona. "It's not like him to miss an appointment. And I know he had a lot of business he wanted to discuss with me."

Throughout the trip, David used his credit cards to pay for the group's meals and lodging, always assuring Jayne and her family that Nassir would reimburse him as soon as they met up.

But by Wednesday night, when they'd been in Europe for nearly two weeks, David ran smack into the reality of his situation. He had treated the others to a two hundred dollar dinner at one of the finer restaurants near Sitges. When the bill came he pulled out a Visa card and sent it back to the front desk with the waitress.

Five minutes later the waitress returned and informed David that the manager needed to see him.

David excused himself and found the manager waiting for him in a small office at the back of the restaurant.

"You wanted to see me?" he said.

"Yes. There seems to be a problem with your credit

card, sir. The representative from the bank said that
you'd reached your limit and that your payments were
past due."

David swallowed and tried to look indignant. "Why,
that's the most ridiculous thing I've ever heard."

The manager nodded in mock understanding.
These Americans were all the same, living on a line of
credit and then angry when their spending caught up
with them. "Sir, regardless of the problems you might
have with the bank, you will have to find some way to
pay for your dinner. We will only accept cash at this
point."

"Of course," David said proudly, doing his best to
sound pompous and slightly offended. "If you would
be so kind as to wait a few moments."

"Definitely."

David walked slowly back to the table. He had hit a
brick wall. There seemed no way around it but to borrow money from Jayne's father. He knew that the others had brought some spending money. He would simply have to tell them there had been a mix-up and that
he would pay Jayne's father back when they got home
to the States. In the meantime, he would have to use
his other credit cards for the rest of the trip now that
he had reached his limit on that Visa.

When he got back to the table, he pulled Richard
aside and explained that apparently the bank had confused his account with another cardholder's and the
restaurant had declined his card. He would need cash
for the meal, he explained. But he would pay the
money back as soon as they got home and he had a
chance to clear up the situation with his bank.

Richard instinctively did not believe David's story.
But he had not had to spend any money on the trip

until that point and he could not leave David with no way to pay for the dinner. He pulled out his wallet and peeled off ten traveler's checks—enough to cover the bill.

Jayne meanwhile watched the scene between her husband and her father with a baffled expression on her face. How could David run out of money?

At that moment a well-dressed man approached them and began speaking rapidly to David in Spanish. David laughed nervously and his face began to redden. The man, apparently the restaurant manager, was clearly waiting for a response and finally David tossed up his hands.

"No comprende," he said, laughing nervously and casting a furtive glance toward Jayne and the others. Jayne was stunned. David was unable to speak Spanish despite the fact that he claimed to have been a Spanish interpreter for Nixon. Later, when they were alone in their hotel room, she asked him about it.

"I thought you were a Spanish interpreter," she said. "How come you can't speak it now?"

"Oh," David said quickly. "That's because they speak a different kind of Spanish here than I used to speak."

Jayne rolled her eyes. "And what about the money? How could the bank make an error on your credit card account?" she asked doubtfully.

David shrugged absentmindedly, hoping Jayne would change the subject.

"David, you're a millionaire. Banks know that kind of thing. All you would have had to do was call them and explain who you are and how much you're worth and they would have allowed you to charge the dinner without another word."

"Jayne, you don't understand how things work," David said angrily. He was, by then, losing control of the situation. He had no money and no way to tell his wife that he was broke. And he still had not been able to come up with a man named Nassir from Kuwait. Suddenly he felt as if his world was beginning to crumble.

"I may not know what it's like to be a millionaire," she said defensively. "But I know that no credit card company would turn down a purchase by a client with your money. I mean, how embarrassing. First you tell us we're going to Europe compliments of Nassir. Then this Nassir, whoever he is, doesn't even show up. And now you have my father paying our dinner bills. This whole trip's one big joke, David. What's going on?"

"You know, Jayne," David lowered his voice, but Jayne could see that he was seething with anger. "You are the most ungrateful woman I've met. Who cares who's paying for the trip? You aren't, are you? Why don't you just be thankful and shut up?"

"Well, who is paying for it, David? I'm really beginning to wonder."

"Fine," he said, his voice rising several notches. "Then just sit here and wonder. I'm going out."

With that, David turned around and slammed out of the hotel room, leaving Jayne in the room alone and furious. She decided she needed to talk to Jodee. Who cared if it cost a lot of money. Nassir was paying for it, right? And anyway, her husband had millions. She picked up the phone and dialed the operator.

That evening—while Jayne spent an hour on the phone with Jodee, voicing her suspicions and sharing anecdotes about her husband—David was down the street in the bar of another hotel. Normally, David was not a drinking man. He enjoyed being sober because it gave him the mental edge over the people around him. When a person was involved in as many lies as David Miller was, he needed every advantage he could get.

But that night, after four straight shots of gin, he slowly began to realize that he would have to tell the truth about certain aspects of his life. For instance, since Nassir did not exist, he would have to come clean with the fact that he, and not the government of Kuwait, had paid for the trip. He would have to tell Jayne that he wanted to impress her and her family and so he had made up the story about Nassir.

Perhaps if he had been more sober, he would have spent his time that evening developing yet another story to explain Nassir's absence. But at that point David was growing tired of lying. Especially about some guy named Nassir who did not exist. Too much effort was required to tell a lie and then cover up when the story proved false.

He might even have considered telling Jayne the truth about their finances, admitting that they were indeed broke and that he had never been a millionaire at any time in his life. But even the gin couldn't convince him to tell Jayne the truth about the money. As long as she believed him to be a millionaire, he acted like he had millions. The fact that he was quickly running his credit cards to the limit meant only that he could no longer spend money as he once had. But as long as Jayne believed him he could still pretend to have millions.

More importantly, he probably could not imagine the anger he would stir in Jayne if he told her the truth about his finances. No, even in his slightly inebriated state he apparently could not bear the thought of telling Jayne he had run out of money.

When he returned to their hotel room late that night, Jayne was sound asleep. He had several more drinks before coming back to tell her the truth about Nassir. Now he stumbled clumsily, struggling to maintain his balance as he groped for the hotel room light and flipped on the switch.

"Jayne," he mumbled softly. When she didn't move, he raised his voice. "Jayne, get up."

She rolled over in bed and sat up, looking groggy and confused. "What's going on?"

David staggered to the bed and sat down near his wife.

She watched him, a disgusted look on her face. "You're drunk, aren't you?" she said, suddenly awake and aware of David's condition.

David nodded uncertainly. "I'm sorry, Jayne," he said, reaching out and stroking her hair. "I'm really, really sorry."

"What do you mean?" Jayne had been worried about where David had gone but now that he was back she didn't want him to know. Where had he gone for so many hours? And why had he gotten drunk? She had never known David to drink and she wondered if perhaps he'd been with another woman. She decided she had to find out. She looked evenly at him. "Where have you been?"

"The bar," he said, slurring his words slightly. "Down the street. Thinking. I'm so sorry, Jayne."

"Sorry about what? Because we fought again and you left? I'm getting used to that, David. Why are you sorry now?"

David shook his head. "Not the fight," he said. "About Nassir."

"Nassir?"

"Yes. I lied about him, Jayne. I'm so sorry."

"You lied about Nassir? About meeting him here?"

"No, no," he said, shaking his head dramatically. "About Kuwait, about Nassir." He paused a moment. "There is no Nassir, Jayne."

Jayne narrowed her eyes. "What?"

"There is no Nassir. No Nassir, no Kuwait deals, nothing. I paid for the trip."

Jayne wondered if she was understanding him correctly. Maybe David was simply too drunk to know what he was saying. "You made the whole thing up?" she asked incredulously.

David nodded. "The whole thing. Wanted to impress you, your family. Impress you all."

Jayne yanked the covers off her body and angrily stood up, staring down at her husband. He looked pathetic, drunken with wrinkled clothes and tears forming in his eyes. "You lied to me, David?"

David wiped away a tear and nodded sadly. "I'm sorry, Jayne. Understand? Please understand."

"Understand what? That my husband is a fraud? That he lied to me and my parents and my sister and my son just so he could impress us? And now you want me to understand?" She spat the words at him, her hands on her hips as her voice continued to rise. "Well, I don't understand. I think you're nothing but a loser, David Miller. A big loser. There is no reason in the world why you should have lied to us about this whole Kuwait thing. We didn't care who paid for the trip!"

Jayne stared at her husband and for a moment she

wondered if she hated him. This was the second time he'd admitted lying to her. "How can I believe anything you tell me?" she shouted. "You're nothing but a cheap liar. You make up so many stories that I don't know what to believe anymore."

David stood up, the alcohol fueling his own anger now. "Listen, I don't need to take this," he yelled at her, pointing an unsteady finger at her face and shaking his fist. "You have no reason to be mad at me. At least I paid for the trip. You should be thanking me, not yelling at me." He pushed her aside and headed toward the door.

Jayne was furious. David had never touched her before during one of their arguments and now he'd gone too far. "Don't ever touch me like that again or I'll report you to the police," she shouted, sitting down on the bed again and bursting into tears. "I'm sick of you."

In the other room, Richard had been wakened by the screaming and climbed out of bed. He had never heard Jayne so upset and he wanted to be sure she was okay.

Richard knocked on their door, but when no one answered it he opened it and looked inside.

"What are you doing?" David yelled at him. "Ever heard of knocking?"

David stormed across the room, pushed Richard aside, and grabbed the doorknob. Then in one sharp motion he yanked the door from its hinges and threw it on the floor. "There," he shouted, looking back at Jayne still sobbing on the edge of the bed. "Now the whole world can look in and make sure you're okay."

David walked angrily past Richard and down the hallway.

"Are you all right, Jayne?" her father asked.

Jayne nodded but Richard noticed how weary she looked. For the next thirty minutes Jayne told her father that David had lied about Nassir and the government of Kuwait paying for their trip. Richard was not surprised, but he knew his daughter had been caught off guard by her husband's lies.

"Honey, I know he's bought you a lot of nice things and taken you on lavish trips," Richard said gently, sitting down beside his daughter. "And I know you think he's wonderful. But I worry about the man. There's something about him that doesn't sit well with me."

Jayne nodded. "I know. But, Daddy, I really wanted this marriage to work."

"It still can, honey," he said. "But right now you don't even know this man you're married to. That's going to have to change if you two are going to work things out. And he's going to have to stop lying to you."

Jayne nodded. She appreciated her father's concern and she thanked him for his advice.

"You can go now, Dad. I'll be all right," she said. "David won't come back until he's thought about what he did."

Jayne was right. David did not return to the room until the next afternoon and by then he was sober and sorrowful for his actions. Still, there was a strain between Jayne and David for the remaining two days of the trip and by the time they arrived back in Orlando, David wondered how he was going to salvage either of his marriages.

He desperately wanted to remain married to both Dorothy and Jayne. He loved them both and was trying his best to please them. But he knew that if he didn't start making good on his promises Jayne might consider leaving him. She already doubted her decision to marry him, David was certain of that. One more disappointment and there was no telling how she would react.

The disappointment came two days after they got back home. Jayne had been anxious to move into their new home and she had been constantly asking David questions about when the financial arrangements would be complete and when they could move their furniture from the storage unit to the new house.

That afternoon in the second week of May, David got a call from the broker. He had taken it upon himself while they were gone to run a credit check on David through one of the local banks. The report showed that David was deeply in debt and late on his payments. When the developer learned about David's credit he decided that if David was unable to pay for the house in full by the next day, his five thousand dollar deposit would be returned and the house would go back on the market.

David thought quickly as the broker explained the bad news. There was no way he could pay for the house without a mortgage loan. And the news about his credit being bad meant that there would be no point in lying to the loan officers about having a business in Florida. No one was going to loan him money without a clean credit report.

"Put it back on the market then and have my refund ready in an hour," David said, pretending to be indignant over the news. "We'll find a house elsewhere."

Jayne had been out shopping when the broker

called, and when she got home, David asked her to sit down.

"We lost the house," he said quietly. "I'm sorry. I guess there was a deadline to have the funds ready and we missed it while we were gone."

The disappointment that raced across Jayne's face was quickly replaced by anger.

"What's going on, David?" she asked. "Do you have the money or not?"

"Of course I do, sweetheart," he said, trying to sound patient and confident. "The timing just wasn't right."

"This whole thing is getting ridiculous," she said, and she stood up, walked into their bedroom, and slammed the door shut. David decided to leave her alone to work through her feelings.

She was angry and frustrated and unsure about what to do next. What if David really didn't have any money? What if he had been lying to her about being a millionaire? By then even that wouldn't have surprised Jayne. She tossed the idea around in her head and wondered if perhaps the only money he had was the salary he was drawing from Disney every two weeks.

The longer Jayne considered that possibility the more she dismissed it. David was spending more money than that, taking her on a luxury cruise and treating her entire family to a European vacation. He must be a millionaire because he was certainly getting money from somewhere.

For much of the next day she spent her time in the bedroom talking to Jodee and wondering why her husband kept making offers on homes and then allowing the deals to fall through.

"Maybe he's not a millionaire, Jayne," Jodee said softly. "Could he be lying about that too?"

"I don't think so. I mean, he must have millions. Otherwise he couldn't have afforded the trips we've taken."

But by the end of May something happened that finally convinced Jayne that her husband did not have millions in the bank.

One afternoon while David was gone on business she got a phone call from a man at the storage unit where their furniture was being held.

"Just calling to verify that the movers picked up the furniture," he said.

"What?" David hadn't said anything about moving the furniture to a new location.

"They took it back to the store, I believe," he said. "That was the order, right?"

"I don't know, I'll call you back," she said quickly. What was happening? Why would they take the furniture back? Within minutes she was on the phone to the furniture store.

"Yes, we have the furniture," the manager said stiffly. "It was brought back to the store a few hours ago."

"But why?" she asked. "We bought that furniture; it belongs to us."

"Your husband made the arrangements, ma'am," he said. "Called and told us he wanted it all brought back. He asked for a complete refund."

Dorothy took a deep breath. "Did he say why he was returning it?"

"Sure did, ma'am. Said he couldn't make the payments on it."

31

His marriage to Jayne disintegrating quickly, David decided to leave Orlando and check in on Dorothy. He no longer knew if she would believe him or not, but he had decided to make every effort to convince her that he had been involved in very dangerous missions, that he was worn out and tired, and that the CIA was responsible for the credit card charges.

Lying had become a full-time job for David by then and he had no choice but to continue making up whatever stories were necessary to keep Dorothy happy. He must have worked desperately hard to keep from worrying about where these lies were leading him and what the future might hold for his two marriages. It was requiring enough mental gymnastics just remembering what life he was living at any given moment.

Three weeks had passed since Dorothy found out that David charged a total of more than thirty thousand dollars on their numerous credit cards. She was desperate to talk with him and hear his explanation for the charges.

After all, most of the charges did not seem to be consistent with carrying on dangerous secret missions for the CIA. There were charges for clothing, expensive dinners in the Orlando area, a cruise to the Bahamas, and costly furniture. Still, Dorothy kept telling herself that there had to be a reason why her husband had purchased those items and then lied about it.

She was so certain that the charges were CIA-related and that the government would provide David with the means to pay them off that she was calling the credit card companies every day or so. Each time, the customer service representatives would tell her that the balance had not been paid and then ask her if she was ready to discuss payment plans.

By the time David showed up in mid-May, Dorothy was frantic with worry. She wondered how much the CIA could put them through. Why were they sending him on cruises? And why hadn't they reimbursed her husband for those expenses? Dorothy wanted to hear the explanation from David.

On the rainy afternoon of May 28, David used his key and walked into the Belle Vernon apartment he shared with Dorothy. He looked worn-out and troubled and Dorothy rushed to his side.

Even with so many suspicious charges on their credit cards, she completely believed her husband and his motives. David had always been faithful and loving, kind to both her and the boys. Not once did she consider that he might have been using the credit cards to pay for an affair—or a second wife. And now that he was home, her first concern was for his safety.

"David, are you okay?" She took his suitcase and led him carefully to the nearest chair. "You look terrible, sweetheart. Where have you been? What's been going on?''

David shook his head slowly. "It's not good," he said.

"What isn't good? Did something happen?"

"No." He sighed. "Not yet, anyway. But I'm in a lot of danger, Dorothy. I'm not sure when it'll pass, either."

Dorothy paused a moment. She didn't want to press the issue, but she needed to know about the credit card bills. If they weren't related to David's job, it was possible someone was forging his signature.

"David, I talked to the credit card companies."

He nodded wearily and rubbed his forehead as if trying to erase the tension strangling his body. "I know, sweetheart. I'm sorry. I couldn't tell you about them before."

Dorothy nodded, more patient and understanding than David dared to hope.

"I've been in so much danger, the CIA wanted me to spend a little time throwing off the terrorists. So I've been in Florida, even spent some time on a cruise."

"Was the cruise part of a mission?"

David nodded, creating the story as he went along. "It wasn't related to the mess in Kuwait and Saudi Arabia, but it was something to take the heat off for a while," he said. "I can't tell you any of the details, but it was important."

"Why didn't they pay for it?"

"Oh, they will," David said. "They'll be reimbursing me any day now. They wanted me to put the charges from the last month or so on my credit card so the terrorists couldn't trace my whereabouts."

"I don't understand."

David continued to massage his forehead and release deep sighs every few minutes. "The CIA thought these terrorists had hired someone to kill me," he said. "They thought the killer was following me based on where I was using my government credit card. So for now they wanted me to use my private cards."

Dorothy nodded. "Are you in danger now?"

"No. Ever since I started using my own credit cards the killer hasn't been on my trail. The CIA is giving me a week to unwind a bit."

Dorothy looked relieved. Finally, David would be spending some time at home.

"Why don't you relax and I'll fix you something to eat. The boys are dying to see you," she said, walking up to him and kissing him gently on the cheek.

She had seen so little of him recently that she had begun to worry about his safety. Then when she'd realized the credit card charges were his, she wondered what kind of danger he might be in. Now she knew and her heart went out to her husband. He worked so hard for his country and the job seemed to put him under so much stress. She wondered if the pressure affected all the CIA agents this badly. She ran her hand through her husband's thick dark hair and smiled at him.

"You'll be okay, David," she said softly. "You're home now."

"Honey, have I told you lately how much I love you?" he said, looking into her eyes in a way Dorothy hadn't seen in months.

For the next week, David and Dorothy existed as they had back in California, when they'd had time for evening walks and romantic dinners out on the town.

David brought Dorothy flowers and held her hand whenever he could. It was a week Dorothy would remember and even marvel at.

Especially in light of what the next week held.

32

In addition to paying for his lavish lifestyle with Jayne in Orlando, David was also still taking care of Dorothy's expenses in Pennsylvania. At first—when he was no longer receiving any money from his business and only a few thousand dollars now and then from his single client in Florida—he had dealt with this situation by taking cash advances. Every few weeks he would take a one-thousand-dollar advance and deposit it into the checking account Dorothy used in Belle Vernon.

As for their savings, Dorothy knew none of the details. David had always told her that he had a great deal of money invested for their retirement years and Dorothy had never pushed the issue or tried to pin her husband down as to where the investments actually were.

"Don't worry, honey," he had always told her. "If anything happens to me the government will take care of you and the boys for the rest of your lives."

Because of this, she never had reason to worry about her personal finances. Whenever she wrote a check the bank honored it, and she and the boys were able to live as comfortably as they always had.

But after spending the first week of June with Dorothy, David realized that it was no longer going to be possible to continue his habit of taking cash advances. Dorothy had not seen the newest charges—including the trip to Europe for Jayne and her family. Therefore, she had no idea that David had actually run up accounts on several cards that now totaled more than forty thousand dollars.

David, though, was very aware of the amount and knew that each of the cards would soon be at their limit. For that reason, he most likely made a calculated decision before leaving Pennsylvania that he could no longer support Dorothy and her sons. Once he'd made up his mind, he drove to the bank, withdrew the funds from their joint account, and then headed for the airport.

With more than two thousand dollars cash in hand, David paid for his ticket and boarded a plane bound for Orlando. He must have known that his actions would leave Dorothy without any money whatsoever. But, he probably reasoned, she had already paid rent for June and she could always get a job as a hairdresser again. Yes, Dorothy would be fine.

In fact, David's biggest concern was himself. As Grant Hawthorne, his former business partner, would later note, David was utterly blind to the way his actions affected those around him. He cared only about maintaining the lifestyle he had created. And if it came down to sacrifice, he would sooner give up his double life than his lavish lifestyle.

David knew that his actions would inevitably end his relationship with Dorothy. Although he was actually more in love with himself than either of his wives, if he had to choose between them David apparently decided he would rather keep Jayne. She was newer and more spunky. It would be a challenge to keep her happy. And although they had been fighting, he hoped that by eliminating the expense of Dorothy he could continue to pacify Jayne until he could get his business going.

He would be sorry to see his double life end, of course. But he believed that once he began bringing in money he would have ample opportunity to meet women. Perhaps one day, when Dorothy was no longer part of his life, he might even marry again. After all, he believed he had been very successful at keeping both wives happy. The problem had been his finances, not his ability to have two wives.

So as David flew from Pittsburgh to Orlando he refused to think about Dorothy's reaction when she discovered she no longer had any money. Instead, he began thinking of ways he could make Jayne happy. He would rent a limousine and take her to dinner and a movie. With his finances becoming so complicated, David felt he deserved a night out. Once he'd made the plan, he leaned back in his airline seat and fell asleep.

The discovery came two days later.

Dorothy had been to the supermarket the same Monday David left and bought enough groceries for two weeks. Later, she had gone shopping and picked up a few pairs of jeans for the boys and some items for the apartment. She had even purchased a few dresses for herself before returning home that afternoon. She paid for all her purchases by check.

The bank called on Wednesday.

"I'm with the department of investigations," the man said when Dorothy answered the phone. "It seems that your account is terribly overdrawn."

Dorothy was silent, trying to make sense of the man's statement. "There must be some mistake. I still have more than fifteen hundred dollars in that account."

The man read her the account number and stated that his records showed a negative balance of several hundred dollars.

"Do you know who's writing these checks?"

"I'm writing the checks," she said angrily. "That account has plenty of money in it."

Dorothy could hear the man punching in numbers on his computer. "I'm afraid your husband withdrew a large sum from the account on Monday."

Dorothy suddenly felt light-headed. David had left for a mission to Israel on Monday, but he hadn't said anything about taking a large amount of cash from their checking account.

"How much money did he take?"

"The balance was two thousand and twenty-three dollars and fifteen cents. He took it all."

Dorothy's mind began to race, trying to figure out an explanation for this latest news. "He must have put some of it in another checking account then. Could you please check your records?"

"Certainly." There was a pause. "No. He didn't open any other account."

Dorothy was desperate to understand what had happened. "There must be some mistake," she said. "Are you sure it was my husband?"

"The man's signature matches the one on file for

David Miller," he said. "Is that your husband, ma'am?"

"Yes," she said, still searching for an explanation. "But my husband left that day on a business trip. He wouldn't have had time to go to the bank. I'm sure this is all just some kind of mistake."

"According to our information, he closed the account at just after one o'clock that afternoon."

Dorothy closed her eyes. David's plane should have left at two that afternoon. "I need to talk to my husband about this," she said, trying to sound composed.

"Well, I want you to know that we've returned four checks since that day. None of them have been paid. I'm afraid someone is going to have to deposit enough money to cover the checks and the service charge for each returned item."

"Yes," she said softly. "I'll be down later to take care of that."

Dorothy felt like she was in shock and she sounded like a robot as she answered the man. She could not imagine why David would close their checking account. And now that he was somewhere in Israel she had no idea how she would pay for the groceries and other items. Without that checking account, she was completely penniless. She had no idea where David's investments were or how to get hold of any money. Especially now that their credit cards had such high balances.

"What time will you be coming in?" he asked.

"Uh . . ." Dorothy didn't know what to say. How could she tell this man that she had no money and no way of reaching her husband? "Let me call you back. I need to get hold of my husband first and then I'm sure I'll be down later this afternoon."

For the next fifteen minutes, Dorothy sat at her kitchen table and tried to imagine what was happening to her life. David had said nothing about taking all their money from the checking account. He had been happy and relaxed when he left for Israel. He had even talked about taking her on a romantic vacation without the boys sometime in the next few months so they could be alone together.

Dorothy decided that her husband's involvement with the CIA must have something to do with his withdrawing the money. But why wouldn't he have told her?

Suddenly she knew what she had to do. Even though David had told her never to contact his office, this was an emergency. If he didn't tell her where their funds were she would be unable to cover the checks she'd written. Then there would be fines and even legal ramifications. She had to talk to him immediately.

She picked up the telephone, called the information operator, and asked for the number of the CIA office in Orlando.

"I don't have a listing for a Central Intelligence Agency in Orlando," the operator said. "The nearest office is in the three-oh-five area code. I believe it's in Miami."

Dorothy was confused. After they'd left Los Angeles, David had told her his office was in Orlando. Why would he lie to her about that? Waves of panic and doubt began flooding Dorothy's body and she had to force herself to calm down.

The explanation was simple. Dorothy and the boys would have been in danger if they ever tried to visit him at the office. So David had lied about the office location as a way of protecting them. That must have been why they had lived in Orlando, also. David had probably wanted her and the boys far away from his actual office.

The more Dorothy worked through the situation the clearer it became. If David's office was in Miami and not Orlando that explained why he had been gone so much of the time while they lived in Orlando. It would have been at least a four-hour drive from their Casselberry home to his office in Miami. Three or four hours of debriefing sessions and eight hours on the road would make for twelve-hour workdays. And that was exactly how long David's days had been back then.

Feeling more composed, she picked up the phone and dialed the Miami number.

"Yes, I'm looking for my husband, David Miller," she said matter-of-factly. "He's an agent."

The woman at the other end paused a moment. "I'm not familiar with that name, ma'am," she said. "I'll connect you with personnel."

Dorothy tried to ignore the urgency she felt as she waited for someone in the personnel department to look up David's file. Finally the woman returned to the phone. "I'm sorry, Ms. Miller," she said. "I don't have a file on him."

"That's ridiculous. Of course you have a file on him." Dorothy was beginning to lose her patience with the woman. Inept people should not be working for the government, she told herself.

"I've searched the computer files and there is nothing on a David Miller," the woman repeated. "I don't know what else to tell you."

Dorothy sighed in frustration. "Listen, he's worked for the CIA for at least twelve years," she said. "Now, I don't know if he goes by a different name when he's on his missions. But somewhere, someone must know his real name."

"All I can do is give you the name and address of the personnel director," she said. "You can submit a formal request in writing to verify employment."

"What?" Dorothy was very angry now. "I need to talk to my husband immediately. There's been an emergency."

"I'm sorry, Ms. Miller," the woman said. "I have no information on him at all."

"Okay," Dorothy said, forcing herself to sound patient. "I know he deals with top-secret missions and I know you can't give that information out to just anyone. But I'll fly there and make the request in person if I need to. I can prove he's my husband. I need to find him immediately."

"I don't think you understand, ma'am. We wouldn't be able to tell you where he was or what he did. But we could tell you if he worked for us," she said. "According to my records, he doesn't work for the CIA and never has."

"That's crazy," Dorothy said. "The file must be under some other name. He definitely works for the CIA. I should know."

"All I can do is give you the address of the personnel director so you can make the formal request."

"Fine," Dorothy said. "But I'll be down at your office tomorrow in person. I need to find my husband right now."

She wrote down the address and put it aside. Then she picked up the telephone and dialed American Airlines. She knew that David would be upset with her for flying to Miami to visit his office in person. But she was absolutely without any money and she needed to know what was going on, why David had taken all the funds from their checking account without telling her. After years of relying on David, suddenly nothing seemed to be making sense. She needed the reassurance of talking to David as soon as possible.

"I want to book a flight from Pittsburgh to Miami leaving tomorrow," she said quickly. "I'll put it on my Visa."

The operator reserved a seat for her and then took her credit card number.

"I'm sorry, Mrs. Miller," she said. "Our computers show that card is at its limit."

Dorothy had been afraid of that. The CIA still hadn't reimbursed David for his recent missions and now their credit cards were nearing their limits. She gave the woman several more credit card numbers, but each was denied because they had reached their credit limit or because the payments were past due.

Finally Dorothy canceled the reservation and hung up the phone. She had no idea what to do next. In fact, she had only one choice. She had to reach David. She forced herself to think clearly, searching for an alternative way to reach him.

Then it occurred to her that perhaps he no longer worked out of the Miami office. Of course not. After all, he'd been promoted several times in recent years and now handled only the most dangerous and secretive missions. He probably worked out of Washington D.C. so that he could be close to the decision-makers and politicians who controlled where he would go for his next mission.

But when Dorothy called the Washington D.C. office of the CIA, David was not listed on their computers either. When she had not located him by the end of the day, she realized she had just one option left. She sat down at her table, took out a piece of stationery, and wrote a letter to the personnel director of the CIA.

She stated that there had been a family emergency and that she desperately needed to know the whereabouts of her husband, David Miller, who had been an agent with the CIA for more than twelve years. She also stated that she had not been able to locate him at either the Miami office or the Washington D.C. office. She finished the letter by requesting an immediate response.

After sealing it in an envelope, she drove to the post office. Because she did not have even fifteen dollars, she could not send it overnight as she would have liked. Instead she found a stamp in her purse, placed it on the envelope, and dropped it in the mailbox.

Then she waited.

Six days passed without any word from David or the U.S. government. During that time she borrowed money from her father to cover the checks she'd written, explaining that there had been a mix-up with David's employer and that she could pay the money back as soon as he returned from his business trip.

But when she finally did hear news about her husband it did not come from the CIA. It came over the telephone from her former neighbor, Merritt Foster.

"Dorothy," she said tentatively, "I don't know how to ask you this."

Dorothy sat down. Something in Merritt's tone of voice told Dorothy that her neighbor was about to reveal more bad news. But after nearly a week of sitting by the telephone she was ready to hear anything the woman might say.

"Just ask me."

"Well." Merritt drew in a deep breath. "Is David seeing another woman?"

Dorothy felt a wave of shock rush over her and she was suddenly glad for the chair underneath her. Her mind told her that Merritt must have a reason for asking such a question. But whatever it was she must be mistaken. David was in Israel, putting his life on the line for his country.

"Of course not," Dorothy said confidently. "Whatever made you think that?" She tried to sound calm. "David's on a business trip overseas."

"Not now he isn't," she said. "Tom and I saw him this morning over at your old house."

"No, you must have seen the renters," Dorothy said, feeling a bit of relief. "We rented the house out a month ago and I guess they aren't around very often. Probably the first time you've ever seen them. In fact, I think the man looks a lot like David."

"Dorothy, listen to me," Merritt said. "The man we saw was definitely David. He had his arm around some blond-haired woman and when he saw us he waved like there was nothing unusual. I wondered if you two broke up. That's why I called."

Dorothy was silent. She had no idea how to respond to her neighbor's news. David was supposed to be in Israel. Unless, of course, the CIA had kept him in Orlando on a domestic mission and he'd been unable to call and tell her. But who was the woman Tom and Merritt had seen?

"Are you sure it was David?" she asked, trying to sound casual.

"Yes. He was just a few feet from us. Oh, Dorothy,

I'm so sorry to have to tell you this. I thought you must have known."

Dorothy struggled with her emotions. She did not want Merritt to think her world was falling apart. There had to be an explanation for everything that was happening. "Was the woman dressed in business clothes? She might have been one of his coworkers."

"No, I would say more like beach clothes," Merritt said softly. "She had on shorts and a tank top. Dorothy, she was kissing David."

Dorothy had heard enough. She needed to work through this by herself. She was certain the woman was somehow related to one of his missions. But there was no way to tell Merritt about David's involvement with the CIA. "Listen, Merritt, there are things you don't know about David. I'm sure there's an explanation for all this, but I just can't talk about it right now."

"Sure," she answered. "Hey, I'm sorry if I upset you. I just had to call you after I saw them like that. You're not mad at me, are you?"

"No, not at all. Like I said, I'm sure there's an explanation for it. I'll talk to you later."

After she hung up the phone, Dorothy began to cry.

Her entire existence seemed to be unraveling at a frenzied pace and she desperately wanted to talk with David. First the credit card charges, which still hadn't been paid for. Then he had taken all the money from their bank account, and when she'd tried to reach him at the CIA office there had been no record of his employment.

Now David wasn't in Israel, he was in Casselberry. Kissing some strange blond woman.

After more than a decade of believing David, Dorothy found it impossible to imagine him capable of deceiving her. There had to be an explanation, and Dorothy was certain it had something to do with his missions. The woman was probably some sort of cover-up. After all, women worked for the CIA also. Perhaps she and David were handling the same mission and pretending to be a married couple while they carried out dangerous tasks for the government. The only scenario Dorothy could not possibly consider was the obvious one. David was involved with another woman.

Dorothy dried her eyes. Whatever was happening to David, he would certainly explain everything when he got home. She was so capable of convincing herself that by the end of the day when she went to get her mail she was actually feeling happy again.

But among the pieces of mail was a letter from the Central Intelligence Agency office in Washington D.C. Dorothy's hands began to shake as she tore open the envelope. Finally she would be able to contact David and clear up this entire mess.

Her eyes traveled quickly over the page and as they did she slowly sank to her knees. The office wanted to notify Dorothy that David Miller did not work for the CIA now and never had in his past. The responding agent thanked her for her inquiry and apologized for being unable to help in her search for her husband.

But it was the last line that made Dorothy start sobbing.

"Apparently," the agent wrote, "you are married to a con man."

Dorothy filed for bankruptcy the next day.

33

It was mid-June and Jayne had long since grown suspicious of her husband. Unlike Dorothy, Jayne did not have a lengthy history of trusting times with David to fall back on. She had known him only six months and because of her past marriages was more skeptical than other women might have been.

But even with her doubts, Jayne loved David. He had been kind to her and unlike other men in her past had shared his most intimate feelings with her. Jayne hoped with all her heart that she was wrong for doubting her husband and that they could get past this stage. But by mid-June she was no longer willing to blindly believe him about anything. Especially after he had returned the furniture without telling her.

Three weeks earlier when David had returned from Pennsylvania he explained to Jayne that he could see no point in paying for furniture that just sat in a storage unit. Besides, he had considered what Jayne had said earlier about every home needing a different arrangement of furniture. They still hadn't found a house, so why keep such costly furniture in storage when it might not even be useful in the home they would someday buy?

After David's explanation, Jayne asked him why he had lied and told the store manager that he had been unable to make the payments on the furniture.

"That's the only way they would take it back," David said simply.

When Jayne still looked doubtful, David had laughed out loud. "You don't think I can't afford it, do you?" he asked. "That furniture was nothing. Honey, I have millions. Remember?"

Jayne remembered that conversation now as she drove to work. She had gotten a job during David's business trip the first week of June and now worked in computer sales. The new job relieved her of her boredom and helped her feel as if she was finally putting down roots again in the Orlando area.

As Jayne drove, she let her mind drift. For reasons she wasn't quite sure of, she still had her doubts about David's job at Disney. She had been in his office and seen his desk with her picture on it. But she still hadn't seen one of his paychecks. From the beginning, David had said that the funds were automatically deposited into their account. And until recently Jayne had believed him. But she couldn't rid herself of the nagging doubts about the situation and now she wanted to find out for herself.

She called her sister, Debbie, when she got to work that day. Debbie always seemed to offer good advice, and even though Jayne was close to all her sisters she thought Debbie would best understand her desire to know the truth about her husband.

"I don't want to check up on him," she explained.

"But I need to know if he's telling the truth. Can you help?"

Debbie agreed. Sandra, the sister who had gone to Europe with Jayne and David and the others, had discussed her dislike of David with Debbie after they'd gotten home from the trip. Debbie knew that Sandra thought David was lying about the job at Disney.

"There's simply no way a person goes to a place like Disney Studios and gets hired at almost ninety thousand a year as an attorney after just one interview," Sandra had told Debbie weeks earlier.

Once, when Sandra had talked to David about his job during their trip to Europe, he had seemed evasive and unable to explain exactly what he did for Disney. But later when Sandra had tried to talk to Jayne about whether David might be lying about his job, Jayne had quickly dismissed the idea.

Now Debbie remembered Jayne's determination to believe David regardless of her sisters' doubts.

"I thought you believed him no matter what," Debbie said.

"I thought so too," Jayne admitted. "But I'm having my doubts. I just need to know for sure."

"Have you called the bank to see if the funds being deposited really are from Disney?"

Jayne hadn't thought of that. "Good idea," she said. "I'll call you back."

Ten minutes later Jayne knew that whatever money David was depositing in their checking account was definitely not coming from Disney. Actually, the little money he had was the result of the lobbying work he'd begun in Florida. But Jayne knew nothing of that. She called Debbie and told her the news.

"What do I do now?" she asked, and Debbie could

tell that Jayne was on the verge of breaking down. "He's lying to me, Debbie. He's lied about everything."

"Well, maybe the money comes from some other company that Disney uses to do payroll," Debbie said. "Tell you what. I'll call Disney and ask to speak to David Miller."

"I've done that before," she said. "They always tell me that he works there but he's out and he'll get back to me. I never leave a number because I don't want him to think I'm checking up on him. He's asked me not to call him at work. The company frowns on personal calls."

"Well, let me do some more checking and I'll call you back."

An hour later Debbie called Jayne at her office. "Bad news, Jayne," she said, sorry to be the one telling Jayne the truth about her husband. "He doesn't work there. I checked it out."

"How do you know?"

"When they told me David Miller wasn't in I asked if I could talk to his secretary. Then I asked her if David Miller was an attorney who had been hired four months ago. I described him and everything, Jayne. She'd never heard of him."

"What did she say?" Jayne hated to ask the question, but she needed to know.

"David Miller is an executive with the company. He's semiretired, he rarely comes into the office, and he's worked for Disney for twenty years. He's also bald."

Jayne sighed loudly and tried to fight the tears that filled her eyes. "What next?"

"I can't tell you what to do," Debbie said, choosing

her words carefully. "But if it were me I'd leave the guy."

"I know, I've been thinking about it."

"Maybe it's time to do more than just think about it. He's lied to you before, hasn't he?"

Jayne was silent a minute as she thought about David's lies involving their trip to Europe and all the house deals that had fallen through. "Yes," she said simply.

There wasn't any way to deny the fact that she had made a mistake in marrying David. Her father had been right; Jodee had been right. And as with her previous two marriages she had been wrong.

Suddenly she wondered about Jake and her first marriage to him. He had been so handsome and so in love with her. In some ways she had never stopped loving him. But they had been too young and after Dillon was born they seemed to fight constantly. Now she wondered if maybe she should have tried harder to make her marriage to Jake work. Then she never would have met David Miller and she wouldn't be in this mess.

"Jayne, you okay?" Debbie asked gently.

"Yeah, I'll be all right," she said. "Hey, it's just one more mistake, right?"

"It's not your fault. The guy's brilliant, Jayne. I've never met a smoother talker."

"I know," Jayne said, her voice cracking as the tears finally spilled down her cheeks. "But I loved him, Debbie. I really loved him."

At six o'clock that evening David came home and walked into their apartment. Jayne had not mentioned house-hunting in the past few weeks because she was too busy with her new job. Besides, as her doubts about

David grew she was no longer certain she wanted to purchase a home with him. And now, in the wake of finding out the truth about his job at Disney, she was fairly certain she no longer wanted to be married to him.

"Hey, sweetheart," he said, walking toward her with his arms open. "You look beautiful!"

Jayne narrowed her eyes and looked disgusted. "Stay away from me."

David recoiled as if he'd been slapped.

"Don't act surprised. I found out the truth, David."

For an instant David wondered if she were referring to Dorothy. But then, that was impossible, because they lived in different cities. He silently congratulated himself on keeping them apart. Whatever lie Jayne had discovered could easily be explained as long as she never found out about Dorothy.

"Have a bad day, honey?" David asked calmly. His disregard for her anger made Jayne furious.

"Shut up, David," she said, walking closer to him as her voice rose several levels. "How could you lie to me?"

"What are you talking about, Jayne?" David tried to sound impatient with her.

"Disney, that's what," she shouted. "The Disney job's all a big lie. Why didn't you tell me the truth?"

"Jayne, for your information, I didn't lie to you at all." When David realized that Jayne was upset about his concocted Disney job he grew especially calm. He had long since developed an explanation in case she checked up on him.

First, he had chosen a company where someone with the same name as his worked. In addition, he made sure the person was semiretired and important enough in the company that he rarely came to the office. That was why he'd had no trouble sneaking into the office, setting up Jayne's picture, and bringing her in for a visit that day several months earlier.

But all along he knew that if she ever tried to find out more information, he would tell her he didn't actually work for Disney. He was actually an independent contractor and Disney used his services on a regular basis.

Jayne stepped back and allowed herself to relax. She had expected David to try to talk his way out of the situation. "You can stop lying to me, David," she said. "Disney's never heard of you. The David Miller who works there is some old guy who's been there twenty years. What do you have to say now?"

David laughed as if responding to a child. "Jayne, that's a different David Miller. I work there as an independent contractor. They use my services, but I'm free to work for other clients as well. So of course I'm not on the Disney payroll or listed with their personnel office. I work for myself, but Disney is my primary client."

Jayne was silent. She was so exhausted from not knowing what to believe that she felt like she'd been physically beaten. Something told her David must be lying about this, but then, what if he were telling the truth? What if she were looking at him through the jaded eyes of someone who had been burned too many times in her past?

"David, this isn't funny," she said softly, tears filling her eyes again. He could hear the resignation in her voice. "I need to know the truth. I don't even care anymore where you work. Really. I just want to know the truth."

David walked slowly toward his wife and circled her in his arms. The spirit had gone from her and even though she was clearly upset, she no longer seemed ready to fight.

"Jayne, I'm telling you the truth. I know I lied to you about that Kuwait thing, but you've got to believe me now. I don't lie to you about serious things like this," he said.

"I'm an attorney. I work independently, but I use an office at Disney. I took you there; you saw your picture on my desk. Do you really think I'd make something like that up? Take you there and break into someone else's office just so you'd believe me?"

"I don't know." Jayne closed her eyes and shook her head. "I don't know what to believe anymore. Why did all those house deals fall through? Why didn't we keep that furniture?"

"Sweetheart, I've explained all that," he said, slowly stroking her blond hair. "Besides, I have good news."

Jayne wiped the tears from her cheeks and looked up at him. As she did, David was struck by her vulnerability. She looked like an orphan, desperately clinging to her desire to believe the man she loved.

David was glad she looked that way and he chided himself for ever doubting his ability to keep Jayne happy. After all, it didn't really matter what lies he told. She loved him. And that would keep her by his side for a long time. David smiled to himself. Women were so predictable when it came to love.

David held Jayne away from him so he could see her clearly. "I've found a house for us," he said.

Jayne did not react to David's statement. She was so confused about what to believe and how to find out the truth that she forced herself not to allow her emotions to get involved with what he was saying. Not until she knew he was telling the truth.

"Aren't you excited?" he asked, seeming to forget the fact that she'd been so upset only moments earlier.

Jayne shrugged. "Tell me about it."

"See, a long time ago, before I found out about the cancer and the inheritance, I lived near Orlando with my girlfriend, Dorothy," David said, deciding that there could be no harm in using Dorothy's real name.

"We lived together in this house I owned in Casselberry. Anyway, when Dorothy and I broke up I leased the house to this couple. But now, years later, they can't make the payments and the house is about to go into foreclosure. I thought you and I could move in there at least for a while until I can find someone else to rent the place."

Jayne was even more confused. Hadn't David said that he had a sister in Orlando who owned a dress shop? Hadn't he said that he'd never really spent much time in Florida? Jayne tried to remember the things they had talked about when they'd first met during that flight six months earlier. But now everything seemed muddled and she no longer could recall exactly what David had said.

"I didn't know you ever lived in Orlando," she said cautiously. She stopped short of accusing him of lying again. After all, he hadn't lied about this, because she had never asked him if he'd lived in Orlando.

"Sweetheart, there's a lot you don't know about me," he said, trying to sound kind. "We've only known each other six months, remember? There are bound to be things about each other that we'll find out only as we grow together."

Jayne nodded but said nothing. She felt worn-out

and unable to sort out the different emotions she was feeling. In some ways she thought that David must be lying to her. Possibly about many things. But she seemed unable to prove any of it. Therefore another part of her wondered if she was perhaps being too skeptical of her husband, making him pay the price for her past disappointments.

"Well," he said when she was silent for nearly a minute. "Can I take you to see it?"

"When?"

"How's tomorrow? It's Saturday. We could go see the house and if you like it we could make plans to move in next week sometime."

Jayne shook her head. Everything was always so immediate with David. They had fallen in love quickly, married quickly, and fought quickly. She wondered if that had something to do with her tendency to doubt him.

"After waiting this long there's no rush," Jayne said. "But I'll go look at it with you."

"It's not anything great, not like the houses we were looking at before," David said. "But at least it's better than living here in the apartment. It would just be temporary until we find something else."

Jayne nodded. That evening she spent much of her time in their bedroom talking to Jodee. She explained about David's job and how she was convinced he'd been lying to her until he had explained everything earlier that night.

"I don't know what to think anymore," Jayne complained, thankful that she and Jodee were still close.

"Sounds like he might be lying about a lot of things," Jodee said.

"But when I ask him about it he tells me something

else and it all seems to make sense. I thought I'd caught him in a lie and then without even thinking about it he had an explanation. How could he make up something so believable so quick?"

"Because maybe he's very good at what he does," Jodee said. "He's a quick talker, remember? You said so yourself."

"I know, but I want to believe him," she said. "Until I can actually prove that he's lying to me, I have to trust him. He's my husband."

In the end, Jayne decided that she still loved David and wanted her marriage to work. Unless she caught him in a lie she would have to let go of her suspicions. Otherwise they would come between her and David and their marriage wouldn't stand a chance of surviving.

The next day Jayne put on a pretty pair of shorts and a tank top and admired herself in their bedroom mirror. She and David had gone to the beach the week before and she still showed signs of a tan. Jayne scrutinized herself and was pleased with her smooth skin and blond hair, which fell softly against the tops of her shoulders. Not bad for thirty-three, she told herself.

When David saw her he whistled proudly. "You look so good I might have to take you back to the bedroom again," David said, leering at his wife's shapely legs.

"No, now come on," Jayne said as she smiled at his compliments. "We have to go look at the house in Casselberry. Remember?"

Jayne felt thankful for her decision to trust David. She had no proof that he had been lying and there was no point in treating him coolly for something he might not have done.

"Okay, you win," he said. "But when we get back you'd better watch out."

She smiled again and looked approvingly at her husband. He looked relaxed and handsome in his walking shorts and polo shirt. But most of all Jayne noticed his eyes—warm and open as if he had nothing to hide. Just like they'd been the day she'd met him.

When they left that afternoon and set out for the Casselberry house, David believed that his former neighbors, Tom and Merritt Foster, would be on vacation. They often spent the entire month of June and parts of July away visiting their family in other parts of the country. He wasn't sure if Merritt still kept in touch with Dorothy, but he didn't want her to know about Jayne in any case.

In fact, had David been thinking more clearly he would never have considered taking Jayne to see the Casselberry house. Because even if she liked it they could never move in. The Fosters would certainly find out about Jayne if she and David were living together across the street.

But, as usual, David was thinking only of himself. By showing Jayne the Casselberry house he could convince her that he was a man of his word. She would no longer doubt his financial worth if he could prove he owned a house so close and hadn't even told her about it. Apparently that was what David intended to prove by taking Jayne by the house that afternoon.

They pulled up in front of the house on Jericho Drive and David got out and opened Jayne's door. As he did, he impulsively put his arm around her bare shoulders and pulled her into a long kiss.

When he looked up, his heart skipped a beat. Across

the street, standing near their car and staring straight at him, were Tom and Merritt Foster. David knew they had seen him kiss Jayne. He waved at them and turned quickly to lead Jayne up the walkway.

The rest of the day, David was not himself. He was distant and cool and several times Jayne had to repeat herself in order to get his attention. She even asked him if he was feeling sick.

But David could not explain the emotion he was feeling. It was something new, something that had not been a part of either of his lives in the past. As he lay awake in bed unable to sleep, his heart pounding in his chest, David must have understood exactly what emotion was responsible for his ill feelings.

For the first time in his life, David Miller was afraid.

34

Before fear became a factor, David would have described himself as an intelligent man, charismatic and handsome, popular with women, and gifted with the ability to make others believe him.

Even in light of his financial failings, his abandoned business, and overwhelming debt, David figured himself to be above reproach, beyond the moral code that average men adhered to. Despite the fact that his double life was crumbling around him, he still thought of himself as a budding politician, with dreams of one day rekindling his connections and running for political office.

Through years of lying and using others to his advantage, fear never seemed to have been a part of his emotional makeup any more than guilt or regret. Those were feelings that strangled other men. Not David.

He was quite satisfied with his life, even that June when it wasn't going exactly as he had planned. He still had his charm and his ability to lie. And with those intact, he probably believed it would not be long before his double life was once again exciting and satisfying.

But now David was afraid. Tom and Merritt Foster had seen him with Jayne and there was every reason to believe that they might share that information with Dorothy. If that happened, it could only be a matter of time before his wives found out about each other. And then there was no telling what would happen. But the possibilities were enough to send David into a terrifying prison of fear.

First, if they discovered each other, Jayne and Dorothy could turn against him, leaving him with no wives. David found his self-worth in his ability to have two wives at once. He apparently could not fathom what would become of him if he lost them both.

But what seemed to frighten him most of all was the chance that they might report him to the police and file bigamy charges. In the past, David had possibly convinced himself that he was not doing anything wrong unless his wives found out about each other. And he had always been certain that that would never happen.

But now that it was possible, he must have worried that if the police knew about his two wives, the press might find out. After all, he did have strong political connections. The media would go crazy for such a story: CIVIC LEADER LIVES DOUBLE LIFE WITH TWO WIVES. The thought horrified David. If that ever happened, his political chances would be ruined. Not only that, but there wouldn't be a woman around who would date him let alone marry him if they knew about his history of bigamy.

In the days after his neighbors had seen him with Jayne, David's mind raced ahead to imagine the worst

possible consequences of what he had always considered to be a harmless double life. The harder his mind
worked at imagining those consequences, the more the
fear began to grow and build, becoming a living,
breathing being that haunted David everywhere he
went.

His fear intensifying each day, David also became
paranoid. Whereas he had always appeared relaxed
and casual even as he rattled off a series of lies, now
David seemed edgy and nervous, unable to think
clearly. Strange ideas began to fill his head and he
found himself suspecting his wives of secretly plotting
against him. There were times when he would hesitate
before walking outside the apartment he shared with
Jayne for fear that Dorothy would be waiting outside
with a warrant for his arrest.

When these suspicions continued to manifest themselves, David began doing several things that were not
in his best interest. First, he began to spend time with
other women in the Orlando area, especially a woman
named Hilda who owned her own business. He knew
Hilda from past business trips and after having lunch
with her one day began spending his afternoons in her
company.

But proof that David was definitely not operating as
smoothly as he once had came during the first week in
July. On a hot and humid Monday morning David went
to a local gun shop and purchased several weapons,
including a semiautomatic rifle.

David was apparently not worried that his wives
might physically harm him, but rather he worried what
they might do to his reputation. Once the guns were
loaded and hidden in the trunk of his car, he must
have decided that he would do whatever was necessary

to persuade his wives to keep quiet about his being a bigamist. Of course, there was still the possibility that they didn't know about each other and never would. But David purchased the guns because he was no longer willing to take any chances. He would defend his double lifestyle no matter what measures might be necessary.

And if that wasn't evidence enough of what David's fear was doing to him, the incident that took place between him and Jayne the next evening certainly was.

After what happened that night Jayne, too, began to grow fearful. But unlike David her fear had nothing to do with her reputation or her concern that she might no longer be able to have limitless pleasure at other people's expense.

Jayne was afraid for her life.

35

The day after purchasing his guns—without apparent concern for the dire financial situation he had left Dorothy in—David Miller went home to tell Jayne the bad news.

David decided to tell her that the people currently leasing the home had caught up on their payments and did not intend to leave. As he expected, Jayne did not take the news well.

"You've been lying to me since the day we met," she screamed at him. "You lied about being an attorney when really you were a lobbyist, you lied about the government of Kuwait paying for our trip to Europe, and you've lied about getting us a house. I'm sick of it."

In the past weeks, Jayne had spoken to her grandmother about her troubles with David and the kind woman had offered to let Jayne live with her if it ever became necessary. She was often out of town on vacations and had left a key for Jayne. With this latest disappointment, Jayne's doubts were rekindled and she decided the time had come.

"I'm leaving," she announced loudly, turning her back on David and storming into their bedroom.

David followed quickly behind her. "What do you mean you're leaving?" He sounded worried and on the verge of tears. Jayne thought he looked pathetic.

"I'm leaving," she said as she pulled a suitcase from her closet and began tossing clothes into it. "I need some time away. I'm not saying we can't work things out eventually. But I'm tired of this. Every time you tell me something it falls through."

Tears began to form in Jayne's eyes and she angrily grabbed pieces of clothing from her closet and threw them into her suitcase. David did not know that she'd had an announcement of her own planned for that evening. One that would have given them cause to celebrate. Now he had ruined all her plans.

She was pregnant. Her period had been a week late and a pregnancy test from the local drugstore confirmed her suspicions earlier that morning. They were going to have a baby.

But now Jayne no longer wanted to tell her husband about the new life inside her. He had let her down again and she did not believe his story about the renters. Jayne had no choice but to wonder whether their entire relationship was nothing more than a series of lies.

David, meanwhile, was searching his brain for some way to keep Jayne from leaving. If she left, it would mean the beginning of the end. After all, his marriage to Dorothy was most likely over. He hadn't spoken with her since he'd left her penniless, but he was sure she was angry with him. Now Jayne was ready to walk out on him. He couldn't bear to imagine life with both of his wives upset with him.

Finally, he decided on a desperate measure. He would tell her the truth about his financial situation and appeal to her kindhearted nature to forgive him and help him get back on his feet. In a matter of minutes David worked out the answers to the questions Jayne would inevitably have about why he had lied about having millions of dollars. When he felt confident about his story, he began to speak.

"Jayne, there's something I need to tell you," he said, and suddenly he began to sob. Tears streamed down his face and he seemed overwhelmed with sorrow.

His outburst took Jayne by surprise. She stopped what she was doing and stared at him. She did not rush to his side as she might have earlier in their marriage. But her heart softened ever so slightly as she watched her husband struggle with his emotions. She said nothing, but continued to stare at him until he was ready to speak.

"You're right, Jayne," he said. His sobbing was becoming so violent she could barely understand him. "I've lied to you. Not about everything. Not about my love for you. But I lied about the money." He paused and began to cry even harder. "Oh, Jayne, I'm sorry."

Jayne was confused and frustrated at the same time. She wondered how many times she would have to go through scenes similar to this one. David seemed to be constantly apologizing for something. "You lied about the money?" she asked. "What money?"

"About having millions of dollars," he said, struggling to compose himself. "I'm not a millionaire, Jayne. I'm in debt. I don't have any money at all."

Jayne's eyes grew wide with surprise and anger. She couldn't believe it. Even when she had doubted her husband's position at Disney and his excuses for allowing the real estate deals to fall through, she never doubted his financial worth.

David continued. "Remember I told you that I spent ten million but saved four?" he asked her. "I lied, Jayne. I spent it all. I have nothing left, no savings account, no investments. Nothing. The only money I have is the money I make at Disney."

"How did you pay for the trips we took, the jewelry and clothes?" she asked. David could tell she was livid and he hoped his plan would not backfire. His admission was supposed to drum up her sympathy and convince her to stay with him.

"Whatever my salary didn't cover I paid for with credit cards," he said, still sobbing loudly. "I've run up my credit cards to the limit."

"Why, David? Why would you lie to me about that?"

"Because I loved you; I still love you, Jayne," he said. His face had become red, his eyes swollen from the severity of his outburst. "You deserve more than the income from an attorney like me. I wanted you to think I was better than that."

Jayne looked sadly at her husband, unable to imagine the guilt he must have gone through after lying to her for so long. Suddenly she was no longer angry at him; she was sorry for him. But not sorry enough to stay with him. She was free to leave now. He had admitted to lying to her and that was all she'd been waiting for. Now she was convinced that there were other lies as well. And even though she still loved him, she knew it was time to go.

"Money doesn't make someone special," Jayne said

softly, looking directly into David's eyes. "Honesty does. I thought I knew you, David. But all I knew was the person you wanted me to know. You were willing to tell me whatever lie was necessary to make me think you were someone you're not."

"But, Jayne, I love you," he cried. "Can't you understand?"

Jayne nodded. "Yes, because I love you too. But I don't know you any better than I did the first time I talked to you."

She turned away from him and resumed her packing, ignoring his crying, which had grown louder.

"You're not leaving, are you?"

"Yes." She stopped packing again and looked at her husband. "There might still be hope for us, David. But I need some time away. Time to figure out what's happened to my life in the last six months."

"Please, Jayne." He sobbed shamelessly. "Don't leave me. I need you."

"No, you don't need me," she said, proud of herself for remaining composed in light of his latest admission. "You need to figure out who you really are. And when you're ready to tell the truth about everything, give me a call. Maybe we can still get to know each other and one day even love each other."

"So you're really leaving?" he asked, sounding incredulous. He could not believe that his plan had failed so miserably.

Jayne nodded. She was sad that the celebration she had planned for that night would not materialize. Of course, eventually David would find out about her pregnancy and probably want an immediate reconciliation with her. But Jayne knew that their child would never be reason enough to return to David. She did not plan to punish the child for her husband's behavior. She would carry the baby to term and raise the infant by herself.

The only way she and David would be able to continue their marriage was if he did some soul-searching during this time away from each other. Then, perhaps when he was ready to be honest, they could be a family. For now she had to think of herself and her baby.

"I'm going to my grandma's house," she said. "You can call me there when you're ready to talk."

She picked up her suitcase and walked past David, who was still sobbing on the side of the bed. The suitcase was heavy but her resolve to leave gave her the strength to carry it down two flights of stairs as if it were weightless. She opened the trunk of the Cadillac that David had bought her and was just about to set her suitcase inside when she spotted several black leather cases.

At first Jayne wasn't sure what they were. But then she unzipped the nearest one and when she saw its contents she let out a loud gasp and quickly placed her hand over her mouth. It was a gun. Slowly she opened each of the other cases and discovered that they, too, held guns.

She felt a ripple of terror race down her spine.

Jayne couldn't imagine why David would have guns. They had talked about owning weapons before and Jayne had thought she'd convinced her husband that they were too dangerous to keep around. He couldn't possibly need guns for his job. And even if he were concerned about his safety there he wouldn't have needed so many weapons.

Afraid to move them, Jayne quickly turned around and carried her suitcase back up to their apartment, where to her surprise she found David watching television. His eyes were dry and Jayne could see no trace of the distraught behavior he'd exhibited only minutes earlier.

For his part, in the time since Jayne had left the apartment, David did not seem to be worried about her decision to leave him. He probably believed it was a temporary arrangement and he would continue to work on her, making her feel sorry for him. Eventually she would come back. In the meantime he would have the apartment to himself.

He apparently stopped crying as quickly as he had started. Then he sat down in the living room and turned on the television.

But now he looked surprised to see Jayne. He thought she had already left for her grandmother's house.

"Did you change your mind?" he asked, trying unsuccessfully to recapture his earlier distress.

Jayne shook her head, her face chalk-white with fear. "What are those guns doing in my car?"

David did not know what to say. He had meant to move the guns to his car before Jayne found them. Trapped and without any means of explaining the weapons, David stood up and approached Jayne with anger in his eyes.

"That's none of your business!" he shouted at her. "They're my guns and you have no right snooping around and looking at them."

"What?" Jayne was taken aback by David's response. "I'm not snooping around. I found them in my car and I want an explanation for them. We agreed a long time ago that we weren't going to own guns."

"I changed my mind," he said sarcastically. "You got a problem with that?"

"Yes!" She was shouting now too. "Guns are dangerous, David. Why did you buy them? Anyway, I thought you said you were broke."

The mention of his financial situation increased David's anger dramatically. "And you said you were leaving," he yelled at her. "So leave. Get out of here before I give you a reason to go."

Jayne could not understand her husband's reaction to her discovery. Her forehead wrinkled in confusion, she raised her voice again. "Is that a threat?"

"Take it how you want, Jayne, but just get out of here," he shouted. Then he brushed past her, went down to the parked Cadillac and took the guns from the trunk. When he got back upstairs he turned to her with hate in his voice. "Leave."

"Why are you mad at me?" Jayne asked, incredulous as to her husband's reaction. She should have been the one who was angry. David had lied to her time and again and now he had purchased guns without telling her. Even after they had agreed that guns were too dangerous to own.

"Because. You don't care one bit for my safety or about the fact that my life has been threatened," he yelled. "All you care about is yourself. So go ahead, run off to Grandma's house. I don't want you around anyway."

Jayne was baffled by the switch in David's personality from desperately needing her to ordering her away. But she had no interest in staying and finding out what he meant about his life being in danger. He was probably lying about that too.

"It's over between us," she said, lowering her voice and trying to regain her composure.

"Fine," he said, returning to his seat in front of the television set.

"I'm serious, David. Don't try to call me or find me. The next time you hear from me it'll be to sign divorce papers."

David shrugged and Jayne turned around and left.

Alone in the apartment, David must have begun to review the situation. Why had he reacted so angrily just because Jayne had discovered the guns? After all, she didn't know why he had bought them. So far, his double life was a complete unknown to both his wives. What was he worried about?

The more he considered how badly he had acted, the more convinced he became that he needed to see Jayne in person and apologize. When he'd made up his mind, he grabbed his car keys and headed for Jayne's grandmother's house in Casselberry.

By then Jayne had decided to confide in her family about how poorly things were between her and David. Her grandmother was on vacation, but she had left the key where Jayne could find it. After she'd allowed herself to unwind, she called her sister, Sandra, and tearfully told her that she had left David.

"For good?" Sandra asked.

"I don't know, Sandy. I want to divorce him, really. But for some stupid reason I still love him. And there's another problem too," she said. Sandra could tell that her older sister was crying and her heart went out to her. She and Jayne had grown especially close since she'd moved back to Orlando and she was sorry to see that Jayne's dreams for a happy life with David had not materialized.

"What problem?"

Jayne paused before breaking the news to her sister. "I'm pregnant. Maybe three weeks along."

"Have you told David yet?"

"No. And I'm not going to either. I wanted to work things out with him but after what happened with the guns I'm not sure I feel safe around him."

"What guns?" Sandra was suddenly frightened for her sister.

"David bought several guns and I found them in the trunk of the car. He says he's in some kind of danger, but I don't know what to believe anymore, Sandy. He's just not the man I thought he was."

As evening neared Jayne also talked to Dillon and invited him to visit her at her grandmother's house. Sometime after Dillon arrived, David pulled up in front of the house.

"Oh, no," Jayne said when she saw him get out. She turned to her son. "Dillon, tell him I can't talk. Tell him I'm sleeping or something."

Jayne rushed into a back bedroom as David made his way up the walkway. Dillon answered the door.

"Mom's sleeping. She doesn't want any visitors," he said, barring the doorway with his body.

It was just past seven o'clock and David knew Jayne could not be sleeping. The idea that she would have Dillon answer the door made David even angrier than he had been before. He pushed Dillon aside and stormed into the house. Dillon was sixteen and quickly becoming tall like his father. But he was still just a boy and no match for David—especially in his angry state.

David walked quickly through the house until he found Jayne sitting on her grandmother's bed.

"You're not welcome here, David," Jayne said stiffly. "Please leave or I'll call the police."

At the mention of law enforcement, David grew dangerously livid. "How dare you tell me what I can and can't do!" he said, his voice low and threatening. "You're my wife and if I want to see you, I'll see you."

He strode across the room until he was inches from Jayne.

"I said leave, David," she said, refusing to be intimidated by him. "Get out of here now."

As David realized the defiance in Jayne's words something in him snapped. He placed his hands around Jayne's throat and began to squeeze until she screamed for help.

"You won't tell me what to do, Jayne Miller." He was seething with anger and he tightened the grasp he had on her neck. Jayne began to choke and gasp for air, struggling to break free of the hold he had on her.

When he heard his mother's screams, Dillon ran to the bedroom and saw that David was strangling her. Instantly he pushed David back, catching the man off guard. David regained his balance and resumed his assault on Jayne. Although Dillon struggled to stop David he realized he needed assistance as quickly as possible. He turned and ran to the nearest phone, picked it up and dialed the emergency operator.

"My mother's being choked to death," he yelled. "Please, send police quick."

When David heard Dillon calling the police, he quickly came to his senses. He backed away from Jayne and stared at her in shock. "Look what you're doing to me, Jayne," he said, his voice barely more than a whisper. "You're making me crazy."

Then he wandered slowly from the bedroom into

the living room and walked out to his car. As soon as he left the house, Dillon raced in to check on his mother.

"Mom!" he said, kneeling by her side. "Are you all right?"

Jayne was crying and rubbing her neck, which was covered with red marks and the beginnings of bruises. She was frightened and sad and fearful for what David could have done to her or the unborn baby inside her if she had been without oxygen for much longer.

She swallowed hard and nodded her head, taking her son in her arms.

"I'll be okay, Dillon, thank you. If you hadn't called the police . . ." She didn't finish her statement.

"Mom, he could have killed you."

Jayne nodded. "He was angry, that's all," she said. "Don't worry, honey, I'm leaving him. He won't be part of my life anymore."

She didn't want Dillon to know how upset she was with David, but she had already decided to press charges against him. By the time the police arrived, David was already gone. Jayne filed a report charging David with domestic violence but refused to get a restraining order against him.

"He won't do it again," she told the police. "It's over between us."

But later that night, when Dillon had gone back to his father's house, David did come back. Jayne had told herself that if David returned she would bolt the door and refuse to talk with him. But as the bruises on her neck developed she became angry at her husband. Now she wanted him to see how badly he'd hurt her. How dare he tell her that he loved her and needed her and then come so close to killing her?

She opened the door a few inches and glared at him.

"Look what you did." She spat the words at him and pointed to her neck. "You could have killed me, David."

"Listen, I came to apologize," he said. But Jayne interrupted him.

"I'm not interested. Just get out of here and don't come back again."

But this time he pushed her aside and shoved her onto the floor. Suddenly Jayne was frightened for her life. There was no one around to call the police and David was clearly angrier than he'd been before.

"You'll be sorry for calling the police," he said, his voice seething with animosity. He pushed her into the kitchen and spotted a four-foot high lockable utility closet.

Completely overcome by rage, David shoved Jayne toward the closet and ordered her to get inside.

"No, David!" she screamed. "Don't do this."

"Get inside or you'll be sorry."

Jayne quickly decided she had no choice and she crawled into the closet. David slammed the door shut and locked it.

"My life isn't even worth living!" he screamed. "All because of you, Jayne."

For the next hour he yelled at her, blaming her for his financial woes, his anger, and his current outburst. He called her names and threatened her and told her he never wanted to see her again.

"You're lucky you're not out here where I can see you," he said. "I don't know what I'd do if I had to look at your face right now. You make me sick. All you ever think about is yourself."

All the while, Jayne said nothing. She was cramped

in a tight cavity eighteen inches deep and four feet high, crying softly and unable to control her shaking body. The closet was dark and smelled strongly of household cleaners and she wondered how long she could survive before passing out.

She had discovered a switch on the door that probably unlocked the closet from the inside. But she knew better than to try to escape from the closet while David was still shouting at her.

Jayne was scared to death and utterly shocked by her husband's behavior. Never had she imagined David to be capable of such abuse. As the minutes passed, she grew more and more frightened. What if he opened the closet and tried to strangle her again? What if the switch didn't open the closet and she suffocated? But the thing that scared her more than anything was David's statement about the guns.

"You know why I need guns, Jayne?" he shouted. "Because I'm married to you, that's why. I bought the guns because of you."

After that, Jayne listened as David walked out of the kitchen and stormed out of the house. She heard a car door shut in the distance and the sound of squealing tires as his car pulled away.

But even though he was gone and Jayne believed he would not come back, she remained in the closet, her heart beating wildly, unable to muster the courage to leave the cramped space.

When she began to feel light-headed and as if she were about to faint, she finally flipped the switch. She had been right about it unlocking the door from the inside and the closet door swung open. She looked at her watch in shock. She had spent four hours in the closet.

She knew at that moment there would be no reconciliation with David and that staying at her grandmother's house was not a permanent solution. She walked slowly toward the kitchen telephone, picked it up, and dialed Jodee in Los Angeles.

"Jodee," she said, her voice weak and unsteady. "It's over. I left him."

"Why? What happened?"

Jayne shook her head. "I can't tell you right now. But I need to know if I can move back in with you."

"Of course," she said. Jodee wondered what terrible thing had happened to cause Jayne to want to leave Orlando. But she knew she would find out eventually. "When are you coming?"

"I don't know. But I can't stay here anymore."

Suddenly Jayne began feeling sharp, painful cramps in her lower abdomen. "I'll call you back," she said quickly and hung up the phone.

Doubled over in pain, Jayne made her way to the bathroom. She pulled down her underpants and saw that they were stained with fresh blood. Gently wiping at the area with a tissue, she sat down on the edge of the toilet and began to sob.

Later she would convince Sandra that she had gotten her period that day and must have been mistaken about being pregnant. But Jayne had taken a home pregnancy test and she knew the truth. At that moment as blood dripped from between her legs, she was certain that she was having a miscarriage, that her tiny unborn child had paid the price for the terrifying hours she'd spent in the utility closet. She closed her eyes and cried as if her heart were breaking.

Her baby was dead.

36

In the month since Dorothy had last heard from David, she had worked feverishly to get their finances in order. In all, David had left her with a debt of more than fifty thousand dollars. Because the accounts were in both their names and she had no idea where David was, she was responsible for paying the bills. She was also without enough money to buy even a bag of groceries.

For that reason, the day after filing for bankruptcy, Dorothy began searching for a job as a hairdresser. A week later she was hired at a small shop near her home and near the boys' school. Since she had already earned her beautician's license in Pennsylvania years earlier, she was able to start working immediately.

When she wasn't working, she spent hours going over their finances—contacting creditors, making payment arrangements, and getting some of the charges written off. She wrote letters explaining that her husband had left her and that she was unable to pay the debt he'd accumulated. And she wrote letters to law enforcement agencies in Orlando and Los Angeles asking if she could file charges against David for leaving her with so many unpaid bills.

There were occasions, in the recesses of Dorothy's mind, when she still believed he worked for the CIA and that one day he would come back and explain the entire situation. But then, why didn't the CIA have any record of his existence? But reality loomed larger with each passing day and by the first week of July she was finally beginning to understand what had happened to her.

The CIA agent who had responded to her inquiry had been right. She was married to a con man. For twelve years she had loved him and given her life to him. And she had believed him. That was perhaps most devastating of all. Every time he'd come home from a business trip unable to explain the covert operations he was involved with, every time he had left her side at a moment's notice to partake in a dangerous mission, it had all been a lie.

Several times since talking with Merritt Foster, Dorothy had wondered who the blond-haired woman was that she had seen with David. But she had convinced herself it no longer mattered. She was probably one of many girlfriends he'd had over the years. And she believed he probably had had several. Why else would he have lied to her about working for the CIA?

In some ways, Dorothy knew she was still in shock. She had cried some and shared her angry feelings with her family. But she had not yet grasped the enormity of the lies David had told her. Her whole life had been a lie.

She remembered the times David would make love to her after what he said was a dangerous mission, whispering in her ear that he had missed her terribly. The hours she had spent worrying about him and the times he had whisked her away from one home to another under the pretense of making sure she and the boys were safe. Every postcard, every foreign country. All of it a lie.

She had told her boys that she and David were having trouble and that he had left her with unpaid bills. But she hadn't gone into detail. Most likely because she was still sorting the details out herself.

She spent hours second-guessing herself, asking herself how she could have been so naive to his schemes. But inevitably she would arrive at the same answer. She knew how it had happened. His lies had been brilliant. And for that reason there were times when she worried about how she would react when she spoke with him next. She fully believed that he would contact her again at some time.

But when he did, would she still be vulnerable? Would he rattle off a believable story to explain the situation and would she find herself believing him? Dorothy shuddered at the thought, afraid of what would happen if he did not come clean with his past lies. She did not know how much more she could take, because she had not yet stopped loving the David Miller she thought she knew. Dorothy decided that whenever they spoke again she would be distant and cautious. After all, the real David Miller was nothing more than a stranger.

The phone call came on July 5.

Dorothy had gotten home from work and was reading a handful of responses from creditors when the phone rang.

"Hello?"

The caller was silent. Dorothy was about to hang up the phone when she heard someone crying on the other end.

"Dorothy?"

It was David. Dorothy felt her heart skip a beat. She quickly sat down and ordered herself to be calm.

"Where are you?" Dorothy's voice was cool and distant, as David expected it would be.

"It doesn't matter where I am. I just wanted to tell you I'm sorry," he said between sobs. "We're in debt and it's all my fault."

Dorothy paused and tried to decide what to say next. There were so many things she had wanted to tell him, so many lies she had wanted to confront him with. But now she was not sure where to begin.

"I've contacted the CIA," she said finally.

"What?" David no longer sounded contrite, but rather frustrated and angry. Dorothy wondered if he had only been pretending to cry. "Why would you do that, Dorothy? I told you never to contact them."

"Don't bother, David," she said. "They've never heard of you."

David sighed impatiently. "They know me by my pseudonym. Not my real name."

"You expect me to believe that? Especially now after you've been gone a month without any phone calls or explanation?"

"I needed some time away to think things through," he said, his voice cracking again with emotion.

"Is that why you started seeing the blonde?"

So she knew about Jayne. David had been afraid of that.

"What?" He was buying time, trying to figure out exactly what Dorothy knew.

"The blonde, David. Merritt called me and said she saw you kissing some blonde near our old house. Why? Wasn't I enough?"

"Like I said, Dorothy, I'm sorry." David cried and once again he sounded deeply upset. "She's nothing, just some girl I met."

"How can I believe you? The CIA hasn't ever heard of you and now you tell me you needed some time away when what you really needed was another woman."

"Dorothy, I've messed up," he insisted. "But the girl's gone. I only knew her for a week or so."

"Wonderful. Is that supposed to make me feel good? Because it doesn't. I'm sitting here trying to wrestle a fifty-thousand-dollar debt and you're in Florida dating some blonde."

David sobbed louder. "I'm so sorry, Dorothy. I knew I shouldn't have used the credit cards. I guess I kind of flipped out."

"Kind of? What are you saying, David? Are all those charges yours or is someone really reimbursing you?"

David struggled to catch his breath. "They're mine. I don't know why, Dorothy. I just went on a spending spree, I guess."

"Who's going to pay for them? I had to declare bankruptcy, you know."

At the mention of bankruptcy, David grew even more upset. "I've ruined everything, Dorothy. Please forgive me."

Dorothy considered what her husband was asking. She thought about his explanation that he worked for the CIA under an assumed name and his apology for spending time with another woman. And she decided that she could not possibly believe him, let alone forgive him. He had devastated her life and she knew at that moment that she could never trust him again.

"No, David, I can't," she said calmly. "It's over between us. I've contacted the police, and if they'll let me I'm going to press charges against you for leaving me in debt."

David stopped crying. "You've talked to the police?"

"No, I wrote them a letter. I'm waiting to hear from them, but they already know everything. How you lied to me about working for the CIA and how you ran up our credit cards so that I had to file for bankruptcy."

"I am not lying about the CIA, Dorothy!" David shouted. "And if you weren't so demanding maybe I wouldn't have been so crazy lately."

Dorothy had heard enough. "Good-bye, David. You'll be hearing from my attorney."

"What's that supposed to mean?"

"I'm filing for divorce as soon as I can afford to."

"But, Dorothy—"

She hung up the phone. She had spent much of the past month wondering what would happen the next time she talked to David and now she knew. He was still trying to lie to her, still making excuses for his behavior. She congratulated herself for not falling for his alibis and she hoped with all her heart that she was doing the right thing. She supposed it was possible that he actually did work for the CIA. But even if he did, he had still cheated on her and left her deeply in debt. That alone was reason enough to leave him.

When David did not try to call back that evening, Dorothy figured she would not hear from him again for a long while. But the next day David phoned again.

This time he was angry from the beginning, screaming at Dorothy and blaming his problems on her. Dorothy listened patiently and waited until David stopped yelling.

"I have nothing more to say, David," she said. "You're a liar and a cheater. We're through." She paused a moment. "With any luck, the police will agree to press charges against you and the next time you call me might be from prison."

Dorothy's words sent David into a blinding rage. "Listen to me, Dorothy," he said, and his voice was so filled with venom that Dorothy could barely recognize it. "You talk to the police and I'll kill you."

Dorothy gasped. She could not believe what David had said. She was beginning to realize that he was not the man she'd thought him to be. But even so, she had never imagined him capable of such a threat. She was silent a moment, trying to decipher whether David was serious about what he had said.

"I mean it," he said again. "I'll kill you, Dorothy." And then he hung up.

Stunned and unsure what to do next, Dorothy sat at her kitchen table shaking. David had been lying to her for the past twelve years, and now that he had been found out he was obviously furious. His schemes were unraveling and he was desperate to keep things together. But would he really kill her? Dorothy remembered David's voice as he made the threat. It had been cold and calculating.

Suddenly Dorothy was convinced David was serious. But the realization only strengthened her decision to involve the police in their affairs. That afternoon she hooked up a tape recorder to her telephone. If David called again with more threats, she would be ready.

His next call came on July 7.

Again he threatened her life, warning her not to report his actions to the police. But this time when he hung up on her, Dorothy smiled. She popped a tiny cassette from the recorder and placed it in an envelope.

Fifteen minutes later she was headed for the local police station.

37

Although she should have been concerned for her own safety, Jayne was worried about her husband. She felt angry and hurt by his sudden violence and deeply betrayed by his lies. But still she wondered where he was and what was happening to him. She thought he might be in need of counseling and even wondered whether they should seek help together and try to salvage their relationship.

"He isn't worth it, Jayne," her sister Sandra had said after Jayne related the incident about the closet. "The guy's a fraud. He might hurt you."

But by mid-July Jayne no longer thought so. She knew that she and David still loved each other, even if their relationship had become unhealthy. In some ways she even thought it touching that he had lied about his wealth. He was only trying to impress her, she reasoned.

Of course, there was no excuse for his violence the week before, and Jayne was still angry with him. But she decided his outburst had been more of a symptom than anything else. The truth had caught up with him and he was struggling to accept the fact that he could not give her everything he had promised.

David's financial situation was so bad that Jayne had contacted the apartment owner and discovered that they were in the process of being evicted. David had apparently already moved out, because the landlord had not seen him since the first of July.

After that Jayne had moved their belongings into her father's storage unit at the U-Store-It in Orlando and promised to pay any rent they still owed on the apartment. She wondered where David had gone and how he would react when he realized his belongings had been moved.

Jayne had already decided that when David contacted her next she would refuse to see him alone. She was spending time living at both her parents' and her grandmother's houses and she had no plans to move back in with David. In fact, she was still considering moving to Los Angeles to live with Jodee.

But before she made such a move she wanted to do what she could to help her husband. He needed to work out his situation and come to an understanding about who he was. Jayne was willing to postpone her future plans until she at least tried to help him through the crisis he seemed to be facing.

He called on July 16 and—as Jayne had expected— begged her to forgive him. He also told her that he had moved to a boardinghouse because he could no longer afford the apartment.

"I know," she said. "I've put our things in my dad's storage unit." She told him that he could get his belongings back whenever he wanted.

"You need help, David," she told him softly. "I know

you didn't mean to hurt me, but you have a bad temper. You've lied to me about a lot of things and you need to work out your problems before there can be anything between us again."

"But, Jayne, I want to see you," he cried. "I love you; you're my wife and I need you."

Jayne thought a moment. Something in David's voice caused her to drop her defenses and empathize with his situation. In the past, the men in her life had not been willing to work out problems in their relationships with her. At least David wanted to try. She decided to give him an ultimatum.

"Get rid of the guns," she said. Her statement was not a request and David knew she no longer felt safe around him after his outburst the previous week.

"I will," he said quickly. "Whatever you want, Jayne. I'll do whatever it takes to make things right between us."

Instantly she developed a plan. "I know what you can do with them," she said. "If you're serious about working things out, then take the guns to my dad's house. I'll call him and ask him to hold them for you."

"Okay, I'll do it," he said.

"I'll let my dad know you're coming. Call me back in an hour to make sure everything's all right with him."

"Okay, Jayne, I will," he said. "Does this mean you'll see me?"

Jayne paused. She had been so hurt by David, so afraid of him when he had tried to strangle her. But she hadn't been able to stop loving him. He was, after all, her husband and she wanted more than anything to make their marriage work. Even in light of his past failures.

"I can't promise I'll see you," she said finally. "But we can talk."

"Will you see me eventually?"

"Probably."

"Oh, Jayne," David said, sobbing softly. "I miss you so much. If you only knew how sorry I am for lying to you and scaring you the other night."

"We have a lot of talking to do," she said, cutting him off. "But first let me call my dad and see if he minds holding your guns."

When Jayne called her father he was frustrated by her request. He told her he had disliked David from the beginning and that he didn't trust him.

"Why does he have weapons, anyway?"

"I don't know for sure, Dad," Jayne said. "But I want him to get rid of them before I agree to see him. Can you keep them at your house?"

Richard could not understand why his daughter would ever want to see David after what he'd done to her the week before. And the idea of his son-in-law having guns further convinced him that David was potentially dangerous. But he quickly decided that if Jayne was worried about her safety he would definitely be willing to store the guns—even though he had never permitted such weapons in his own home. At least then David wouldn't have access to them.

"I don't like the idea, Jayne," he said. "You should forget the guy. But if it'll make you feel safer I'll keep the guns."

Jayne thanked him and when David called later that hour she told him that her father was waiting for him.

"I'm on my way," he said. "Jayne, I think everything's going to work out for us. Really."

"This is a start, David," she said. "Let's just take it slow."

After David hung up he must have been relieved. Everything was working out much better than he had expected. Dorothy did not know that he was married to Jayne and Jayne had no idea he had another wife in Pennsylvania. Maybe he really didn't need the guns after all. Besides, he really did love Jayne and he wanted to work things out with her.

He must have congratulated himself on telling Jayne that he was living in a boardinghouse. In truth, he was living with Hilda and doing some part-time work for her company. She was a wonderful woman and he was greatly enjoying her company. He had told her that he and his former girlfriend had broken up and therefore he needed a place to live. Hilda had been more than willing to let him move in with her and he was convinced that she knew nothing about either of his marriages.

That afternoon he told Hilda he needed to go out for a while. He checked to make sure his guns were still in the trunk of his car, then he made his way to Richard Leebrick's house in Sanford. As he drove he found himself again thankful that the fear he'd been plagued with was finally gone. It had disappeared as soon as he realized his wives did not know about each other.

But when David pulled up in front of the Leebrick house on Crow's Bluff Lane, he began to shake, his body breaking into a sweat. It was back. As quickly as it had gone, the fear that had eaten away at him had returned.

He was suddenly afraid. He must have wondered what he was doing getting rid of all the guns. What if he were wrong about Dorothy and Jayne? What if they really did know about each other and they were only pretending not to know so they could trap him? He looked toward the house and saw that Richard had opened the door and was waiting for him.

He forced himself to smile, then casually climbed out of the car and opened the trunk. He picked up three of his four guns, carried them up the walkway, and handed them to Jayne's father. The man did not remark about the missing gun. He did not know how many guns David had and neither did Jayne.

But after he thanked Richard and got back into his car, David relaxed. Everything would be okay—even if Jayne and Dorothy ever found out about each other and tried to destroy him. He had saved himself one means of protection. Just in case.

A 9 m.m. handgun.

38

In late July Richard and Janice Leebrick left Sanford and flew to Virginia to visit their son, Rick, who was sick in the hospital. The visit lasted nearly a month and the entire time Richard was crazy with worry. But not for his son.

Richard was worried about Jayne.

The longer he thought about David Miller and the guns he'd turned over that July afternoon, the more he believed the man might be dangerous. Certainly if he'd found a way to get three guns he could find a way to get others. Richard was convinced that the fact that he was holding the weapons at his house offered absolutely no security for Jayne.

One night toward the end of August, Richard sat straight up in bed and called Jayne's name out loud. He and Janice had been staying at a motel, and that night they turned in early, just after eight o'clock when visitor's hours at the hospital were over. It was 9:30 P.M. Janice was still asleep beside him and Richard nervously glanced around the dark room, unsure of what had woken him.

Then it came to him. He'd had a nightmare. Something about Jayne being in trouble. Yes, that was it. David was trying to kill Jayne. He tried to shake away the horror of the dream and fall back asleep but his heart was racing and he lay in bed with his eyes wide open. An uneasy feeling of anxiety had come over him and he could not shake it. Something kept telling him that Jayne was in trouble.

Finally, Richard picked up the phone next to his bed. He had to talk to Jayne and find out if she was okay. She was staying at their home, so he dialed his number and waited. It was busy.

Richard stood up and began to pace the motel room. What if something had happened to Jayne? What if David had broken into the house and forced himself on her? What if he had found the guns and done something crazy and then left the phone off the hook?

He was nearly frantic with worry when he picked up the phone again and redialed his number. This time the answering machine came on.

"Listen, this is Dad," he said, his voice filled with concern. "I'm at the motel. Jayne, please call me when you get this message. I don't care what time it is."

Then he tried to fall back asleep.

Not until early the next morning, on August 24, did Jayne finally return his call.

"Jayne!" he said as soon as he heard her voice. "You're okay!"

Jayne paused a moment. "Of course, Dad," she said. "Is everything okay?"

Richard sighed and forced himself to relax. He had

shared the dream with Janice the next morning, but he had been unable to sleep for most of the night and now he was drained. "I had a dream last night and I thought David might have done something to hurt you. I had to call and see if you were all right."

"I'm fine," she said again. "Come on, Dad. Don't worry so much."

"Well, sweetheart, I just don't like that man," Richard said. "He's trouble, Jayne. Believe me. I know I have those guns, but last night I was sure he had other guns that he didn't give me. Be careful around him, Jayne. You don't know what he's capable of."

Jayne thanked her father for his concern and assured him that she was fine. But after she hung up she felt guilty. In the month since her parents had left for Virginia, she and David had been talking more frequently despite her family's concerns. Although she was still upset with him for lying to her, she had agreed to talk to him and eventually to visit with him. In her opinion he was making progress and finally coming to terms with who he was.

He had managed to keep his job at Disney through all the turmoil in his life and he had made plans to rent a house near Sanford after he repaid the debts he'd accumulated. Jayne was actually quite proud of him.

The night before, while her father lay worried sick in the Virginia motel room, she had been busy having dinner with David. Afterward, the two wound up spending the night together. She had ignored the phone call and hadn't received the message until she woke up. Now David was still in the shower.

She thought about her father's dream and his suspicion that David still carried a gun. He must be wrong, she told herself. David had willingly turned his guns over to her father. If he had wanted to keep them, he would simply have said so. No, Jayne was positive David did not have access to any guns. He was not interested in weapons; he was interested in her and in working through their problems.

The water continued to run in the back bathroom and Jayne tried to put aside her father's warning. Suddenly she had to be sure about the guns. She grabbed David's car keys from the counter and walked out to where his car was parked. Opening the trunk quickly, she glanced around for any sign of a gun. In the back, underneath a towel, Jayne noticed the handle of a small dark suitcase. She looked back toward the house to be sure David was not watching her and she opened the case.

Inside was a small handgun.

Jayne's mouth fell open and she stood there several seconds staring at the weapon. Her father had been right. David was still lying to her, still making her believe he was someone he wasn't. She closed the suitcase and marched into the house.

By then David had come out of the shower and was drying off in the bedroom when Jayne stormed into the room.

"How could you, David?" she yelled.

David turned to her, a blank look on his face. He and Jayne had not fought in so long that he wondered what her problem was now.

Jayne did not wait for David to respond. "I thought you were really trying to change!"

"Jayne, get hold of yourself," David said calmly. If he got angry, the situation would only escalate.

"I went out to your car to see if you had any laundry

that needed doing," she lied. She didn't want him to know about her father's suspicions. "There's a gun out there, David. A handgun! You told me you gave your guns to my father."

David smiled. "Oh, that," he said. "Yes, I meant to give that gun to Dad a long time ago. But then he left for Virginia and I never got a chance."

"No, I'm not buying that," Jayne said, shaking her head and turning to leave. When she got into the living room she yelled at her husband. "Get your things and leave. I'm sick of your lies."

"Jayne, listen, honey, I can explain everything," he said, and for reasons she did not understand Jayne found herself listening. "I overlooked the gun when Dad took the others. I forgot about it."

Jayne glared at him doubtfully. "David, you better be telling the truth about this. I've had it with your lies. If you don't get rid of that gun right now I don't ever want to see your face again."

"You want me to give it to you?"

"No!" Jayne shouted. "I don't know where my father keeps the other guns and I don't want to be responsible for it." She was still very angry. "Take it to the police station. They'll hold it for you."

"What?"

"The police will hold weapons for you. I read it somewhere in the paper. Take the gun there and bring back a receipt."

David considered the situation he was in. He desperately wanted to keep the gun in case he needed it at some future time. But there would be no point in planning for the future if he didn't get rid of it. He knew from Jayne's anger that she would not be satisfied until he had done as she asked and taken it to the police station. Besides, he could always get it back later.

"Okay, sweetheart," he said softly. "I'll take it down and give it to the police."

Jayne opened the door and waited for him to leave. "Do it now, David. I've had it with all these guns and everything. I still don't know if I believe you. How could you forget about a gun?"

David shrugged. "Let up a little, Jayne. I'll get rid of it, okay?"

"I'll be waiting for the receipt."

David walked past her without saying another word. Jayne had become terribly demanding. But even as angry as she had become at him, he still loved her and hoped they could save their marriage.

As he had promised, David drove to the Sanford police station and checked the weapon in with Officer Guy Brewster. He explained that his wife was uncomfortable having the weapon around the house and that he would not be needing it again until he could purchase a locking gun closet.

Brewster took the gun and gave David a receipt.

Later that night, David brought back the receipt and told Jayne he was returning to his room at the boardinghouse. Not long afterward, Sandra called. Jayne told her about finding another gun in David's car and how he had agreed to take it to the police.

"Jayne!" Sandra was astonished by the story. "You don't think he actually took it to the police, do you?"

"Relax, Sandy. He brought me the receipt. It's definitely from the police department. He doesn't have the gun anymore."

"But, Jayne, he could still have other weapons. You

just don't know with this guy. I get the feeling he's been lying to you from the beginning."

"That was before," she said, trying to convince herself as well as her sister. "He's trying to change, Sandy. I got pretty mad at him when I found the gun, but he didn't seem to mind. It's like he's willing to do whatever I want him to do as long as I don't leave him. He really wants to work things out."

"I hope you're right," she said. "But I get a creepy feeling about him. Please be careful."

Jayne saw very little of David during the next few days. She thought he was busy with his job, but actually David was suffering from a severe case of anxiety. He worried constantly that Jayne might try to frame him or that she would find out about Dorothy and tell the press that he was a bigamist.

At least when he'd had the gun he knew he could protect himself. If either of his wives ever threatened to destroy him he would have the ability to destroy them first. But not without a gun.

As a result, David was having trouble sleeping and eating. He was losing weight and his roommate Hilda had commented that he wasn't looking well. He knew he had to get the gun back, but he was apparently worried that the police would be suspicious if he claimed it so soon.

He decided he needed some time away from Jayne to sort out his feelings and try to allay his fears. He called her on August 28 and told her he was taking a week-long business trip to Los Angeles.

"Is everything okay?" Jayne asked. Something in her husband's voice sounded distant and strained.

"Yes, things are just busy at the office. I'll miss you,

honey. I'll call you at your father's house as soon as I get back."

As she had been in the habit of doing lately, Jayne believed him. She was convinced that his days of lying were behind them and that once they rebuilt their relationship they could continue on in their marriage and possibly even have children one day. Jayne had decided never to tell David about the possible miscarriage she'd had. She knew he would blame himself and she didn't think he was strong enough to handle the guilt. Especially now that he was working so hard to make things right between them.

David had no reason to lie to her now, Jayne told herself. She knew the truth about his finances and his temper. Therefore he no longer had anything to hide. He had taken so few business trips lately that Jayne did not for a moment doubt that David was indeed leaving for Los Angeles that evening.

She learned the truth two days later.

Sandra had offered to take her to dinner and they had driven to Orlando so they could go to Jayne's favorite steak house. Sandy was driving and they were five minutes from the restaurant when they stopped at a red light.

Suddenly, Jayne turned toward her right and looked directly into her husband's eyes. They were the eyes of someone filled with hatred, someone trapped and dangerous. In David's eyes at that moment Jayne saw something that was brutally honest. In her opinion, David looked like he wanted to kill her.

Sandra had noticed David's car beside them and she looked puzzled.

"What's he doing in town? I thought he was in Los Angeles."

But Jayne was unable to talk, terrified by the look in her husband's eyes. The light turned green and David raced through the intersection, speeding off ahead of them.

"Sandra! Stop the car!" Jayne screamed. "Please, stop. Turn around. I have to get out of here; I have to get home."

Sandra looked at her sister, confused by her reaction. Jayne was clearly terrified.

"What is it, Jayne?"

"Sandy, he wants to kill me. Please take me home. I can't believe it. He's going to kill me!"

Sandra did as Jayne asked and turned the car around, heading back toward Sanford. "What's all this about?" she asked.

By then Jayne had started crying, nervously looking behind them every few seconds as they drove. "Did you see his eyes?"

"Not really," Sandra said. "As soon as I saw him he was already starting to drive away."

"He's not supposed to be here. He told me he was going to Los Angeles for a business trip. Don't you see?" Jayne sobbed. "I caught him lying again. He knows I'm onto him and now he's going to kill me!"

"Jayne, come on. It's going to be okay," Sandra said, trying to calm her sister.

"No! It's not okay! I saw his eyes, Sandy," Jayne cried. "He's going to kill me."

That night there was nothing Sandra could do to pacify her sister. Finally, they drove to the police station and Jayne filed a restraining order against her husband. The police had record of the charges she'd filed two months earlier against him and now she had no problem obtaining the order. Jayne gave the police the phone number and address of David's boardinghouse.

"We'll be sure he gets this first thing tomorrow, ma'am," the officer told her.

Jayne nodded and turned to leave. She was angrier than ever and terrified at the same time. David had violated her last bit of remaining trust. He had also made a fool of her. Now she was finished with him.

Still terrified about what he might do to her and about how many guns he might still have, Jayne went back home to her grandmother's house. It was well after midnight before she fell asleep.

The next morning, red-eyed and tired, stricken with anger and anxiety, Jayne decided there were still too many unanswered questions about David Miller. The time had come to know the truth. She searched the phone book and an advertisement caught her eye.

When you must know—for peace of mind, it read. Jayne called the number alongside the ad and made an appointment for September 1 with Bob Brown, private investigator from Seminole County.

David, meanwhile, was suffocating in a blanket of fear. Jayne knew he had lied. Now, he reasoned, it was just a matter of time before she found out about Dorothy. It was inevitable now that Jayne knew he had lied again. Especially after she had been so kind and forgiving in the past few months. David imagined she would probably go back to the Casselberry neighborhood and ask the Fosters about David's past. Then she would find out about Dorothy.

The thought terrified him beyond belief. He needed to get his gun back. There was no other solution.

So that night, just a few hours after she had come in and filed her restraining order, David went to the Sanford police station and retrieved his 9 m.m. handgun.

"Got the locking closet." He smiled at the officer behind the desk and signed the release form. He hoped the explanation would keep the police from growing suspicious.

"Thanks for keeping it," he said, and walked out to his car.

Once he had the gun safely in his trunk, he returned to Hilda's and fell into a restless sleep. The next day, an officer approached the house and handed David a paper that ordered him to stay away from Jayne.

At that moment, despite the gun he carried with him, David's fear began to completely consume him. If she were going to get the police involved, then she intended to ruin him. David was certain of it. He was discouraged because she had left him just one choice.

He would need to destroy her first.

39

The moment Jayne stepped into the office of investigator Bob Brown she knew she had done the right thing by calling him. In addition to numerous degrees, certificates, and commendations, Brown had a sign on his wall that read, "God is greater than any problem I have."

Jayne figured that if the investigator lived by those words, she had to be on the right track. She told him about her estrangement from David, his threats and lies and how frightened she was that he might harm her.

"Our marriage is over, Mr. Brown," she said. "But I still need to know the truth. About his job at Disney, his time away from me. I need to know who he really is."

Bob nodded. "I understand. Why don't you tell me what you know and we'll go from there."

After Jayne left, Bob sat for several minutes at his desk pondering Jayne's desire to know the truth about her husband. He had become a private investigator because of cases like this. Other private eyes might feel the same way, but for vastly different reasons. Domestic cases were numerous and for the most part simple to solve. Typically, private investigators who handled domestic cases enjoyed digging up dirt and making money on other people's inevitable misfortunes.

Bob was nothing like those investigators.

In 1969 Bob Brown was nearly thirty years old, with what seemed like everything going for him. He had a happy home life and he was one of the most successful detectives in the Seminole County sheriff's department. But over the years Bob had handled a number of domestic cases in which feuding between family members had escalated to the point of violence and even murder.

Time and again Bob wondered what might have happened if someone had intervened earlier. Perhaps if the victimized family member had been able to see the early danger signs the tragedy could have been averted.

Bob began praying about his desire to help these people. He had been a Christian for most of his life and he drew daily from the strength and guidance God provided. Late that year Bob decided that he was being guided toward a career as a private investigator. He opened up his own office in December 1969, and began seeking out the people he felt led to help.

From the beginning Bob made his mark by being different from other investigators. He was kind, soft-spoken, conservatively dressed, and he said grace over his meals at restaurants. He was not interested in his hourly fees as much as he was intent on restoring relationships in broken families. When clients could not afford his fees, Bob often charged them far less than

the going rate in order to help them. People oftentimes mistook Bob for a preacher and were inevitably
surprised to learn his true occupation.

As word got around about Bob and his concern for
people, clients began making their way to his office in
steady numbers. There were hurting men and women
who hired him to see where their spouses were spending their spare time. When Bob would discover another man or woman in the picture, he would offer to
confront the cheating spouse. Many times the unfaith-
ful partner would be willing to end the affair and work
with his spouse on mending their marriage.

When Bob realized his distraught clients were seeking counsel from him, he made a point of seeking professional training. He enrolled in marriage and family
counseling courses through his church and became a
certified counselor.

Perhaps he might have been satisfied to work in such
a role permanently if it weren't for his considerable
talent as an investigator. His significant ability brought
dozens of missing-persons cases to his office door. He
solved most of them in a matter of weeks.

His secretary, Donna McConnell, once said that Bob
had the ability to make people nervous if they had
something to hide.

"He has a way of moving about undetected, finding
keys to old locked closets and turning up bones that
some prefer remained buried," she said. "Bob is not
one you would want on your trail, because he has a bad
habit of not letting go."

In 1978 Bob was hired by a woman whose son was
missing. Police had shelved the case and any leads regarding the boy's whereabouts seemed to have been
exhausted. Over a period of three months Bob located

a number of informants until he finally found the bodies of the boy and one of his friends in a desolate swamp hundreds of miles from the place they had last been seen. His investigation led to the arrest and conviction of two men who had murdered the boys and stolen their car.

When news reporters asked Bob how he had been able to find leads when others had given up, he credited his faith in God.

"I prayed about every lead I came across," he would say unashamedly. "My faith has always been my guide."

Over the years Bob's genuine concern and considerable abilities caused him to develop a clientele most private investigators might only dream of. By September 1, 1991, the day Jayne Miller first met with Brown, he had eight full-time investigators working for him and various correspondents throughout the world.

Normally he might have passed Jayne's case on to one of his other investigators. But something in Jayne's sad brown eyes reminded him that he had opened his business because of people like her. He told her he would handle the case himself, charging her $200 for the initial week of investigation.

Now, alone with the information Jayne had given him, Bob began making phone calls. The discoveries were easier than he had hoped.

Jayne told him that David owned a house on Jericho Drive in Casselberry. Bob ran the information through the county assessor's office.

"Whose names are on the deed?" he asked. Several minutes passed before the representative returned to the phone with the answer.

"David and Dorothy Miller."

Next he contacted the Department of Motor Vehicles and gave the operator information regarding David's license plate.

"Who's it registered to?"

The operator punched in some information on his computer. "Registered to David R. Miller and Dorothy Miller."

"Is the registration current?"

"Just renewed last month."

And so, minutes after Jayne had left his office, Bob knew more than Jayne had ever imagined. David had recently been married to another woman. Because the DMV registration was current, he suspected that David might still be married to Dorothy. If that was the case, the man would be a bigamist.

He waited until the next morning to call Jayne at her grandmother's house.

"Hello, Jayne," he said softly. Jayne had asked him to call her by her first name. "I have some information for you."

Jayne was thrilled and terrified at the same time. She hadn't expected the investigator to find anything out so quickly. But now that he had she was afraid of what he might say. She leaned against the kitchen counter for support. "Go ahead."

"Well, it seems that the house in Casselberry is owned by David and Dorothy Miller," he said.

Jayne felt as if she'd been punched in the stomach. "Dorothy *Miller*?"

"Yes. Both their names are on the deed."

Jayne's mind raced as she tried to remember what David had told her about a woman named Dorothy. Oh, yes. She had been an old girlfriend and he had lived with her at the house. Jayne was sure that was what David had said.

"Are you sure it says Dorothy Miller?" Jayne asked.

Bob paused a moment. He had been through these types of conversations so many times. Even after suspecting someone they love, most of his clients were shocked to learn that they were right about their loved one having lied to them.

"That's the name on the deed," he said. "There isn't any other name for her."

"I see," Jayne said. Why hadn't David told her he had been married to Dorothy? Jayne closed her eyes and tried to shut out the sick feeling that was coming over her. She forced herself to speak. "Anything else?"

Bob cleared his throat. "Yes. I checked with the DMV and David's car is registered to David R. Miller and Dorothy Miller. Jayne"—he paused again—"the registration is current."

"Current? What does that mean?"

"I could be wrong," he said. "But I think it means he was still married to her as recently as last month."

"What?" Jayne shrieked. "That means he would have been married to both of us at the same time. Is that possible?"

"You said he travels a lot, is that right?" Bob asked gently.

"Yes." Jayne thought of all the trips he had taken since their marriage in February. "Yes, he travels all the time. And the other day I saw him driving around Orlando when he was supposed to be in L.A."

"I think it's quite possible, then, that he may still have a wife in some other city. He may even still be seeing her."

Jayne was silent a moment, shocked by the investigator's suspicions. How could it be possible? David had loved her and needed her as no other man ever had. Could he actually be married to another woman, someone he was still spending part of his life with? Jayne could not imagine the answer. Then she had a thought.

"Maybe he was married to her a long time ago and just never changed the information on the deed or at the DMV?"

"I don't think so," Bob said. "The DMV information is usually correct as long as the registration is current. But it's possible David broke things off with Dorothy before meeting you and just never bothered to file for a divorce."

"Still, isn't that bigamy?" Jayne was horrified at the thought that David might have been married when she met him. He had said nothing about having a wife or going through a divorce. And when he had mentioned Dorothy he referred to her as an old girlfriend.

"Yes. It's against the law to be married to two women at the same time," Bob said simply. "You would be within your rights to press charges against him if you wanted to. But let's wait awhile first. I still want to find out about his job at Disney and a few other things."

"Okay," Jayne said, still reeling from the news.

"I don't think you should confront him with all this yet," Bob advised. "Let's wait until we know everything there is to know. Okay?"

"I'll try. But I can't promise anything," she said. "If he calls me I'm sure I'll say something."

"I understand. But don't let him know you're working with me or it'll be very difficult to find out anything else."

Jayne agreed and hung up the phone. She walked

slowly to the sofa and sat down as tears filled her eyes. David had lied to her all along. Here she had thought he was the most honest and open man she'd ever met. He had confided in her and seemingly shared his innermost feelings with her and she had trusted him.

Now she had to admit the truth. He was a liar and a con man. He had pretended to be an unmarried millionaire, a man recovering from terminal cancer. And all of it had been nothing more than a lie. She hadn't been the love of his life at all. She had been the focus of some kind of twisted scheme. Jayne wondered why he would marry her if he was married to someone else. After all, there hadn't been any rush. They could have lived together first or dated a while longer as he worked to finish things with Dorothy.

Jayne weighed her options that morning and decided to visit the local library. During the next few hours she looked up the legal definition of bigamy and discovered that she could have her marriage to David annulled, since it had never been legitimate.

She decided to set the process in motion and called an attorney when she got home that afternoon. She made plans to pick up the paperwork required for an annulment and then she lay down on the sofa. At just before six o'clock that evening the phone rang.

It was David.

Forgetting the advice from Bob Brown, Jayne verbally laid into her husband, accusing him of being a bigamist and informing him that she knew about Dorothy. In a state of panic, David insisted that Jayne tell him where she had gotten her information.

"It's on the deed to your house, David!" she shouted. "Anyone can get the information. It's public record."

David drew in a deep breath and struggled for an explanation. He had never faced a challenge that loomed as large as this one. But suddenly he found the answer. "That doesn't mean she's my wife, Jayne," he said, instantly calmer than he'd been moments before.

"What?"

"I told you we lived together, didn't I?"

"Yes!" she yelled. "You said she was your girlfriend."

"She was," he insisted. "But when you live with someone for several years you become common-law husband and wife. That doesn't mean Dorothy and I were ever actually married."

"Don't lie to me, David!" Jayne screamed, and she started sobbing into the phone. She was so tired of being confused by his stories and the conflicting elements she always seemed to discover later.

"Jayne, why would I lie about this?" he said, no doubt forcing himself to sound calm. "Of course the house and the car list her as Dorothy Miller. After living together a certain amount of time the state automatically assumes you to be husband and wife. It's just a technicality so that if you ever go your separate ways the property has to be divided equally."

Jayne rubbed her forehead with her fingers and tried to clear her thoughts. David's story made sense to her, yet she knew she would be crazy to believe him.

"Why didn't you ever tell me her name was on the deed to the house?"

"I did," he said confidently. "Back when I took you there. Remember? I'm sure I told you she owned the house with me. You must have forgotten."

Jayne felt weary. She could no longer remember what David had said about the house. Maybe he was right. Maybe he had told her that Dorothy owned the house with him. She tried desperately to clear her confused thoughts.

"So you're telling me you never married her?"

"Of course not, Jayne," he said, finally allowing himself to relax. "If I had married her I would have divorced her. I mean, I wouldn't marry you if I was still married to someone else. She's been out of my life for years."

"Why haven't you changed the information on the car or the house?" She was still suspicious. But her information seemed much weaker than it had before he called.

"I keep meaning to do it," he said. "But there's been a lot going on in my life. We moved to Orlando, I got a new job, we've been having problems. It just hasn't been a priority, I guess."

David paused a moment. "Jayne, why did you get a restraining order against me?"

Jayne started crying again. David was making so much sense that she wondered if perhaps she were going crazy. Maybe she had incorrectly read the look in his eyes the other night. It was even possible that David had only returned from his business trip earlier than he'd planned. Maybe he really did love her like he said he did.

"I was afraid, David," she said, and he was satisfied to hear the resignation in her voice.

"Of what?"

"Of you. You looked like you hated me when I saw you in your car that night."

"Jayne, I was angry because you didn't even say hi," he explained. "I got back from L.A. early and when we ran into each other like that I thought you'd be happy. But you looked like you were angry at me."

"Why did you speed away so fast?"

"I don't know," David said weakly. "I guess I thought you and your sister were driving to meet some guys. I was jealous that you were going out without me."

Jayne thought about her husband's explanation and realized it made perfect sense. But she was still afraid, still unsure if what he was saying was the truth.

"I need some time by myself, David," she said. "I have a lot on my mind."

"Well, if it makes you feel any better, I'll take care of changing the deed and the car registration today."

"Fine," she said. She was mentally exhausted when she hung up the phone. An hour earlier she had been convinced that her husband was a bigamist. Now she was no longer sure. In fact, his story sounded completely believable.

The next morning she called Bob Brown and told him what David had said about living with Dorothy long enough to be considered married by common law.

"I don't know, Jayne." Bob was doubtful. Although he had not ever investigated a case in which one partner was a bigamist, he had a strong suspicion that David Miller would become his first. "I'll keep checking."

"Thanks, Bob," she said. "I'll be waiting."

40

Merritt Foster was completely baffled about David Miller. She had spoken with Dorothy since telling her about seeing him with another woman. According to Dorothy, David had lied about his actual occupation and had left her with a considerable debt. He had even threatened her life.

None of this was consistent with the man she and her husband had thought they'd known. David had always loved Dorothy and her boys unconditionally. He had doted on them, allowing their needs to come before his. Merritt even remembered several times when he had just gotten back from a business trip and less than an hour later he would be outside playing ball with Dorothy's boys.

Months had passed since she and Tom had seen David, and when they discussed him they agreed that he must have suffered a mental collapse. There could be no other explanation for his recent actions.

But when they finally did see David again, on Saturday, September 7, he seemed fine. By all appearances he was every bit as mentally balanced as when he and Dorothy had lived across the street.

Never did they suspect the truth, that David was on the verge of a nervous breakdown.

The people renting the Miller house on Jericho Drive had moved out at the end of August and now David suddenly had no way to make the mortgage payment. He was still working part-time for Hilda's company, but he had not done any lobbying in months and had finally run out of money.

He had decided to check out the house and make sure it was clean and in good living condition and then he intended to turn it over to a management company, which he hoped would find renters by the first of the month.

The idea that David would be concerned with making his mortgage payments when his life was falling apart around him was proof that he was not as clear-headed as he had once been. Although David was going through the motions of existing—waking each morning at Hilda's house, showering, dressing, and eating, even checking on his property and trying to make extra money at her company—his mind was consumed with the terrors of a fear he could not escape.

What he could not stand was the idea that one of his wives would make his bigamy public. The possibility of that was causing David such tremendous fear, it seemed to be gradually strangling him. If the police or the press ever found out about the fact that he had two wives, he would be finished.

He apparently had no intention of letting that happen. For this reason, he still kept the loaded 9 m.m. with him everywhere he went. He had it with him on September 7 when he drove up in front of his house on Jericho Drive and proceeded to spend thirty minutes checking the premises.

At the same time, Merritt Foster looked out the window and saw David's car.

"Tom!" She yelled for her husband, who was in the backyard cleaning their swimming pool. "Quick! Come here."

Tom put the pool sweeper aside and went inside the house.

"What's wrong?"

"Look! David Miller's car. I wonder what he's doing there?"

Tom shrugged. "None of our business," he said. He and David had not kept in touch since the Millers had moved to Pennsylvania, although Merritt had kept him informed about what was happening to Dorothy. He had nothing to say to David and turned back toward the pool.

Merritt, however, was too curious to let the opportunity pass. She waited until she saw David locking up the house and then she went outside to greet him.

For several minutes the former neighbors made uncomfortable small talk. Then Merritt asked him about Dorothy.

Suddenly, David did not know what to say. All his life he had been able to lie on cue, creating complicated and believable explanations for his actions and almost always convincing people he was telling the truth. But now, as Merritt looked at him inquisitively, he appeared overwhelmed.

His fear seemed to push and poke at him, choking off his ability to breathe. At that moment it must have seemed to David that if he were not at least partially honest with this woman, perhaps his fear would kill him. He struggled with the words and began to cough.

"Are you okay?" Merritt asked. She thought David was suddenly acting very strange.

"Yes." David caught his breath. "I'm fine."

"Well, like I was saying," she said again. "How are things with Dorothy?"

David had no choice. He needed to tell the truth. He could no longer keep lying to everyone he met. The burden of keeping his stories straight while battling his constant anxiety was apparently too much to take. He would tell her as much of the truth as he could, he decided.

Of course, by telling Merritt the truth about Jayne he risked the very destruction he so constantly feared. But perhaps by then David was so exhausted from battling his private demons that he subconsciously sought an end to his double life. Whatever his reasons, David cleared his throat and began spilling the truth to Merritt.

"Things aren't good, Merritt," he said quietly. "Dorothy and I separated."

Merritt already knew that much. She was looking for details. She waited for David to continue.

"Actually, you remember the woman you saw me with?"

Merritt nodded.

"Her name is Jayne. We got married last month. Right after the divorce became final."

"You what?" Merritt was shocked by David's admission. She had spoken with Dorothy the month before and the woman had said nothing about being divorced from David. Dorothy was angry with him and planning to divorce him, but as far as Merritt knew neither of them had actually filed the paperwork.

"I married Jayne," David said nervously. "I knew you'd be disappointed. You and Dorothy were very close."

Merritt stared at David in disgust. "How could you do that to Dorothy?"

"You don't know the whole story, Merritt," David explained. "It wasn't all my fault."

Merritt shook her head. "That's not what I hear. How could you leave Dorothy with all that debt? And then run off with another woman?"

Merritt continued to watch for some sign of remorse in David's face. There was none.

"Look, Merritt, I made my choice. I'm in love with Jayne and she's my wife. There's no point in crying over the past," David said, moving anxiously toward his car, in a hurry to leave.

He probably had hoped to feel a sense of peace after telling Merritt the truth. Instead, he felt worse. He seemed terrified that the moment he left she would call Dorothy and tell her about Jayne. What had he done by telling the truth? David had no answer for himself, but he wanted very badly to leave before he revealed any more of the truth.

Merritt, however, seemed intent on continuing their conversation. "Dorothy loved you, David." She was sickened by David's lack of empathy toward his ex-wife. "How could you?"

David shrugged and opened his car door. "That's life, Merritt. See you later."

Merritt said nothing as she turned around in a huff and stormed back toward her house. Ten minutes later she was on the phone to Dorothy.

Since tape-recording his death threats in July, Dorothy had been suffering from a mixture of emotions including deep and bitter frustration. The Belle Vernon police had said there was nothing they could do with her taped conversation unless David actually acted on his threats. In the meantime, they suggested she stay away from him if possible.

During the past two months Dorothy had tried endlessly to understand why David lied to her for so many years. She analyzed their good times trying to remember any sign that David's loving words had been anything but sincere.

But no matter how many times she relived their past, searching for clues that he had been lying to her, she came up with none. For that reason it was even more difficult to deal with the reality of her current situation.

Things were no better now than they had been when she first learned the truth from the CIA. She no longer felt any love for David, but rather an intense hatred. And she was finally beginning to convince herself that she had never even known the man she'd spent so much of her life with. He had left her in financial ruin, but even worse, he had left her with no explanation, no answers for her myriad questions.

So on the good days Dorothy went from morning to evening without breaking down and crying. But there were far more bad days than good and Dorothy wondered when the nightmare David had abandoned her in would ever end.

She had just gotten home from work at the beauty salon that Saturday when Merritt called and explained that she had something important to ask her.

"When did you and David finally get the divorce?" she asked.

"Divorce? We aren't divorced yet," Dorothy said, puzzled by Merritt's question. "I'm going to file but I have to get my finances figured out first."

"So you and David are still married?" Merritt was baffled by this latest information.

"Yes. Why?"

Merritt sighed and told Dorothy that their renters had moved out and David had come by their old house to check on it.

"We got to talking and he told me you two were divorced," she said. "Dorothy, that's not all he said."

"What else?" It was just like David to be lying to Merritt. He seemed to lie to everyone he spoke to.

"Remember the blonde I told you about?"

"Yes, what about her?"

"Well, I don't know if it's true or not, but David said her name is Jayne and that they got married last month."

Dorothy was shocked. "What? He said he was married to her?"

"Yes. I don't know, Dorothy. I mean, it seems like it might just be another of his lies. Maybe he made the story up." She hadn't meant to upset Dorothy and now she searched for an explanation to pacify her friend.

"But what if he didn't? If he married her last month while he was still married to me, that would make him a bigamist."

"I know," Merritt said softly. "I didn't think you two were divorced yet. That's why I called."

"What do I do now?" Dorothy moaned, trying to maintain her composure.

She was not surprised to learn that David had spent

the past two months with Jayne. But the nerve of him, marrying that woman while he was still legally married to her. Dorothy could feel herself growing even angrier at David. Suddenly she hoped he had married the other woman. That way she could press charges against him for being a bigamist. Maybe he would even have to serve time in prison. Dorothy hoped so.

For the next hour Dorothy and Merritt discussed the options Dorothy had. In the end they agreed there was very little they could do since they had no way to reach David or verify whether he really had married Jayne.

"Just try to stay calm, Dorothy," Merritt urged her friend. "I'll call you if I hear anything or if he comes back around here."

When Dorothy hung up the phone she sat down and wrote letters to the police departments in Orlando, Los Angeles, Belle Vernon, and Las Vegas—the city she and David had been married in. She asked their advice about filing bigamy charges against her husband and she notified them that she was looking for him. Finally, she asked them to notify her if they heard from him.

She didn't know if her letters would do any good. But she could not simply sit back and wait until he called her again. Notifying the police was the only solution she could think of.

41

Bob Brown had discovered two things in the days since he had last talked to Jayne. First, David did not work for Disney, either as a staff member or as an independent contractor. Disney had never employed him or paid for his services at any time.

Second, Bob had uncovered a detailed phone bill in David Miller's name from March 1991, just before renters began taking over payments on the Casselberry house. One number—in Belle Vernon, Pennsylvania—had been called several times that month.

Bob knew he could be wrong. But his suspicions told him that Dorothy lived in Belle Vernon. If that was true, then whatever his relationship with the woman, it was still continuing one month after he married Jayne.

Since David had lied to Jayne about working at Disney and about taking business trips to Los Angeles, Bob figured he had actually been visiting Dorothy in Belle Vernon. What he had not yet figured out was how David had made enough money to live such a double life and how he had explained his absences to Dorothy.

Of course, he could find out the answers if necessary. But he would need Jayne's permission to continue the investigation, since he had concluded his initial work.

He called her on September 11 with the news.

"I'd be happy to call the Belle Vernon number and continue my investigation, but there will be additional fees," Bob explained.

"No, thank you anyway. I'll take it from here," she said firmly. "If Dorothy lives in Belle Vernon, I want to talk to her myself. I'll call you and let you know what I find. I would still like your help in filing bigamy charges against David if it becomes necessary."

Although David had tried to contact her, Jayne had not spoken with him since early in September when he had made her feel like a fool for accusing him of being married to Dorothy. For days afterward, she believed he might still be telling the truth. His explanation seemed possible enough. Besides, it gave her a way to shut out the pain she would feel if he really was married to another woman.

But after she discussed the matter with Sandra and her friend Jodee in Los Angeles, Jayne had a change of heart. Both her sister and her friend thought she would be crazy to believe David after all the lies he had told her. In light of their advice, she again became angry and distant toward her husband, convinced that he was lying to her.

When he had tried to call during the past few days she refused to talk to him. There were times in the past week when he had called her every ten minutes, demanding to talk to her. But she had steadfastly refused, telling herself that she would not speak to him until Bob Brown had completed his investigation.

Now she finally had something to work with, some way to figure out the truth. She took the Belle Vernon phone number from Bob and waited until that evening to make the call.

The phone rang three times before someone picked it up.

"Hello?" It was a woman's voice. Jayne could feel her heart pounding wildly and she considered hanging up.

"Uh . . ." She hesitated, unsure of what to say. Finally, she had to know whether the woman at the other end was also David's wife.

"This is Jayne Miller, David's wife," she said deliberately. "Who's this?"

There was a long pause before the other woman spoke again. "This is Dorothy Miller, David's wife."

42

The conversation between David Miller's two wives that Wednesday night lasted more than an hour. During that time they expressed no animosity toward each other, agreeing that they were both victims of a self-centered con man who had nearly pulled off perhaps the greatest scheme ever.

Before they hung up, Jayne found out that David had actually been visiting Dorothy when he had told her he was going to Los Angeles for business. She also discovered that until he had left Dorothy in debt and taken the cash from their checking account, they had lived as husband and wife—sleeping together, sharing intimate secrets, and seeming to be in love with each other.

Dorothy, meanwhile, learned that while David was supposed to be carrying out covert operations and dangerous missions, he had actually been with Jayne, at least for eight months. When he had claimed to be especially busy with missions in Kuwait because of Operation Desert Storm, he was in fact using the time to marry Jayne and take her on lavish vacations. Dorothy also learned about David's previous job as a lobbyist and about his extensive political connections in Los Angeles.

Although both women cried during the conversation, they were for the most part composed and calculating. Having been badly scorned, they now wanted revenge. Together they made a plan to fly to Las Vegas and press bigamy charges in Clark County—where both their marriage licenses were currently filed. Unfortunately there had been no failsafe in the county system to prevent from being married to more than one person at a time. David had taken advantage of the relative ease by which a person can exchange vows in Las Vegas. But now they would see that justice was served. They would finalize their plans the following Monday.

Three days passed and David was frantic with worry. He could not understand why Jayne was refusing his phone calls. Could she know that he was lying? Had she found out that he actually was married to Dorothy? If so, what was she doing with the information? David was unable to sleep or eat and he was desperate to know what she was thinking.

And what about Dorothy? Had Merritt called her and told her about Jayne? For all he knew, his wives might even have spoken with each other.

The possibility must have driven David crazy. His fear continued to consume him. It had become his constant companion, leaving him not even one moment of rest throughout the day or night. Each morning his fear pushed him out of bed and forced him to check the headlines—just to be sure the press didn't yet know about his two wives or his double life.

Finally, by September 14, David could stand the fear no longer. It was time to face the situation and find out exactly what Jayne knew. He drove to her grand-mother's house and when the woman told her that Jayne was not home, he asked to come in and use the phone.

David knew Jayne's habit of writing in phone books. He had begun to suspect that she might be using a private investigator. How else had she found out about Dorothy's name being on the deed to the house? Now he intended to check the elderly woman's phone book to see if there were any signs that he was right.

The woman hesitated a moment. "I don't think Jayne would want you in here," she said. "But if you just need to use the phone, I guess it's okay."

Jayne was staying at her father's house. She had not yet told him about David's being a bigamist, but she knew she needed to break the news soon. She planned to meet with Bob Brown on Monday to discuss the spe-cifics of filing bigamy charges. Then she would leave the next day for Los Angeles. She had already booked a flight and made plans to move in with Jodee. From there she would eventually fly to Las Vegas to meet Dorothy and file the charges.

She had nothing to take with her to L.A. except the few belongings in her father's storage unit. David had spent all her savings and had left her with nothing. But she still had her future. She would try to get her old job back and eventually her life would be in order again. She could hardly wait to leave. Just being in the same city with David Miller made her sick to her stom-ach.

But David knew none of Jayne's plans as her grand-mother ushered him inside her house and toward the phone.

"Do you have the yellow pages?"

The woman reached into a cupboard and handed him the thick yellow book. David flipped through the pages until he came to the section on investigators. Suddenly his eyes lit up. One name was circled in red ink and notations were made alongside it. *Bob Brown and Associates: When you must know—for peace of mind.*

David memorized the number and pretended to make a phone call. When he was finished he got in his car and left.

For an hour he drove aimlessly throughout the town of Casselberry. His teeth rattled, his hands shook, and he felt like he was suffocating. There seemed to be no way to calm his racing heart.

This is crazy, he told himself. How could she have hired an investigator? But he knew the answer. She was onto him. He was finished; his entire life was over. Jayne would certainly know by now that Dorothy and he were still married. And she was probably in the pro-cess of telling the media.

After driving for an hour he wound up in front of the Fosters' home on Jericho Drive. He knew they dis-approved of his marrying Jayne, but he needed to talk to someone he could trust. He walked up their side-walk.

"David," Merritt exclaimed as she opened the door. "What's wrong?"

Tears streamed down David's face and he shook his head, unable to speak. Merritt had not yet heard back from Dorothy and she was unsure about what the woman might have found out. Merritt called for Tom, and when he appeared David finally spoke.

"Tom, I'm at the end of my rope." He sobbed. "Can I talk to you? Just for a little while?"

Tom led David into the house, offered him a tissue, and took him out back by the pool. Merritt stayed in the house. David would be more honest if the conversation was between him and Tom.

For three hours David cried and spilled out his feelings, if not the truth, about his situation. He told Tom that he was considering killing himself and that he did not know what to do about Dorothy and Jayne.

"They're going to ruin me, Tom," he cried.

Never once during the conversation did David mention that he was married to both women. Nor did Tom ask the question. He only listened and tried to convince David that he still had a reason to live.

Later he would testify that when David left that Saturday afternoon he was upbeat and happy, determined to seek counseling and to take one day at a time as he worked through his problems. But psychiatrists would argue that at this time, he was near his breaking point.

He didn't know when he would next see Jayne, but he hoped it was soon. He needed to deal with his fear before he had a heart attack or a stroke or simply died from the anxiety that was constantly assaulting his body.

Dorothy might be a problem too. But Jayne was the one who had hired a private investigator. Therefore, if he could eliminate her, he would no longer have to fear her revenge.

It was such a shame that it had come to this. He really had loved Jayne and if she hadn't been so curious they might have been able to work things out. Now that would be impossible.

When he got to Hilda's, there was a message from Jayne. She wanted him to come to her father's storage unit the next day to get his belongings. She would call him in the morning to make arrangements.

As David read the message, he may have smiled to himself despite his terrible anxiety. Relief was bound to come soon.

That Saturday night Jayne spoke with Dorothy and then later with Bob Brown. She told them that she was moving to Los Angeles on Tuesday, but that first she was going to take David's things out of her father's storage unit and give them back to him.

"I don't want his things," she told them. "I want him completely out of my life."

When Dorothy and Bob Brown learned of Jayne's intentions they grew concerned for her safety. David would be feeling trapped and quite possibly desperate. In light of that, they offered her the same warning.

Stay away from David. He could be dangerous.

43

On the hot, humid morning of September 15, 1991, Jayne Miller broke the news to her parents about David's other wife. She assured them that she was leaving him and moving back to Los Angeles. Then she called David and left a message on his answering machine directing him to pick up his things by 3 P.M.

Because she didn't want her parents to worry, she assured them that she would remove David's belongings and be gone before he arrived. Actually, Jayne had other plans. This would be the last time she ever saw him and she intended to use the opportunity to her advantage.

Jayne was going to ruin her husband. He had lied to her, cheated on her, and made a mockery of the emotions she held dear. He was not simply going to waltz out of her life after what he had put her through. And she wanted the satisfaction of seeing his face when she told him of her plans.

First, she would press bigamy charges and notify the press of his double life. Next, she would expose his questionable political connections, which she had learned about when going through his things a few days earlier. She did not understand exactly what David was involved with, but it certainly seemed illegal. Jayne would let the authorities decide.

Then, after she told David of her intentions, she would leave him and never look back. She had already booked a flight to Los Angeles and in forty-eight hours she would be thousands of miles away from David Miller.

Driving her red Hyundai, Jayne left her parents' home sometime after noon. She stopped at a convenience store for a wine cooler, then drove to the U-Store-It at 2905 Orlando Drive and parked the car in front of Building B-4, Unit 18.

For the next hour Jayne sifted through David's belongings, placing each box outside the unit before returning inside for another. When she had removed everything that belonged to her husband, she returned to her car and opened the wine cooler. The temperature was already hovering near one hundred degrees and the drink was refreshing. Jayne sipped it slowly, hoping it would help calm her nerves.

Then she waited.

At ten o'clock that morning David Miller left his bed at Hilda's home and drove to her office. There he worked out a financial arrangement with general manager Jeremy Patel, who with a coworker would meet at the U-Store-It to help move David's belongings. Jeremy called the man, Jay Flesher, and the two agreed to meet at the storage unit at just after three that afternoon.

Then David drove to the Fosters' house.

For the second day in a row, he spent three hours pouring out his feelings and fears to his former neighbor.

In Tom Foster's opinion, David seemed distraught and confused and quite possibly suicidal. Again he refused to say whether he was actually married to both Dorothy and Jayne. But through the course of their conversation, David certainly gave Tom the impression that he was living the life of a bigamist.

This time, though, when David left at 2:30 P.M., Tom did not feel as confident about David's state of mind. He even wondered if David might kill himself. For hours after David left, he and Merritt considered calling the authorities before agreeing that they weren't even sure where David had gone. There was nothing they could do.

At 2:45 P.M., Orlando resident Jason Herget pulled up next to Jayne's car in front of Unit 17 at the U-Store-It on Orlando Drive. He had a list of things to do that Sunday afternoon, but first he needed to go through his belongings and locate some documents. As he climbed out of his car he noticed a pretty blond-haired woman wearing shorts and a T-shirt sitting on the car beside him. She was reading a book and drinking a wine cooler.

"Hi," he said, and smiled at the woman, noticing the boxes stacked up outside her unit. "Moving?"

Jason had never seen the woman before, but she had beautiful features and a golden suntan that had made him look twice at her. But there was something sad in her eyes and Jason wondered what had made her so unhappy.

"No," Jayne said. "I'm waiting for my husband to come get his things. I'm leaving him."

"I see," Jason said, understanding her sorrow.

"Actually, I have a restraining order against him," Jayne said. She had finished her wine cooler and she was feeling talkative. "But I'm going to wait for him anyway."

Jason looked at his watch. "Well, I'd better get to work. I have a bunch of things I need to find." He hesitated before turning away. "Hey, you be careful, okay?"

Jayne nodded and watched Jason disappear into his unit.

At 3 P.M., Jayne was still sitting on the hood of her car when David pulled up forty feet away. He glanced beside him and saw the loaded gun. This was Jayne's last chance. He climbed out and began loading boxes without saying a word to Jayne.

Jayne watched in disgust as David moved his things. When it became obvious that he wasn't going to say anything she began to speak.

"You're such a jerk, David!"

David glanced up at her as he walked past with an armload of boxes. "Shut up, bitch."

"I don't have to shut up! You're the one who married two women. How could you, David?"

David felt his heart skip a beat. Jayne knew the truth.

"I can do whatever I want!" he shouted.

David's fear was completely out of control and he no longer intended to lie to her. He was finished with her. She had the ability to ruin him and he wanted her out of his life. One way or another.

"You know, I really thought you loved me! But you're nothing more than a con man and a coward, David Miller!"

"Don't blame me, Jayne," David sneered at her. "You were stupid enough to marry me."

Jayne climbed off the car and moved closer to David. "You're going to be sorry now!" she screamed.

"Are you threatening me, Jayne?" David glared at her. Then he waited to see what her intentions were.

"You bet I am! I'm pressing charges against you, David. Bigamy is against the law, in case you don't know. And remember all those nice political connections you had in L.A.? They're all going to find out you had two wives, because I'm taking this story to the media. And then you'll be ruined, David. Just like you tried to ruin me."

Jayne stepped back, proud of herself for sharing her plans with David. He looked horrified and for a moment Jayne enjoyed his fear. But instead of crying or backing away from her, David came closer.

He began to scream at her, unleashing a chain of profanities and blaming her for destroying him. As he continued to yell, Jayne began to grow fearful of David. She had not expected him to react so dramatically.

She turned around while he continued his tirade and headed toward her car.

Jason Herget had been trying to ignore the loud fighting going on just outside his unit. He heard the woman shout something about another wife and then the man seemed to lose control. He glanced around the corner to make sure the woman was okay. She was heading toward her car.

She's leaving, Jason thought. Just as well. The man

seemed very unstable and he didn't want anything to happen to the pretty blonde. He listened as she shut her car door but instead of driving away she continued to fight with her husband. The screaming between them grew louder with each passing minute.

At 3:25 P.M. Jeremy Patel and Jay Flesher pulled up near Unit 18 to help load David's belongings. They realized immediately that David and his wife were in the midst of a very loud argument.

"Better steer clear," Jeremy muttered to Jay, and the two men walked toward the stack of David's belongings without saying a word to the fighting couple. They had taken one load of boxes to the cars when they suddenly saw David reach into his wife's car and hit her on the face.

Jayne reeled backward in her seat as David hit her. She began sobbing, stunned beyond belief. She had never thought David would actually strike her. Now she ran her fingers over her face and realized she was bleeding badly from her nose.

She opened her car door and fell to her knees on the sweltering pavement. "How could you, David?" she sobbed, wiping the blood from her face and staring at her husband in shocked fury. David moved back several feet and watched as his wife struggled to her feet.

"I'm calling the police!" she said between sobs, moving slowly back into her car and turning the key in the ignition.

David had heard enough. He walked back to his car, leaned into the passenger side and pulled out his 9 m.m. Jayne was finished.

Jason Herget heard the woman crying and wondered what was happening. He looked around the corner, saw that her husband was returning to his car, and figured he was finally leaving.

But just then the man reached into the car and grabbed a gun. He cocked the barrel and walked quickly toward his wife, who was crying and trying frantically to put her car in reverse. For a moment the man stood staring at his wife through the driver's-side window.

Then he turned and stared at Jason, the cold-blooded stare of a man about to commit a heinous crime. Before Jason could react, David turned again toward his wife and pulled the trigger six times.

"No!" Jason screamed as he dove back into his unit. He was terrified by what he had just seen. Suddenly he heard another shot ring out and he held his breath. He thought that he would certainly be next.

His coworkers watched horrified as David coolly stared at his wife and began to shoot her through the car window. He showed no emotion when he finally stopped, but began to walk slowly around the car toward the passenger side. Then he raised the gun again, aimed it at Jayne's slumping body, and shot one final time.

Jeremy could not believe what was happening. As the general manager for Hilda's company, he had known David for several months. But he had no idea what the man was capable of and now that he had shot his wife in broad daylight he might turn the gun on them.

He watched as David lowered the gun and stared vacantly into the bullet-ridden car. Jeremy had seen enough. He moved quickly behind the cars and came up behind David, taking him by surprise and snatching the gun from his hand. David turned, looked vacantly at Jeremy, and with one final glance at his wife's car, he wandered aimlessly away from the unit, disappearing around a corner.

Still holding the gun, Jeremy turned and raced toward his car, where Jay was still standing motionless in shock. Using the vehicle's dispatch system, he immediately called the 911 emergency operator.

"There's been a shooting!" he shouted, rattling off the address of the storage area. "Hurry! We need an ambulance."

He put the gun inside his car and raced back toward Jayne.

Jason Herget heard someone calling the police and decided it was safe to exit his unit. He saw that a man was already heading for the woman's car and that her husband had disappeared. No longer fearing for his safety, he ran to the woman.

"Quick, help me with this glass!" Jeremy said, and Jason moved in alongside him and began to remove pieces of the car window from Jayne's bleeding body.

Jason reached for Jayne's wrist and felt her pulse. It was weak but steady and suddenly he could hear her gasping for air. The woman needed artificial respiration, but a bullet had pierced her cheek, leaving her face almost unrecognizable. CPR would be impossible.

"Let's straighten her up," he said. "She can't breathe."

They struggled to get her into a sitting position and then they quickly tilted her head back to clear her airway. As they did, she made two sickening gasps, struggling desperately for air.

Then suddenly she was silent.

"Come on, sweetheart," Jason said, helpless to do anything for the woman. "Hold on!"

Blood was still seeping through her T-shirt and Jason resisted the urge to turn away. She had a gaping hole in her shoulder in addition to the one in her cheek. And her chest was a mass of torn flesh. He figured that she had probably been pierced by each of the seven bullets her husband had fired.

Suddenly, David leaned around the corner and stared at the men working on his wife.

"Is she dead or what?" he said calmly. Both men were struck by the lack of remorse in his voice. Just then sirens began to sound in the distance and David turned and again disappeared from sight.

When he had heard the sound of gunfire, U-Store-It manager Brian Higa closed the front gates and locked them. Then he picked up the telephone and called 911. When he was told that a shooting had already been reported at that location he looked around nervously. Whoever had fired the shots would have no way out except through the front gates. He hung up the phone and waited.

At 3:45 P.M., with the sound of sirens growing constantly louder, Brian spotted a man moving toward the front gates as if he were in a trance. The man did not have a gun and Brian was unsure if the man coming toward him had fired the shots or perhaps witnessed the shooting.

"My wife has been shot," the man said in a monotone. "She's probably dead. Call 911."

At that moment, several police cars pulled up outside.

David watched as the police made their way into the compound, their guns drawn. He wondered why they thought they needed their weapons. He would not hurt anyone, not anymore. He sat down on the pavement as an officer came toward him. For the first time in months he could not feel the presence of fear inside him. He could not feel anything.

Lieutenant Roland Hamilton saw the man sitting just inside the gates. "Stay with him," he said, motioning Officer Mike Barnes toward David. Then he ran down the driveway toward Unit 18.

David looked at the police piling out of their cars and he put his hands in the air. Officer Barnes moved toward him and noticed that the man seemed to be calm and coherent, aware of what was going on around him.

"Lay down on the ground!" he barked, aiming his gun at David. When David was facedown on the ground, the officer handcuffed him quickly and waited for further instructions.

Meanwhile Lieutenant Hamilton directed various officers toward the crime scene and then ran quickly toward the victim's car. After seventeen years of working homicide scenes the lieutenant looked at Jayne's body and knew they were in trouble. He motioned for the paramedics and two men ran toward the car.

At 3:56 P.M. paramedics from the Sanford Fire Department began working silently on Jayne's body, searching for signs of life. They pulled her from the car, ripped off her T-shirt, and applied their electric heart starter paddles to her chest. For ten minutes they worked furiously to restore life to Jayne's devastated body.

By 4:07 P.M. they had stopped trying.

"There's nothing we can do," one of them said to the nearest police officer. Then he placed a yellow tarpaulin over Jayne's body. "Call the coroner."

Jason Herget had been watching the paramedics, hoping there might still be some way to save the woman's life. Then he watched in horror as the paramedics covered her body. Jason hung his head and began to cry for the woman he had barely even known.

She never had a chance.

44

Richard and Janice Leebrick were sitting down for Sunday dinner when a uniformed officer knocked on the door.

"It's a policeman," Janice said, looking at her husband strangely and willing away the terrible thoughts that had suddenly come to mind.

But if Janice was looking for strength, she was not going to get it from Richard. He knew instantly what the officer's presence meant. Something had happened to Jayne. He felt his heart breaking as he stood up and forced himself toward the front door.

Janice followed a few feet behind her husband. She, too, was thinking of her second daughter, always so determined to get what she wanted. Janice remembered how pleased she had been when Jayne moved back to Florida. Having her so far away in Los Angeles had always been hard. Especially in light of how close she and her daughter had grown during the hard times Jayne had experienced after Dillon was born.

But Janice, like her husband, had disapproved of

David Miller from the beginning. There had been something shady and false about the man and for the past several months she had worried about Jayne's safety. Now she hoped with everything inside her that this visit did not involve Jayne.

Richard opened the front door.

"Yes?"

"Mr. and Mrs. Leebrick?" the officer asked, and Jayne's parents nodded. The officer swallowed. These visits were never easy and he dreaded the job he was about to do.

"I'm afraid there's been a shooting," he said. "Your daughter Jayne has been killed."

Janice reeled backward. "No!" she screamed as the officer stood uncomfortably on the porch. "No! Not Jayne."

Richard put his arm around his wife and hung his head, tears rolling slowly down his cheeks. After a moment he looked up at the officer. He had to know the truth. "Was it her husband?"

The officer nodded. "They had a fight at the storage unit. He shot her in front of three witnesses. We have him in custody."

Richard closed his eyes tight, his body shaking as he silently began to sob. He remembered when Jayne was a little girl, pigtails and skinned knees and wanting her daddy to make everything okay. And later when she had gotten married the first time to Jake. Beautiful and radiant in her wedding dress with the future ahead of her. Even though she was so young, he had never been more proud of her.

Janice moved closer to her husband, bending down and clinging to him in a desperate attempt to survive the heartbreak.

They stayed like that a long time, oblivious to the officer outside. He needed to tell them where her body had been taken. Someone needed to identify her for the coroner. But that would wait. Now, at this moment, they needed each other.

By 10 P.M. Jayne's entire family had gathered at the Leebrick house and everyone was in a state of shock. Jayne's sister Sandra felt like a part of her had died. Jayne had become her closest friend in the months since she had moved back to Orlando. But still she found the strength to make the necessary phone calls. Jodee was first on the list.

Jodee Bowen was visiting with her boyfriend when the phone rang.

"Hello?" she said.

"Jodee, it's Sandy," she said through tears. Jodee knew instantly from her voice that something was wrong.

"What is it? What's happened?"

"It's Jayne. David killed her. He shot her in front of a bunch of people." She began to sob and Jodee felt herself growing faint. "Oh, Jodee, it's so awful. I'm so sorry."

Jodee's throat felt like it had closed off, and she was unable to speak. Instead she listened to Jayne's sister sobbing on the phone as tears began to spill from her eyes.

"Are you sure?" she said after nearly a minute had passed.

"Yes," Sandra cried. "She's gone."

Jodee could not believe it. She had begged Jayne to leave Orlando sooner. Everything Jayne had told her about David lately indicated that he was capable of harming her. But she had wanted to meet with the investigator first and work out the details of pressing bigamy charges against David. She had been ready to start her life over. Just two more days and she would have been safe. Jodee hung up the phone, put her head down on the table, and began to cry.

Bob Brown was in his office early Monday morning when the phone rang. It was Officer James Bell of the Sanford Police Department with news that Jayne had been killed by her husband.

Bob's heart was heavy as he listened to the details of her murder. He told the officer that he would be willing to make a statement for the record if necessary, then he hung up.

Alone in his office, Bob prayed for Jayne's family and wondered why she hadn't listened to his warnings. For a long while he sat at his desk, staring out the window and agonizing over whether there was something he could have done to prevent Jayne's death.

Suddenly he realized that there was someone else who needed to know. He pulled a file from his desk drawer and sifted through it until he found what he was looking for. Then he picked up the phone and dialed Dorothy Miller's number.

She was about to leave for work when the call came in.

"Hello?"

"Dorothy, this is Bob Brown. I'm an investigator in Orlando, Florida."

"Yes, Jayne told me about you. I think she's told you, we both want to press charges against him for bigamy and—"

"Dorothy, wait," Bob said, interrupting the woman. "She's dead. David killed her yesterday afternoon."

Dorothy's face grew white and she sat down on the side of her bed.

"Is he in jail?"

"Yes. There were three witnesses, so don't worry. He isn't going anywhere."

When Dorothy hung up the phone she called work and told the receptionist that she wouldn't be in. For the rest of the day she existed in a state of shock. The man she had married, the man she had lived with and made love to and trusted completely had murdered someone. He was worse than a liar and a con man. He was a killer.

Time and again as the day passed she was haunted by the same two thoughts. First, that her daughter, Brandi, had been right about David all along. And second, that it could have been her.

News that David Miller was in jail on first-degree murder charges did not reach Los Angeles until Wednesday. On that day, the L.A. *Daily News* ran an article under the headline LOCAL CIVIC LEADER ACCUSED OF MURDER.

But not until September 22, one week after Jayne was killed, did David's political friends and associates learn the whole story. On that day, the *Daily News* featured a picture of David on the front page under this headline: THE DOUBLE LIFE OF DAVID MILLER: UNRAVELING WEB OF DECEIT REVEALS A MAN FEW KNEW.

When Grant Hawthorne read the article he was saddened but not surprised. He had shared an office with David and he knew many of the lies the man told. Grant did not think David was the devil incarnate.

Rather he thought of David as a man who found out he could juggle three balls successfully, so he added a fourth and then a fifth. But when he found himself juggling twelve balls he suddenly looked up and panicked and the balls came crashing down on his head.

The opinions of others who knew David were not nearly as kind. People like Ed Cholakian and clients of David's felt angry and betrayed by the lies he had told them. They wondered what kind of evil man might marry two wives and then kill one in an effort to protect his selfish double lifestyle. Many of them were forced to realize that they had never known the man.

Senator Alan Robbins, himself only two months away from being indicted for extortion and racketeering, expressed shock over Jayne's murder. While he did not discuss the fact that David had carried on business in his Sacramento office, he did say that he and David had been friends for six years and that they had jogged together.

"To say I was surprised by this would be an understatement," the senator was quoted as saying. "Certainly he was somebody I thought I knew well enough that if somebody had told me this story and I had not read it in the paper, my response would be, 'Oh, come on, you're kidding.' "

And in Sardis, Ohio, the small town where David had grown up, Maxine and Russell Miller turned off their telephone and kept their sorrow to themselves. In the past few days they had been deluged by phone calls from numerous print and television reporters. But they did not want to talk to anyone. They had no answers, no explanations for their son's behavior.

They were sorry that David had killed Jayne, sorry that her parents had lost their second-oldest daughter. They understood that pain. Because after learning the truth about their son, it became obvious that the boy they had loved and raised no longer existed either.

But even though they were shocked by their son's actions, they still felt an obligation to him. They had saved some money over the years and decided the best way to help David was to get him the best legal counsel available. In the weeks after Jayne's murder they researched attorneys in the Orlando area until they found a man whose legal talent caused his peers to talk about him in hushed tones.

His name was Leon Cheek.

45

Leon Cheek was a defense attorney who did not believe in no-win cases. He had represented hundreds of clients since opening his own law practice in 1972 and only four times had his clients been convicted on all charges.

During that time he had developed a reputation as a clean fighter, a hard-working attorney who researched his cases to the letter. He was handsome and spoke with a deep, resonant voice that drew attention to his six-foot-five frame and gave him a presence that dominated most courtrooms. When closing arguments were given, other attorneys often marveled at his ability to make his client's criminal actions seem understandable given the circumstances.

For these reasons, he had become a formidable opponent for deputy district attorneys throughout Seminole County. If there was one thing Leon had learned in his years as an attorney, it was to never take a case at face value. Once the facts had been studied, there was almost always some point of law to explain his client's misdeeds.

The case involving David Miller was no exception.

Leon had carefully studied the details of how David had shot his wife seven times, killing her in front of three eyewitnesses, and he knew immediately that there was only one legal explanation for his client's actions.

David Miller had been temporarily insane.

By Florida standards, a person is considered temporarily insane for criminal purposes if they meet three qualifications. They must not know what they are doing at the time of the crime and they must not understand the consequences of what they are doing. Most importantly, they must not know that what they are doing is wrong.

After interviewing David and watching his reaction as he answered certain questions, Leon felt certain that David met every one of the qualifications. Next he needed a psychiatrist who would examine David and find the same thing to be true.

Leon chose Dr. Michael Gutman.

If anyone would be able to determine that David had been temporarily insane at the time of Jayne's murder, Dr. Gutman would. Early in his training as a psychiatrist, Dr. Gutman began to specialize in forensic psychiatry—which often involves diagnosing the criminally insane.

He graduated from the University of Miami Medical School in 1960 and moved to central Florida in 1966, where he set up an office on prestigious North Orange Boulevard in Orlando. But from the beginning he spent at least as much time in the local courts. For more than twenty years, Dr. Gutman had been the paid expert witness in as many as three criminal cases per week. During that time he had given official testimony for nearly fifty felony cases.

The first time Dr. Gutman examined David Miller he discovered two disorders that would not have surprised anyone who had spent time with him. First, David was suffering from depression.

Next, Dr. Gutman determined that David was experiencing a narcissistic personality disorder. According to the American Psychiatric Association's *Diagnostic and Statistical Manual of Mental Disorders,* 3rd ed. *(DSM-III),* this condition occurs when a person suffers from at least five of the following symptoms:

1. Reacts to criticism with feelings of rage, shame, or humiliation even if not expressed.

2. Is interpersonally exploiting; takes advantage of others to achieve his or her ends.

3. Has a grandiose sense of self-importance; exaggerates achievements and talents. Expects to be noticed as special despite lack of appropriate achievement.

4. Believes that his or her problems are unique and can be understood only by other special people.

5. Is preoccupied with fantasies of unlimited success, power, brilliance, and beauty.

6. Has a sense of entitlement, unreasonable expectation of a favorable treatment; assumes that he or she does not have to wait in line with others who must do so.

7. Requires constant attention and adoration; always fishing for compliments; desires to be associated with people of power or people in the public eye.

8. Lacks empathy; is unable to recognize and experience how others feel.

9. Is preoccupied with feelings of gratifying self.

10. Is preoccupied with feelings of wanting more than what he or she already has.

In Dr. Gutman's professional opinion, David's narcissistic personality disorder was a textbook case because he did not exhibit five of the symptoms. He exhibited ten.

But none of that was enough to prove David had been temporarily insane at the time of Jayne's murder. What convinced him of that was something that in David's case had grown out of his depressant disorder.

By medical definition, depression can in rare cases lead to a condition called dissociation. When this happens, the mind separates and compartmentalizes certain events so that they occur only in a portion of the mind. An extreme result is multiple personality disorder, in which a person can be one person one day and someone entirely different the next.

The danger of having such a split or multiple personality is that occasionally something will happen that causes the person to black out a segment of his life. Dr. Gutman believed that this had happened to David in the moments before he shot and killed Jayne. If it had, then David would have met all three qualifications for the legal definition of being temporarily insane; he would not have known what he was doing, the consequences of his actions, or whether his actions were right or wrong.

The doctor based his opinion on one simple detail. Not only did David not remember any of the details of Jayne's murder—he also did not remember being married to a woman named Dorothy.

46

Deputy District Attorney Maryanne Klein did not begin to prepare in earnest for the people's case against David Miller until six months after Jayne's murder. That was when she returned from maternity leave and discovered she would be up against Leon Cheek.

Maryanne had worked opposite Leon several times in the past and she had nothing but respect for the man. She knew he intended to prove that David was temporarily insane at the time of the murder. She had also heard Dr. Gutman testify in the past and she was certain he would be convincing.

Aware of what she was up against, the prosecutor contacted three psychiatrists to interview David in an effort to prove that contrary to Dr. Gutman's opinion David had been quite sane. Maryanne had analyzed the accusations against David and had even spoken to Dorothy. And while marrying two wives and leading a double life was not indicative of a well-balanced person, Maryanne did not believe David was insane, even temporarily. She believed, as did a number of her potential witnesses, that David had purposefully killed Jayne before she could expose his double life and bigamy.

Maryanne did not know how the examinations by the three doctors hired by the state would find David, but she felt certain that at least one would find that he had been sane at the time of the murder.

While she waited for their reports, Maryanne spent quite a bit of time with Jayne's parents. She learned that Jayne had been especially close to her father and that the couple was willing to spend whatever time necessary to see that David was convicted of first-degree murder.

Their dedication initially came into play that summer when Leon Cheek tried to arrange a plea bargain in which David would be found guilty of third-degree murder. In Florida, such an agreement must be worked out between the defense, the state, and the victim's family, although ultimately the decision is made by the two attorneys.

Janice and Richard Leebrick would not for one moment consider such a deal. They called and visited Maryanne almost every day, begging her not to settle for less than taking the case to trial and charging David with first-degree murder. They attended every court date and meeting involving the potential plea bargain until finally the idea was dropped and a trial date was set for December 7, 1992.

"Good news," Maryanne said when she called the Leebricks and told them of the decision. "The case is going to trial. Oh, and we got the reports from the doctors. They believe he's got problems, but they think he was sane at the time of Jayne's murder."

Richard had answered the phone and he felt tears

spring to his eyes. He had been suffering from heart trouble since Jayne's death and the idea that David might be given a light sentence was more than Richard thought he could bear. And now that they had doctors willing to testify against David, everything seemed to be going their way. He swallowed hard and cleared his voice.

"Thank you, Ms. Klein," he said. "But the good news won't come until he's convicted."

David, meanwhile, had grown despondent while awaiting the outcome of his case in the John E. Polk Correctional Facility in Sanford. He was on a constant suicide watch, and whenever he spoke with his attorney he seemed to accept the fact that he would be serving time for killing his wife.

Dr. Gutman interviewed him several times and always found David to be forlorn and very serious. He moved slowly and deliberately, as if he were preoccupied. He also spent a great deal of time crying, which to the doctor especially seemed to indicate that David was suffering from a mental breakdown.

Of course, Dr. Gutman did not know that David had cried on a regular basis whenever it was helpful since he had been a young man. Normally when a person falls into depression after committing a crime it is because he is suffering from guilt. But in David's case it seemed more likely that he was feeling sorry for himself and his ruined reputation.

When he was alone in his cell, David wondered how everything had fallen apart. He had only wanted what he deserved—an exciting life with Jayne. He had been kind to her, paid her expenses and given her everything she wanted. Why had she turned on him? Why had she threatened him? How could anyone blame him for what he had done? David could find no answers.

As the trial date drew near, Dorothy, too, was in constant contact with the prosecutor and her assistant, Trisha Piedrahita. Dorothy wanted to be sure that the case included David's bigamy, even though Maryanne knew they might have trouble introducing that fact in court.

"He killed her because she knew the truth," Dorothy insisted during one of her conversations with Maryanne. "She was going to expose him."

"I know," the prosecutor said, trying to assure David's other wife. "But you have to know that the defense will fight tooth and nail to keep that from coming out in court."

"What are you saying?"

"I'm saying I'll do my best," Maryanne said. "I want the jury to know he was a bigamist just as badly as you do."

Jury selection began on Monday, December 7. Leon Cheek had hoped to fill the jury with men, who might be able to relate to David's inability to decide between his two wives—just in case the judge allowed the information about his client's bigamy to be introduced. But in the end the jury had far more women than men and Leon could only hope they would be compassionate.

The trial began two days later.

That morning the court seemed to vibrate with energy and excitement. There were numerous members of the media represented among the crowd of people milling about outside the courtroom, each of them hoping to hear about David's bigamy.

A few feet away from the crowd, Dorothy waited in the hallway looking angry and beautiful in a conservative skirt and blouse. The state had flown her to Sanford in hopes of allowing her to testify about talking to Jayne and learning that they were both married to David. She forced herself to be calm. If things went well, she was about to get her revenge.

Jayne's friend Jodee waited nearby. She would be a witness for the state regardless of whether the issue of bigamy was allowed in court. Jodee knew about David's previous violence and how desperate Jayne had been to leave Florida and get away from him. She held back tears as she stared out the window. For the past year she had done little more than cry for her best friend. She would do this last thing for Jayne and then she would move on with her life.

In the courtroom, in the back row, Janice and Richard Leebrick sat solemnly holding hands and giving each other emotional support. They had sought help by joining a group for parents of murdered children. But there were times when they wondered how they would go on. Together they watched as Maryanne Klein entered the court. They liked the prosecutor and knew she was capable of getting a first-degree murder conviction. They watched anxiously and waited for the trial to begin.

The first order of business involved the issue of whether testimony regarding David's bigamy would be allowed in court. The jury was excused and then the judge listened to arguments regarding the issue.

Leon argued that his client's bigamy had nothing to do with the murder.

"Jayne and David got into a fight over his belongings, and when things got too heated he experienced a form of insanity and he killed her," Leon explained to Judge Norman Brock during a private session between the judge and the attorneys. "Introducing the bigamy would defame my client's character and prevent him from getting a fair trial."

Maryanne disagreed adamantly.

"The reason they were fighting was because Jayne had found out about David's other wife. She was threatening to take the story to the media," she said passionately. "His being a bigamist is crucial to this case because he killed her to protect his reputation."

The judge thought over the two arguments and made his decision. Testimony about David's bigamy would be allowed and the jury would decide its importance. It was a crucial victory for the prosecution and Maryanne had to refrain from openly smiling in court.

At 11 A.M. the prosecution began its case by presenting the three men who had witnessed David shoot Jayne. Next, there was testimony from the officers who reported to the murder scene and remembered that David had shown no emotion or remorse as he was being arrested. After that, Maryanne put the coroner on the stand to prove that Jayne's body had been hit by seven bullets and that whoever had shot her had definitely intended to kill her.

On the fourth day Dorothy Miller took the stand and revealed for the first time that David had been married to her while also being married to Jayne.

"And did Jayne also know that her husband was a

bigamist?'' Maryanne asked, standing as far from Dorothy as she could so that the jurors could hear her question clearly.

"Yes. We spoke to each other the night before she
was killed. We were both going to press charges against
him.''

"Do you know when Jayne planned to press charges
against her husband for being a bigamist?''

"On Monday.''

Maryanne feigned a surprised reaction to Dorothy's
answer. "She was killed on Sunday and she had been
planning to press charges against her husband the
next day?''

"Yes. That's right.''

The few spectators in the courtroom began mum-
bling to each other and Richard Leebrick squeezed his
wife's hand tightly. The connection had been made.
Obviously Jayne had told David of her intentions and
that was why he had killed her.

The prosecution also heard from Tom and Merritt
Foster that morning. The Fosters testified that David
had visited their house on Saturday and Sunday and
had left their presence only hours before killing Jayne.

"David was very depressed and he kept saying that
Jayne and Dorothy were going to destroy him,'' Tom
Foster said.

"Did he mention that he was a bigamist?'' Maryanne
wanted the jury to hear the word as often as possible.

"No. He just said he didn't think life would be worth
living if Jayne and Dorothy ruined him.''

"Thank you. No further questions.''

The case was moving along quickly and by midday
on December 12 the prosecution concluded its case.

Maryanne had refrained from putting the three psychiatrists on the stand because she thought they would make a greater impact as rebuttal witnesses. She knew the defense would rely heavily on the testimony of Dr. Gutman and she intended to use the state's three doctors to repair the inevitable damage Dr. Gutman would do.

As Maryanne expected, the entire defense was built around Dr. Gutman's testimony. He took the stand that afternoon and testified about David's mental problems, including his narcissistic behavior and his depression, which had led to a split personality and a memory blackout involving the murder.

"It is my opinion that David Miller does not remember the events leading up to and during the murder of his wife," Dr. Gutman said. "Without such a knowledge of the events he could not have been aware of his actions and whether they were right or wrong. He was, therefore, legally insane at the time of the murder."

After rattling off a paragraph of credentials and citing professional sources upon which his opinions were based, there was very little Maryanne or Trisha could do to discredit his statement.

Instead they waited until their doctors took the stand two days later. Testifying one after the other, each of the three doctors stated that after examining David they had determined him to be depressed but definitely sane during the murder.

Maryanne watched the jury's reaction as the doctors' opinions contradicted that of Dr. Gutman. They did not seem affected. Suddenly Maryanne worried that the doctor for the defense had made the greater impact on the jury.

That night Maryanne agonized over the case and what she might do to further convince the jury of David's guilt. She could not imagine the horror Jayne must have felt in the moments before her death. Watching as her husband walked forty-four feet from his car to hers, pointing a gun at her face, she had to have known he was going to kill her.

The picture of those last minutes of Jayne's life continued to weigh on the prosecutor until finally, just before she fell asleep, she decided what she was going to do. It wasn't something she did often—in fact, she had never done anything quite like it before. But it was the only way to show the jury how intentional David had been in killing Jayne. Maryanne smiled as she fell asleep. Her doubts about the case were gone.

Closing arguments began the next day.

Leon spoke carefully and confidently as he used his closing argument to paint a picture of a desperate man in far over his head.

"He wanted to make things right between himself and Jayne," Leon said, looking deeply into the eyes of the women on the jury. "When she told him she was leaving him for good, he snapped."

Maryanne listened intently and watched the faces of the jurors. Normally by this time in a trial she could tell which way the jury was leaning. But in this case it was impossible to tell. Leon Cheek was making a good case for David's insanity and was trying to use David's bigamy to his advantage. He argued that any man who would be married to two women at the same time had to be crazy.

Finally, it was her turn and Maryanne hoped the plan she had devised would work. She stood up and matter-of-factly reminded the jury that Jayne was killed the day before she had intended to press bigamy charges against her husband. She talked about David's self-centered behavior and how callous he had been in lying to Jayne about every aspect of his life.

Then she refreshed the jury as to the definition of first-degree murder.

"A person needs only to have enough time to formulate intent," she said slowly. "That does not mean a person needs to be thinking about committing a murder for days before it happens. Some people might need only a few seconds to decide that they want to kill someone. In Mr. Miller's case he had at least thirty seconds.

"You have heard eyewitness testimony that it took thirty seconds for David Miller to pick up the loaded gun from the front seat of his car and walk forty-four feet to the place where he began shooting."

Then Maryanne picked up Exhibit 3—the unloaded murder weapon—walked to the back of the courtroom, and turned back toward the jury.

"I have measured out forty-four feet, the distance David Miller walked from his car to Jayne's. There are forty-four feet between this spot and the jury box. I am going to walk that distance and I want each of you to imagine if Mr. Miller might have had enough time to make that decision to murder."

Maryanne turned toward the judge. "If it please Your Honor, I would like perfect silence for the next thirty seconds," she said.

"Fine," he answered. "There will be no talking or noise for the next thirty seconds."

Each second ticked methodically off the clock as Maryanne stood motionless, still holding the gun at her side. When fifteen seconds had passed, the jurors began to move around uncomfortably in their seats. Finally, thirty seconds had gone by.

"I believe that is long enough to formulate intent," Maryanne said. "Imagine how it must have been, what the defendant must have been thinking as he took thirty seconds to walk those final forty-four feet." She paused a moment and raised the gun, aiming it at the jury box and locking eyes with the jurors.

Then the prosecutor began walking with angry determination across the courtroom toward them.

"You're not going to ruin me," she shouted.

Ten feet. Then twenty.

"I'll get you for this! I'll kill you!" she screamed.

Thirty feet.

"You'll never threaten me again, you won't live to tell anyone the truth!" Maryanne was shouting at the top of her lungs, storming closer and closer to the jurors.

Forty feet. Forty-four feet.

Maryanne stopped, anger blazing in her eyes and the gun still raised toward the jury box.

The effect was chilling. Suddenly every juror could feel what it must have felt like to be Jayne. They were there beside her, sitting in her car and looking down the barrel of David's gun.

Maryanne slowly lowered the gun and looked carefully, sadly, at each juror individually.

"The prosecution rests."

The moment Maryanne sat down she knew she had done the trick. Normally she frowned on courtroom antics, wanting the jury to decide the case on the facts. But in this case there seemed to be no other way to demonstrate to the jurors exactly how much time had passed as David Miller deliberately walked up to his wife and shot her.

Of course, Maryanne was convinced that David had been planning Jayne's murder all along. Otherwise he would not have been carrying the gun. But in order to win a first-degree murder conviction she needed only to prove that he had formulated the intent to kill. Even if it had happened in those final thirty seconds.

From where they sat in the courtroom, Jayne's parents, her two sisters, and her brother were thrilled with the prosecutor's closing argument. They, too, had worried about the outcome of the trial. But after Maryanne had reenacted the final moments before Jayne's murder, they felt they could visibly see the jury make up their minds.

Leon Cheek was experiencing a sinking feeling in his stomach. He had not expected such a dramatic closing argument from the prosecution and he could only hope that the jury would respond to it unfavorably. He knew there was a strong chance they would find David guilty of second-degree murder. But he dared not imagine that they might convict him of murder in the first degree. Now he watched anxiously as the jurors rose from their seats and made their way to a private room to begin deliberating.

The jury deliberated for only three hours. At 4 P.M. that afternoon, when the foreman announced that the jury had reached a verdict, Maryanne Klein felt a surge of hope. If they had needed only three hours to reach a decision, then there was a good chance the verdict had gone the prosecution's way. She sat down nervously and waited.

David sat at the defense table next to Leon Cheek.

Throughout the trial he had looked dejected and incapable of masterminding the double life he had lived. He wore a dark suit but he looked unkempt and distracted. Not once did he make eye contact with Dorothy or the other witnesses.

Richard and Janice sat in the back row of the courtroom as the jury filed in and the bailiff prepared to read the verdict. Sandra, Debbie, and Rick sat nearby, as did Jayne's friend Jodee Bowen, each remembering special times with Jayne and praying that the verdict would bring her memory the justice it deserved.

And across the aisle, sitting alone with her anger and twisted memories was Dorothy. She stared at the back of her ex-husband's head and wondered how she could have trusted such an evil man. But she knew she was not to blame for believing him. He had lied to everyone he met and not one person had doubted him enough to imagine he might be living a double life. She had long since officially divorced him and knew that when the trial was over she would be free from him forever. She narrowed her eyes and waited for the verdict.

The bailiff took the slip of paper from the jury foreman and cleared his throat.

"The jury finds the defendant, David R. Miller, guilty of first-degree murder as charged. . . ."

Suddenly bedlam broke out in the courtroom. Although the spectator section was not completely filled, those who had attended did so because they had something personal at stake.

Richard and Janice clung to each other, tears streaming down their faces. After a moment, their children joined the embrace. There would be years of struggles ahead, days when it would seem impossible to go on without Jayne. But at that moment they reveled in the fact that justice had been served.

"Wherever she is, she's happy now, she can rest," Richard said softly. "My little girl can rest."

Then he turned toward the jurors, who were receiving a formal dismissal from the judge. "Thank you," he said loudly enough for several jurors to hear. "It's good to know that someone understands how we feel."

Dorothy listened with deep satisfaction as the verdict was read. David deserved what he would be getting. First-degree murder carried with it a term of twenty-five years to life without the possibility of parole. David had made a mockery of their marriage, and worse, he had emotionally scarred her children.

Dorothy looked one final time at the man she had been married to and then turned and left the courtroom. She had a phone call to make.

Since discovering that David was a bigamist, Dorothy and Brandi had regained the relationship they had shared when she was a little girl. Now, in light of David's conviction, her heart went out to Brandi for all the years Brandi felt hurt by David. And after what David had put Dorothy through, Brandi had found it in her heart to understand and forgive her mother for siding with David so often in the past.

Still, Brandi was terrified of David. Since David's arrest she had been suffering from terrible nightmares in which she thought David was trying to kill her. She believed that if he was ever set free, he might indeed come after her or Dorothy. Simply because they knew the truth.

Dorothy knew about her daughter's fears and she

walked quickly toward the pay telephone outside the courtroom.

"Hello?"

"Brandi, it's me, Mom," she said, and only then did she begin to cry. "It's over, sweetheart. He's guilty of first-degree murder."

Brandi screamed at the other end as if she'd just been notified of winning the lottery. Dorothy laughed through her tears.

"He's going to have to serve at least twenty-five years, honey," she said. "I thought you'd want to know."

Brandi thanked her mother and later went to dinner with her boyfriend to celebrate. That night she read the entries she'd made in her journal so many years earlier. When she was finished, she put them away and smiled. David Miller was finally out of their lives. She turned off the lights and went to sleep. And for the first time in more than a year she slept peacefully.